For my daughters, that they may see what is possible, and heal the suffering that my decisions and actions have caused them, as every parent, being human, cannot but inflict upon those they love most.

Foreword

22:51 – 9 June – 2020
São Paulo – State of São Paulo – Brazil

Let me start by stating that everything in this book is true, as it happened, according to how I remember it.

My memory is not perfect, and so the exact order of some events may not be accurate, but I've no concern over that.

The events themselves happened exactly as described, to the best of my recollection. However, I readily acknowledge that any other individual that was present at any of these events, may remember an exact same event slightly differently, somewhat differently, or completely differently. No two of us in this world will remember the exact same event exactly the same way, for each one of us perceives and interprets our reality in accordance with the complete summation of our knowledge, experience, skills, senses and instincts built up over a lifetime of second by second occurrences, choices, and consequences, which have both fed into and shaped that very ability to perceive.

Some of the people that I write about in this book will be able to identify themselves no doubt, however, I have left off last names because it is not my purpose to publicly identify anyone, and I have further avoided using first names where I wanted to take particular caution to leave individuals unidentifiable, such as my daughters.

I do this because, ultimately, this book is not about any other person; it is solely about me. It is about my fifty-year thus far journey through life as I remember it, my suffering throughout this life to this point, that caused by others and that caused by my own decisions and actions, how I came to seek to heal, and the realizations and methods that enabled me to do so.

This book is solely about my life, the way that your life is solely about you. Sure, others play parts, some large, some smaller, many seemingly inconsequential, but epitomically, they are not sharing your existence with you; they are each living their own complete, entirely separate existence.

When you are born, you go through that experience alone.

When you die, no one else shares your dying experience with you.

Sure, others, a mother at minimum, will be present at birth for example, but they as well will be perceiving the event of your birth through their own individually developed and completely separate and unique perception.

Why did I write this book?

1. *To complete my healing*: As Buddhists say, to be human is to suffer. And they are not wrong. We have all suffered somewhere in our lives. Some more than others to be sure. But I believe, and am writing this book to share the belief, that we can heal from any

trauma, be it from childhood or from any other time in our lives up to and including the present.

I believe that I have been able to heal from the most traumatic events and experiences in my life to date, though I expect that I will continue to have realizations about other events throughout whatever time I have remaining in this existence.

2. *To explain my actions to people that I have caused to suffer:* I have exercised poor judgement consistently throughout my life. I have caused suffering to countless people, both intentionally and accidentally. Being human, one cannot go through life without making errors, and at least some of those erroneous decisions that must inevitably be made, will have consequences that will cause suffering in others.

   By writing this book, I am attempting to explain to each person that I've included in this book and that I have caused to suffer in any way in my life, why I made the decision that led to their suffering, so that they can decide whether or not they need anything further from me to heal.

   I am not seeking forgiveness; I am offering to do what is both wholesome and appropriate to help anyone heal from their trauma and leave it behind in the past, where it belongs.

I believe that every single trauma that we experience or have experienced in our lives can be healed; It was meant to be a lesson, not a life sentence.

3. *To posit my fellow beings that it is possible for each one of us to heal the childhood and life traumas that have in fact created us, if we simply acknowledge to ourselves that this healing is possible*: I believe that I am strictly an average person, no more gifted or capable than anyone else. Sure, we all have varying skills and abilities, be the root reasons genetic or cultural, but the ability to heal is innate to every living being.

Further, it has been my experience that, in order for one to truly heal, that healing must be lead by the person that the trauma occurred to. They are the only person who knows exactly how and why trauma occurred, who was involved, and is the only one that can thus determine both how to heal that trauma, and when that trauma is sufficiently healed.

Introduction

01:44 – 10 June – 2020
São Paulo – Brazil

I do not claim to have any special knowledge, skills, senses or abilities, nor to have experienced any event that no one else has ever, or will ever, experience in this universe. I am not special. Not in any 8-billion-humans-on-this-planet sense of the word anyhow. But I am special to me. Because I only have me. And this is my life. And I have more lessons to learn, if I can heal my psyche and make it stronger for the further challenges that may yet come.

Since I am not special, and have no special knowledge, skills, senses or abilities unpossessed of my fellow humans, and since I have not experienced any unique event unavailable to any others, I believe that anyone can change their circumstance as I did, to any degree that they believe to be necessary and wholesome. To do so, one simply has to realize and acknowledge that reality, and acknowledge all the reasonably possible costs of that change. Then, they can decide whether or not the most reasonably extreme price is one they are willing to pay.

I believe that this is what I have done. At a precariously pivotal moment in my life, I realized the price that I would have to pay to live out the rest of this existence in a productive manner. And I believe as a result of my decision to pay that price, just over twelve years later, I have been able to heal from the relevant major traumas in my life to date, and I want to share the general process of how I did it.

Please hold no illusion or delusion that what worked for me will work for you or someone you love, because it can't. I am different than any other individual on this planet; we are all born to different parents, we are inducted into different tribal worldviews, customs, practices and beliefs, and we each have experienced a unique stream of events in this lifetime, in a particular order, that is not impossible to be duplicated by another human's experience per se, but is definitely so mathematically improbable, as to likely be unique thus far in the existence of this universe, and likely for many more to come. The unresolved trauma in each one of us leaves a unique trauma fingerprint upon our psyche, and we each are the only person then that can see that traumaprint.

However, I do hope that part of what occurs when one reads this book, is that the reader comes to understand all of me, my traumas and my experiences, and thus comes to understand the process that I went through to heal myself, and through this, it is my sincerest intention that the reader see that what I did is not special or unduplicatable.

Each and every person can produce the same or similar result, by focusing all of their waking attention upon discovering and/or determining the first thing or things that need to be addressed, and once that is done, beginning and never stopping to search all the heavens above, and hells below, for a solution that might work for them.

We each are the only one in the universe that knows <u>exactly</u> what we have experienced, and <u>how</u> and <u>why</u> those experiences caused trauma upon our psyche and soul, and so we each are the only entity in the universe that can determine what is needed to heal ourselves.

The views, perceptions, interpretations and beliefs that I put forward in this book are purely my own, developed over the almost fifty-one years of my life.

I do not claim that they are right, only that they exist, and that I choose to believe them.

I welcome any chance at wholesome discussion about any.

PART I: Canada

Chapter 1

19 November – 1969
Winnipeg – Manitoba

"The two most important days in your life are the day you are born and the day you find out why." – Mark Twain

If asked, I would request that you call me Micheal.

I was born late in the year on the above date to a typically lower-class, mostly English and French family of that time. I was their first child. My mother claims that I was planned, but I frankly don't believe her. And that is fine. Some things are just irrelevant.

Never look a gift horse in the mouth, as Grandma used to say.

We lived in the city, though exactly where I can barely recall. I remember at one time living in a three-level, rectangular-shaped apartment building with an inner courtyard, where I could run perpetually in a circle.

I also recall the school where I went to preschool, as it was directly across the street from that apartment. I feel that I could probably still pick out the metal chain-link fencepost that I got my tongue stuck on in the middle of winter for the very first time. This was not a traumatic occurrence, and a surprisingly common one amongst children born in winter climes.

And while I really have no idea what that part of the city was like at the time, knowing that both my parents were very young, my mother being twenty-one and my father being twenty, and both lacking higher education or trade skills, at least back then, I hold no delusions that our home was one of the most simple for that time. I know now that my father worked for a time bagging groceries, and though I don't know whether or not my mother was working, I suspect not, as that was the custom back then.

I have a fluctuating number of earliest memories; the first being of a turd floating in my bathtub, I'm going to say produced by my mother's second child, my younger sister, who was less than one year of age at the time, myself not being yet three. I remember being mystified by the floating cucumber. I'll tell you a touch more about my sister later, but suffice to say she weathered the tempest of our upbringing far better than I did, and today is a vibrant, generous, beautiful inside-and-out being with the loving capacity of several supernovas.

In what I am going to call my next sequential earliest memory, I am running with my mother's father down the gravel road somewhere outside the home that my grandfather has built, and in which his many children would grow up. I am looking up at him, laughing and beaming with love, as he runs backward and I run forward with all the might my little three-year old legs can muster, trying to keep up with him but failing thrillingly. I can still hear my own laughter and can still feel that absolute joy.

After that one, I am with my family at a sandpit outside the city called by some *The Oasis*, and I've badly cut my foot on a piece of glass in the water as I was playing. I still have the scar today.

The next earliest memory after that is again of my grandfather, and would be the only other one that I have of him. He is on his deathbed in the hospital in the city. He had survived World War II, having served as a gunner in Europe, only to die of inoperable brain cancer in his early forties. While I was really too young to recognize the significance of this event, it would be what I recall as the first major event to affect my life.

My next earliest memory is of being cared about; one of the few times that I would ever remember feeling this way for the next thirteen years or so. My sister and I are in the back seat of my parent's car, which I believe was some sort of yellow hatchback, heading who knows where. Both of my parents, who are sitting in the front seats, are turned around and looking at me with concern. One of them instructs me to read a sign by the side of the road, and when I am unable to, they correctly determine that my eyesight is deteriorating and that I need glasses. Thick ones.

My next memory is of almost dying. It is winter and my sister and I were sleeping in the back seat of that little yellow hatchback again while Mom drives alone. I wake suddenly. Judging by the dark sky well-lit by streetlamps, the hour is late. The street is slick with snow and ice. We are likely going home.

We are going through a large cement underpass, I believe the one at Main and Logan, when a man suddenly steps out from behind one of the cement pillars holding up the underpass, and directly into the path of our car mere feet away. I remember that vision to this day, frozen in time, viewable for inspection by my consciousness. I don't recall if I understood his intention at that tender young age. I just remember the scene.

Mom panics and slams on the brakes, swerving around the lost soul as our car goes spinning and spinning on the icy road, until we hit a snowbank and came to an abrupt stop. To my best recollection, the man simply disappeared into the snowy darkness.

The last earliest memory that I have is of one of my mother's younger brothers bribing me with Kraft Dinner to put his penis in my mouth, while he lay flat on his back on the couch in the living room, and my sister watched television mere feet away.

I remember that he was circumcised, and I could barely fit the tip of his seemingly large penis into my small mouth. I did my best to follow his instructions, but I guess I did not do well enough because he only gave me a single noodle of Kraft Dinner, and ate the rest himself. I don't believe my sister got any though.

And this is the only memory of this type of event that I have. At least that I have now; this memory did not surface until sometime in my early thirties. One day, the memory was just there. I was drinking a lot at the time for reasons that I will get into later.

When the memory first surfaced, it was hazy to me, and frankly I don't recall when exactly that occurred. All I know is that at some point in my early thirties, I realized that I had this seemingly new memory that I couldn't recall previously, and at some point in time, I convinced myself that it must have been a dream that I had had sometime in the recent past, one of the rare ones that I remembered, and that possibly the dream was reoccurring, because it resurfaced now and then over the next decade or so.

It wouldn't be until the age of forty-eight that my new psychiatrist would advise me in my first session with him, that this is commonly how memories of sexual abuse manifest later in life; like a long ago, just remembered dream, or nightmare.

Chapter 2

"Mother is the name for God on the lips and hearts of all children."
- Eric Draven, The Crow (1994)

A short time after, Mom's father died of brain cancer. To put it simply, her world was shattered.

She worshipped him.

And with the abrupt death of this kind, devoted, steely, seemingly indestructible example-setting man, the up-to-that-time seemingly pleasant existence simply ended for my sister and me.

Shortly after my grandfather's death, my mother and father separated, and my mother fled the city with me, my sister and her mother, all packed into that little yellow hatchback that, unbeknownst to us, was on its last legs.

I was about five, my sister thus two-ish. I can't recall what time of year it was, or what the road conditions were, as the hour that we abruptly departed was very late, and we drove on into the night, and I slept.

However, I do recall the car breaking down in the middle of nowhere.

Mom was sobbing uncontrollably and all but hysterical by this point, and I would decades later learn that this was

15

likely her first of many mental collapses throughout her life. But it was the time that impacted me the most, for I was about to make my very first attempt at making my mother happy.

We are in the repair garage, waiting for our car to be repaired.

I do not recall how we got here. All I know is that Mom, and thus my whole world, is sitting in a chair against a wall, sobbing uncontrollably. This is the first time that I have seen her like this, and I feel like my heart is being torn from my chest.

Grandma sits beside her calmly by contrast, I believe holding my baby sister as she slept.

I am standing directly in front of Mom, about eight feet away, facing her. If I could take a snapshot of this memory and show it to you, it seems to me that it would likely resemble one of those glorious painting in the Vatican, if you have ever been, of a beautiful, glowing angel, slumped over in her chair, sobbing as if Heaven itself had broken apart.

And it hurt like nothing I had every felt before. And I knew that I needed to do something, anything, to sooth her heartache that I could clearly feel in my chest, for she was my universe, and I did the only thing that I could think to do.

I walked up to her, put my arms around her, and said, "I love you, Mom."

She hugs me, and then cries harder.

I have failed, and my mouth is suddenly bitter with bile at the disappointment I feel in myself, in my inability to make the very core of my existence stop crying.

Mother is the word for God on the lips and hearts of all children, and it is at this moment that I first feel imperfect, that my love for my mother is not strong enough to make her whole in her clearest hour of need.

And genesised at that very moment, hot like a star exploding into existence within my breast, was a hate of my failure, and thus of myself.

I could know it at the time, but this hate of myself would be stoked by events constantly over the next few decades, sometimes into a burning fury, and at other times into a feeling of such eternal, energy-devouring hopelessness, as to cause me to not-infrequently lament the utterly bleak, lonely and searingly painful eternity of this existence.

13:09 – A Summer Day – 1974
Somewhere outside of Neepawa – Manitoba

For the next period of time, we floated around I seem to recall. We lived for a short spell in a farmhouse or two in the countryside. My mother had a passion for horses, and we kept several over those early years, as well as chickens, goats, dogs, and likely more.

We lived for a year in a haunted house, and this would leave quite an impact on me in terms of my first fledgling belief in a spiritual world of some sort.

I will always recall the first time that we drove up to that house. The countryside was prairie farmland as far as the eye could see in any direction, golden wheat fields glowing under a clear blue sky, and green patches of woodland dotted the landscape.

We turned right off of a gravel road leading a mile or so back from the highway, and were immediately confronted by the eerie, two-story monstrosity about fifty meters or so from the road.

The first thing that I noticed was the large wooden door, set smack in the middle of the two-and-a-half story wall facing the road. It stood out starkly because there was no staircase leading down from the door, nor were there any windows. It seems to me a gaping maw, flimsily shuttered by a seemingly translucent wooden door, all covered in a flaking, cracking, once-white yellowish paint.

I learned may years later that a large balcony had originally covered the entire front of the house about a century previous, but had collapsed during a party, killing several of the attendees, if I recall the story correctly.

As we entered the property in the vehicle, a large rectangular garden could be seen stretching out behind the house which sits on the left side down the property line. Leading down the property line on the right was a rickety shed facing in toward the house which was immediately followed by a wooden chicken coup that was completely wired in. Bringing up the rear quite a ways back on that right side was an old, dilapidated, once-red sun-cooked gray barn, which kind could typically be seen all over those prairies.

As you faced it, the right side of the property was lined with trees as a windbreak, and these ended at the rear of the property behind the barn. On the left side of the house at the front corner was a single large tree, with a very thin string of thin trees and bushes stretching down the property line to the back.

On the other side of that stretched oil-black farmland and far as the eye could see.

Now, life at this point was unremarkable, but I was developing some weird habits that I now put down to the abrupt, unexplained and inexplicably painful departure of the only father figure that I had ever, and would ever, have or allow in my life.

For example, I began to eat dry dog food.

I have mentioned that my mother kept animals, and at this time was breeding German Shepherds. She would soon begin breeding whippets, and I remember Tweakers, our first dog, racing alongside the car as we tore down a gravel road, my mother racing him mayhaps with hopes of selling him.

He was such a happy dog, always smiling, and I loved him fiercely.

When I started kindergarten, I would sneak into the library after lunch, and go through the trash cans placed sporadically amongst the bookshelves, and eat pretty much any discarded food that I could find.

Half-eaten sandwiches where my favorite.

We were predictably poor, and while I never remember going hungry, except during the countless nights where I was punished for some minor offence or other by being denied sustenance, we basically ate sandwiches made of peanut butter and jelly, bologna or sometimes Kraft Cheese Whiz, and those partially eaten sandwiches that I devoured from those garbage cans tasted marvelous, hinting that a better world existed for at least some of my schoolmates, and I hungered deeply to know more of it.

Anywho, back to the allegedly haunted house.

Almost from the very beginning, all of the adults claimed to know that the house was haunted. What that meant to me at that age, I recall not, but what I do recall is that all of the adults were on edge, right from some the start, about some types of frequent occurrences in the house.

Occurrences so alarming as to cause one of my mother's brothers, a strapping fearless young man at that time, to sleep with a kitchen knife under his pillow, every single night.

Occurrences during the short time that we lived in that house included clear steps on the above floor when no one was up there, shadows moving under the closed bathroom door, clearly visible as you sat in the tub, and someone calling your name, and when you found the only other person in the house, they had been sleeping.

My mother would relate to me years later the most frightening of all of the stories from the short time that we lived in that house.

She was napping on the couch one day in the living, when she suddenly awoke.

Standing before her was a clear apparition of an older man. She could see him, but she could also see through him. She related to me her fear at this ghostly vision that simply stood there, staring down at her with a sorrowful expression, as she lay on the sofa.

He then simply disappeared.

While I noticed none of this at the time, three curiosities from that time in particular I do remember very well to this very day.

The first was that I slept on the top bunk of a bunk-bed, with my sister on the bottom bunk, until the age of fourteen or so, and in that house, and only in that house, I fell (or was distinctly pushed) out of that top bunk, five feet to the wood floor below, on a regular basis, and never once hurt myself.

I would simply wake up and climb back up the ladder into bed.

And this could happen several times in one night.

At other times, someone would tuck me in sometime in the middle of the night, but when I asked my Mom the next morning if she had done so, she couldn't seem to recall.

However, the third was the most disturbing, and still haunts me to this very day.

Sometimes I would hear music outside of my second story bedroom, and would distinctly hear people chatting loudly, as if at some party. In the morning, I would ask Mom who had come by, because I would have loved to have gotten up to see them, and her answer was always the same:

"No one came by, and I went to bed early."

It was not until years later that I would learn about the house's tragically fatal history.

Mom soon found a boyfriend, a John Denver type I want to say. We moved out of that alleged haunt and into a similarly-sized house with him in Minnedosa, Manitoba. I recall it had a small backyard.

We had a homing pigeon that Mom had rescued off the side of some road, and when it healed and flew away, it would return to the house every couple months to let us know that it was still alive.

I went to kindergarten in this town, which was when I started eating food out of the garbage. A few years ago, I ran into a schoolmate from those days who worked in an upper-end men's clothing store that I frequented from time to time, and he confirmed to me that I seemed like any other normal student at that time.

I remember those days quite fondly in fact. Mom was happy most of the time and would burn sandalwood incense while Grandma's Feather Bed played on the record player. Life was peaceful for that year, except for the time that my sister and I sat in the back of that yellow hatchback, while Mom and her boyfriend went grouse hunting in the woods.

My mom was very attentive of me on that day; before they left the vehicle, she instructed us to remain quietly in the car so as not to attract any bears that surely lived in the woods. As the eldest, Mom instructed me to honk the horn in a particular pattern, should a bear try to get at us in the car.

And wouldn't you know it, one came along about two hours later while my sister and I lay crouched and still in the hatch.

Well, we heard one anyhow. We never did actually see the bear, you see. As we lay silent, the car suddenly started to bounce up and down on its shocks, and we definitely heard something growling quite low.

Following my mother's instructions to the "T", staying very low in the vehicle, I reached slowly into the front and honked the horn in the prescribed pattern.

The car immediately stopped bouncing around and something shuffled off growling into the trees.

My sister and I held each other while we waited for the adults to return and save us, which they did quite a short time later, to our happy relief.

Breathlessly, I told Mom, beaming with pride, that I had followed her instructions and saved my sister. I even showed her again exactly what I had done.

And Mom smiled at me and laughed.

And I was happy.

During these years, my sister and I would rarely get to see our father, if ever.

This would leave me defenseless for the hunters that would soon begin to haunt me ceaselessly.

Chapter 3

Early Summer – 1976
Brandon – Manitoba

*"When you're in pain, that's when you learn who you really
are. That's when you focus, sharp like the point of a knife."*
– Unknown

We abruptly moved out of that peaceful town sometime
later and into a small, low-rent duplex with my mother's
mother in a quiet part of Brandon, the second largest city
in the province.

Two houses away, there was a small park with a couple
swing sets, some monkey bars, a large sandbox and plenty
of green grass. I would live here for nearly eight years.

I was terrified for all of them.

My sister and I hadn't seen Mom for some months, and we
didn't know why. We were never told anything about
anything, really.

When mother eventually did return, she had changed. She
no longer smiled. At all. At anyone.

I learned years later that her boyfriend, and one of her
brothers' wives, ran off together in the middle of the
night, while they visited us in Minnedosa right before we
moved. My mother suffered her second mental
breakdown, and had likely spent some time
institutionalized for what I will hypothesize was

depression, for I too would fall under the shadow of that for the next forty years of my life, beginning all too very soon.

I have one insightful memory from that time.

 I'm five or six years old, and my mother has brought me over to the next-door neighbor's duplex, and we are all watching TV in his living room.

My mother and the neighbor are sitting on the couch, with me a couple feet closer to the TV and off to the right side, sitting on a rug.

On the television, farm pigs are being hauled off to be slaughtered for meat, and their terrified squeals bring tears to my eyes as I watch, horrified.

At this point, both my mother and the neighbor look at me curiously; neither say a word to me though.

When I can't take the horrifying squealing anymore, I ask my other if I can go back home. She nods and I get up, walk out of the house and across the twenty feet of gravel to our front door, enter the house, go to my room, close the door and cry for those pigs that had done nothing wrong but exist in the wrong place at the wrong time.

Not too long after we moved to Brandon, we would begin to see our father kind of regularly.

Sometimes he would drive out to Brandon to pick us up, and then take us to visit our family in the city for the weekend. Sometimes mom sent us to the city alone on the Greyhound bus.

These visitations would vary in frequency over the years, sometimes monthly, sometimes much, much less.

Whenever Dad would drop us off at home in Brandon late Sunday, I would usually try to get my mom to come out and talk to him, or for him to come in for a cup of coffee, before he started the two-hour drive back to the big city.

That tactic never worked though, and each time I failed to get my parents back together again, my young, innocent heart broke just a little bit more.

It was around this time that my mother graduated from using the occasional slaps across my hands or behind, or spankings across her knees, to using at first the wooden spoon across my palms.

As I grew, this escalated when the pain became insufficient to make me cry out and/or my mother broke the wooden spoon across my palms (though it may have been sister's palms...she was always far tougher than I).

Regardless, out came the belt, or perhaps it was the clothes-iron cord, or perhaps it was the horse whip or the riding crop, I'm not really sure. But down came my pants and across her knees I went, but this time, for all intents and purposes, my mother lashed a non-lethal weapon all across my bare back, buttocks and legs, ten, twenty or thirty times in a row, with greater force than was required to break a wooden spoon.

When I wailed loudly enough, and/or she was satisfied, I was unceremoniously flipped back on to my feet and instructed to pull my pants up myself, while my entire backside screamed in agony, and my little willy hung out humiliatingly for any who might be present to see.

"The person that you will spend the most time with in your life is yourself, so you better try to make yourself as interesting as possible." – Unknown

September came that year, and I went off to grade one to Valleyview School, now known as Valleyview Centennial School.

That was when the loneliness started.

For I was never to be accepted at this school. Ever. By anyone. Not a single person the entire seven years. I had no friends. I played alone. Until my very last year of elementary school.

I was called four-eyes for most of that year and the next. The reader may recall that from the age of three or four, I had to wear thick eye-glasses, typically referred to as coke-bottle glasses.

I still have pictures.

It made me a target.

As a result of not having a father to teach me sports or self-defense, I had absolutely no coordination or confidence. I couldn't throw a ball. I was gangly and thin. I was always picked last for sports teams. Girls would get picked before me. It was humiliating to my young psyche.

But these were the good times of elementary school.

At that time, I walked to school mostly by myself, as my sister was yet too young to start school. Twenty minutes was the journey, which I made four times a day.

And that was when I started to talk to myself. Not in some mind-slipping sort of way, but just because I had no one else to talk to.

My favorite TV show at the time was *The Benny Hill Show*. This was an early slapstick-comedy show from the UK, and most episodes would feature at least one scene with naked breasts, which I am sure any boy of that age would be at minimum highly curious of.

I certainly did not complain about seeing them.

However, it was not for these brief flashes of nudity that I mostly watched the show whenever I was allowed to, but rather for the British accents that the comedians spoke with. I have no idea why, but I was fascinated with these accents. I would practice them day in a day out while walking to and from school, and by the time I was nine years old, I could do a very impressive Queen's and cockney accent.

I constantly worked over the years on expanding my repertoire.

In grade two, I first heard my inner voice, the one that I would label many decades later as The Watcher.

I am visiting two doors over at the babysitter's house.

She is about fifteen, with large breasts. We are wrestling on the bed in her bedroom and half-accidentally, half on purpose, I grab one of her breasts, fully expecting to get smacked for it.

But surprisingly, she stops wrestling and lays still.

I touch the other one fully.

She does not move.

I then move to touch her special area over her thick jeans, and The Watcher speaks in our head and chest equally.

"Micheal, we should not be here."

I look up at her face; she is still lying prone on the bed, but she has lifted her head up slightly off the bed, and is looking down at me expectantly.

I hastily make some excuse, get off the bed, leave the house, and go home.

I never said a word to anyone.

And she never babysat me again.

In grade four, the boys started calling me "Hardon", which was a clever play on my last name. I was a penis with glasses, they said. And they picked on me. And then they bullied me. I became the go-to target for what I felt at the time must have been every single bully in the entire school.

Recess quickly became a hell. I learned to run out of the class first, as soon as the bell rang, so that I would be first out the classroom door and thus early out the school doors.

I became a runner, an Ethiopian chicken for all intents and purposes, which was a joke I learned about this time: What is the fastest land animal in the world? An Ethiopian chicken, because it was well known at that time that Ethiopia was struggling though a terrible famine, and that any chicken in the country that remained alive had to be damn fast to survive.

So I would run out the school doors, turn right and run down the left side of the school property, about one hundred and fifty yards, all the wat to the rear property line.

A chain-link fence enclosed the entire property.

Here, I would lie low in the grass, peering back up the field to the school, as students flowed across the playground and field. Even though I wore glasses, my prescriptions were always up to date and I could usually see just fine, and I would scan the crowd for the frequent aggressors, and move about the field and playground stealthily in a manner to best avoid detection and entrapment.

Many times though, I was successfully hunted down, or other students ratted me out. Regardless, I would always take varying degrees of damage from punches to the head, kicks and elbows to the balls, head locks, toe stomps. They would spit. They would trip me or push me down. They would take my glasses.

After the school bell signaled the end of each recess each day, I was sometimes able to bet back into the school untouched. Small, not-unpleasurable victories, but it became a true running of the gauntlet for me.

I realized very quickly that I was most likely going to take damage of some kind getting back into the school after recess. It was unavoidable; when the end of recess bell rang, all of the bullies knew that I had to get into the school, and they would frequently wait by the only way back into the school after recess, a double set of metal doors with large glass windows that opened outward on the right side of the building, as you walked up to it through the parking lot.

My tolerance for pain got pretty high pretty quickly. I was not a sissy to whine or whimper or cry or beg too often (for sometimes that was a useful strategy), but there were usually just too many to take on myself, and so my goal swiftly became to simply minimize the damage that I took each time that I entered the school.

After some weeks or months, I believe that my mental development began to slow, for I started having trouble with my studies as even during class, with a teacher always present, the bullying never ceased.

Slaps to the back of the head, paperclips sent flying from elastics bands that they all carried, pokes in the back from newly sharpened lead pencils.

One student would go up the front of the classes and pretend to ask the teacher a question, and on the way back past me to his seat, with his back to the teacher so that she could not see, he would shoot a spitball directly into my face or hair, and high five the others after as I wiped it off in silent humiliation.

No other student ever stepped in all of the years that I was hunted at that school. No teacher ever stopped them. And this told me that what they did to me was okay, that this was the way it was supposed to be. That this was my role in this place; to be ceaselessly hunted. To be called a penis with four eyes. That I had no value to them, or to the teachers for that matter, except as target for anyone that wanted a little fun.

And they always had fun.

12:54 – 12 June – 2020
City of São Paulo – State of São Paulo – Brazil

I have not thought about these events since I left that hell.

As I sit here, a fifty-year-old man, my heart is pounding, my hands are shaking, my face feels hot, and every nerve and fiber of my physical being is humming at an extremely high frequency.

I am trying to light a stick of incense, but the incense end is shaking back and forth so much that I must hold the stick in the middle to light it successfully.

Even though not even a single cell from that ten-year-old body remains in me physically today, clearly, my body remembers this trauma.

The reader may wonder why I didn't tell anyone and try to get some help.

Well, the answer is simple.

I never told my mother because she never asked. I thought that this was normal, that this was the way it was supposed to be at this school, because it never happened at the other schools, and it started on day one here.

Additionally, next chapter, the reader will very quickly understand why I never trusted my mother ever again with my physical and mental welfare, never mind with problems that I had at school.

And I never told the teachers because I didn't have to; they all knew. They saw what was going on every single day and did nothing. I imagine that someone at sometime must have helped me, but seriously, I don't remember a one. So the system at that time failed me, though I acknowledge that bullying was not high on the radar for teachers in the 1970s at it is now.

Chapter 4

Spring – 1977
Brandon – Manitoba

"Live a good life. If there are gods and they are just, then they will not care how devout you have been, but will welcome you based on the virtues you have lived by. If there are gods, but unjust, then you should not want to worship them. If there are no gods, then you will be gone, but will have lived a noble life that will live on in the memories of your loved ones." – Marcus Aurelius

Without warning or explanation, my sister and I are woken up one particular Sunday morning and unceremoniously packed off on the church bus to Sunday School at Calvary Temple. My mother is not particularly religious and rarely if ever attended with us, with the exception of perhaps Christian holidays.

I love Sunday School. Everyone is so kind to me.

And I don't get bullied by my compatriots.

I begin to get up even earlier Sunday mornings and bike down to the church, have breakfast with all the bus drivers (quiche was my favorite), and then ride one of the bus routes.

As the bus rounded the city picking up other children, I would stand by the front doors of the bus, and whenever the bus pulled up to a residence, I would run to the appropriate door, ring the doorbell or knock on the door, and escort all the kids onto the bus.

Everyone liked me and I felt so important, so useful.

And I had done this all on my own.

Typically, after the Sunday school class was over, all the children joined the adults in the worship area to receive that week's sermon, which invariably at least touched on accepting Jesus into your heart, and being saved by the Lord.

I remember being fascinated by the particular culture at this church; each Sunday when the sermon was finished, the priest invited any saved members of the congregation to "bear witness" to the power of the Lord. This, by a country mile, was by far the most interesting part of the entire six-hour morning for me, because you never knew what was going to happen.

Someone might break out in glorious song. Someone else might relate a miraculous event that had occurred recently. A person might suddenly fall to their knees, loudly praising the Lord for answering their prayers.

Or, and my personal favorite, someone saved by the Lord might suddenly burst forth with a heavenly message in a language that that individual assumedly did not speak. They called it "speaking in tongues", and I was desperate to be so blessed, for as the reader may recall, I had grown particularly fascinated with different accents.

But most of all, I want to be saved by the Lord because I wanted to be accepted as I was, and to be loved for what I was.

Autumn – 1979
Brandon – Manitoba

"I have come to understand, and accept, deeply, and with certitude, that I have been born into a world, a life, that will not let me be whole." – Robin Hobb

The bullying intensified over that year and into grade five, and I started to struggle in my studies. My grades were dropping, and my mother was becoming concerned about that.

I remember having frequent panic attacks at school, where my right shoulder suddenly become quite pained and I could not breathe well. I remember one such attack in the middle of the school year that was so bad, I actually went up to my teacher and told her that I could not breathe. My mother was called, and she took me to see the doctor.

They found nothing wrong.

It was also that year that I was successful trapped by hunters while I was trying to get into the school after a recess.

The hunters had me surrounded me on all sides through the tight crowd of elementary students in which I was caught, and as the entranceway into the school narrowed to the span of the two outward-opening doors, one hunter was just outside the doors ahead of me and had me right in his sights. The crowd was carrying me inescapably towards him, but I desperately managed to move off at a rightward slant as I was carried forward by the crowd.

I arrived at the right-side wall, which extended out from the main building to form a ten-foot rain cover of brick, just in time to avoid being swept right into the bully's waiting fists. I had turned my back to the wall so that I could see any incoming attacks, and my right shoulder was jammed up against the metal and glass door that was held open by the mass of ingoing student bodies.

Right behind the door was about a foot of open space between it and the brick wall, and I immediately knew that if I could get into it, I would likely be able to remain out of the reach of the hunters.

Have you ever surprised a wild rabbit in a fenced-in backyard? They instantly bolt for the nearest hole in the fence, no matter how impossibly small it is, and they will force their furry bodies through that hole in a blink of an eye. I've seen this in recent years, but at the time I had not. But I became the rabbit; I forced my body through that six-inch opening with the strength of absolute panic.

Unfortunately, not all of me made it.

I managed to push the door away from the wall with a sort of bench press move, and slid my back to the right along the brick wall in behind the door, but as my torso slipped through the narrow opening, my left forearm was trapped horizontally between the brick wall the metal and glass door, with my left wrist caught palm out and fingers pointing up to the ceiling.

The mass of student bodies slammed the door on my forearm as I slipped in, badly sprained my left wrist, with which I wrote (I throw right-handed).

Gritting my teeth against the pain, I waited behind the door until all of the students had gone in and the recess teacher had herded the bullies off to class. Then I slipped out from behind the door and into school and headed for my homeroom, satisfied.

That could have gone a lot worse.

I failed grade five because, the official explanation was, my cursive was too underdeveloped to be allowed into grade six.

It was humiliating. I was devasted.

And then horrified.

The following September I was in a new homeroom with a new homeroom teacher, and all the boys last year who had been younger than I and thus not a threat on the playground, were now one year older and a threat.

And why reinvent the wheel when you have a perfectly good sap already being the unofficial school anti-mascot?

I got pretty decent at threat avoidance. I knew all the backyards and backlanes with bushes for hiding in over the entire twenty-minute walk home, which I had to make four times a day. My school had no lunch program at that time, and frankly I preferred going home for lunch as any food or money that I might bring to school would be quickly and efficiently confiscated by the bullies post-haste, if any were waiting for me at the entrance to the school when I arrived in the mornings.

I established multiple escape routes out of the school (the best one by far was a building emergency exit that you had to go through the teachers' lounge to get to), and sometimes I would take a completely circular route home if I caught wind that an ambush was in the making, which was a frequent occurrence, as hardon-hunting season extended annually from September, through to the end of June.

I developed a sixth sense, a "spidey-sense" if you will (guess what I watched on TV every day at noon), which warned me when one or most often more my compatriots were paying undue attention to me, such as watching just a little too closely if I am leaving the classroom to go to the toilets.

As the year wore on, I had to run any expanded route home, because arriving home late from school to do my homework this second year of grade five had become...problematic.

I had to be home fifteen minutes after school ended to do any and all homework that I might have. If I was late, I had to write first fifty, then one hundred lines in a paper notebook specifically designated for this purpose. If I committed any kind of transgression at home, I had to write lines. If I didn't ace a test, I had to write lines. And if I didn't write the lines well enough, I had to write more lines.

I wrote an awful lot of lines in the first couple months.

It was very calming.

However, as the bullying intensified at school, my mother grew increasingly unhappy with my scholastic performance and my quiet, listless behavior at home. I was working on perfecting my threat avoidance strategies at school, but it took some not-inconsiderable time and innumerable failures to do so, each for which I paid a varying price in physical and emotional suffering.

Up to this point in my life, while my mother had employed corporeal punishment on a not-irregular basis, I guess it seemed to be providing her with the results that she was hoping for, as she decided that this disciplinary method had the best potential of getting me off that path of failure at school.

Thus, when it became clear to my mother that writing lines was not providing sufficient impetus in me for the improvement in my scholastics that she desired, the physical beatings intensified beyond what she already had been subjecting me to since her boyfriend had betrayed her in Minnedosa.

I typically would then be sent to my room for the night without dinner.

I had no safe haven from that time forward.

I was on constant hypertensive alert at school, my spidey-senses always on maximum every moment of every day because of the constant threat of physical assault by bullies, and I was terrified at home of my mother, because there was simply no escape from her.

Summer – 1980
Brandon – Manitoba

"Don't get high on your own supply." – Elvira Hancock, Scarface (1983)

To get me out of the house that summer, my mother suggested that I get a job with Dickie-Dee selling ice-cream.

I was still pretty scrawny, and the some of the hills in Brandon were quite steep, but I enjoyed the challenge of getting that refrigerator-on-wheels up and down the hills all over town.

I did, however, develop one small problem; I became unable to resist eating the ice-cream myself.

And I began to gamble.

Approximately 1 in 4 of the various delectable treats yielded a free ice-cream; once one ate the ice-cream, they simply licked the little wooden stick clean and, if they were lucky, the words "FREE ICE-CREAM " would be branded on both sides of the stick at the end, where the ice-cream had previously been.

Slowly at first, but with increasing frequency over the summer, my resistance to the idea that I might find a free ice-cream, and thus a free-sugar hit, intensified, and I pushed the warnings out of my head, and I did in fact get high on my own supply.

As the summer wore on, I was finding less and less money in my pocket at the end of the day.

Then one day late in the summer, I was out on the Dickie-Dee bike and I got caught in a torrential downpour. Since I was closer to home than I was to the Dickie-Dee depot, I made the brilliant decision to take the bike home and store the ice-cream in the downstairs freezer overnight.

I even asked my mother to lock the freezer.

Sometime between the Benny Hill Show and bedtime, I figured out how to pick the freezer lock.

By morning, I had eaten most or all of the ice-cream.

I was not invited back to Dickie-Dee the following year.

"Survival is the ultimate ideology." – The X-Files

I passed that summer catching frogs in the perpetually water-filled ditch, down at the end of our bay and across the main road connecting all the bays. Just past the ditch, a chain-link fence closed off the entire ditch, water, trees, bushes and all, from the railroad tracks on the other side.

Sometimes I hung out with a neighborhood boy across the street from us. He was one of the few people that I felt safe with because he was younger and even scrawnier than I was, and had a huge belly, even though he was a string bean. We saw him frequently with his shirt off, and he had a huge scar running over the top of his belly that was about six inches in total length.

He claimed that he had fallen on a shovel when he was younger, and we all believed him.

Once the summer passed and I started my last year of elementary school, I was being bullied at school any day that I was unsuccessful at threat avoidance, and was being physically abused at home with increasing intensity and frequency, by the very person that was supposed to be keeping me safe from harm.

Mother had grown to use a single phrase every time that she came into my room to exercise her warped sense of facilitating character growth in me; after I had pulled down my pants, and before she began to lash me, she would say:

"This is going to hurt me more that it hurts you."

I believed her at the time, after all, she was my mother.

I don't know exactly when I first noticed it, but sometime early that last year of elementary school was birthed, deep within my chest, a sudden red-hot fury any time that I thought anyone was going to attack me, whether at school or at home.

At school, I became quieter and quieter in class, and during my days and nights at home, I came to feel a deep, ever increasing fury that begged to be let out whenever I was physically or verbally punished.

It was during that time that I began to punch walls.

I don't know when exactly the first time was, but I do know that my mother attacked me verbally in some way, as she was ever critical. I felt the unfairness of it all, and I was angy at her for it, and the fury that had been growing deep in my chest burst forth, and without thinking, I punched the wall in front of me with all the might my skinny eleven-year old arm could muster.

And then I froze in absolute terror; I was going to get a lickin', I knew it.

But surprisingly, my mother just stared are me darkly for a number of seconds, and then just walked away.

I continued to do this whenever I could not contain the fury.

She continued to let me.

That esoteric victory was very short-lived, however, as it was at this point that mother dearest began to change her tactics to include deliberate mental abuse of her eldest child.

Domestic terrorism I calls it.

On one particular day no different than the last, she snapped, and rather than assaulting me physically, she simply sent me to my room to wait for my beating.

Which never came.

She has discovered, I surmise, that a whole evening of me agonizing in my room in sheer terror, waiting for the door of my bedroom to open so that I could see what the implement of the day was, was just as effective as, if not more effective than, actually giving me the beating itself. But this new disciplinary method was much less tiring on her arm, as I had hit puberty during the summer on a road trip to British Columbia, to visit my mother's brother who was having some sort of family difficulties, and my pain threshold was again increasing.

My mother perfected her new disciplinary method over the fall. One might wonder why she continued to punish me if I had successfully passed the second year of grade five.

Again, the answer was simple; beatings had proven to be an effective tool at getting me to do my schoolwork, which meant that she was vindicated in her use of that unethical and immoral disciplinary method for any purpose that she desired.

Though, cringingly, that wasn't the worst part of that fall.

My mother, feeling mentally stronger, started attending Brandon University, and began dating.

The first man that she attracted quickly showed his stripes.

He drove her home one early date, however, he was not satisfied with the "see you tomorrow" that she ostensibly gave him, and demanded to come in for a night cap. My mother was able to jump out of the car and run the ten feet or so into the house and successfully lock the door behind her.

I am asleep.

The door to my bedroom suddenly bursts open, and I am startled instantly awake as my mother picks me right up off the top bunk, drops me on my feet, half-drags me, half-carries me down the twenty foot hall and around the corner to the locked front door, and shoves a baseball bat into my hands.

Totally baffled, I note that one of our kitchen chairs has been placed with the chair back against the door, and the chair back top rail jammed up under the doorknob, ostensibly to make it harder to kick the door in.

I look out the window of the thick wood-paneled door and see headlights on high beam shining directly at the door, so I cannot see anything at all.

But I can hear a vehicle running.

I look back at my mother, uncomprehending of the horrifying danger that we are all in.

She stares back at me. Her eyes are wild, and I recognize this look. I've felt it on my face when I have been corned by hunters, and it is immediately clear to me that my mother is terrified.

I look back out the window.

She tells me that a man is out there and wants to get inside the house, and that I must not let him get in. I turn back to her, and the disbelief must have been clear in my eyes, for she yells at me;

"DO NOT LET HIM GET IN THIS HOUSE, DO YOU UNDERSTAND?!"

I understand.

Strangely, I feel calm. I do not feel the terror that I would normally feel when hunted at school or disciplined at home.

I say nothing to her.

I simply turn back towards the door, raise the bat up so that it is clearly visible through the window, and wait.

"Very little worth knowing is taught by fear." — *Robin Hobb, Assassin's Apprentice*

The man never tried to enter the house.

After about twenty agonizing minutes, the running vehicle shifted into reverse and whoever was out there left, and I went back to bed.

A few weeks later, mother dearest started dating a man from Nigeria, who, it turned out, was more than willing to take on the role of chief arm-swinger for her.

To me, he was a huge 9'4", wide-chested black man and he absolutely blotted out my bedroom light when he came in that first time to fulfill his new responsibilities on an eleven year old, scrawny, half-panicked child that was not of his bloodline (he was/is a tribal prince).

And this is what he said:

"This is going to hurt me more than it hurts you."

I shit you not. My mother's own words vomited right out of his mouth. He then told me to pull down my pants, he placed me across his knees, pinned my head in his arm pit with one massive arm, and started hitting my backside with his thick leather belt in the other.

I began to urinate freely after the first strike.

His arm didn't break rhythm.

Chapter 5

I was assaulted a handful of other times by that man who would eventually go on to become an elementary school principle in a number of schools across Canada, though never again did it reach that violent level, thankfully.

My backside was horrifying the next day and for weeks after; black, blue, yellow, green and red where the edges of the belt had broken my skin. There was blood, but not free flowing. It was excruciating to sit at school, and all but impossible to sleep in my bed.

Oddly, when the beatings ended somewhere toward Christmas that year, I was never informed that my overlords would not be employing this particular disciplinary method again, and so when I transgressed and expected the normal punishment, the nights hiding in my closet in terror of what should have been coming continued until we moved out the that house.

Grade six was mostly the same as the previous year. My threat avoidance skills continued to improve, I was hounded at home to do homework, and from time to time I still received beatings from my mother's boyfriend, but like I said, though the worst was over at home, I didn't know it, and so my senses always remained hyperactive.

What was different about this school year was that I made my first genuine friend. His name was Greg, and he lived about ten houses away on Westaway Bay with his mom, his younger brother Bradley, and his sister, Angela.

Greg and I connected because we were both hunted by the same bully all that year, a big cruel brute whose name escapes me. Since we lived so closely together, we made the dangerous commute to school and back again together whenever we could, presuming that there was safety in numbers. We did find some reprieve from the bullies when we numbered two and not one, but we still had to keep an eye out. Like I said, we had attracted the attention of a particularly devoted bully, and on the dozen or so occasions that year when he actively hunted us, we always managed to escape.

The adults in my house began hosting parties quite often in our basement. There was alcohol and drugs consumed regularly right in front of me and my sister, and we quickly clued in to the fact that during these frequent events, all the adults, including my mother and her muscle, didn't give a single squirt about what my sister and I did.

So we joined right in.

With the dancing, not the alcohol and drugs.

To this day, I cannot sit down if Electric Avenue by Eddie Grant is playing.

Last Day of Elementary School – 1981
Valleyview Elementary School – Brandon

"As the sun begins to set, the lowly scavengers reveal themselves." – Dexter Morgan

Grade six went by fairly quickly it seemed to me, definitely far better than most, particularly since I was not lonely anymore.

Greg and I did most things together; caught frogs in the ditch at the end of the bays, put pennies on the railroad tracks, and then collected the wickedly warped and flattened out copper with glee after a train had run over them.

We hung out a lot at the local golf course, played hide and seek at a park past the golf course, skipped rocks across the river there, and searched for, collected and then sold lost or abandoned golf balls.

The last day of school arrived, and very early in the day I remember that my spidey-sense was tingling more than ever before; I quickly pieced together that an ambush had been set for me after school, and this chilled me to the bone, as my tactical mind very quickly realized the implications;

I would not be able to get back into the school once I left.

All of the school doors would normally be locked at the end of the shortened school day at noon, and all of the teachers would typically leave early.

As the day wore on, I got an increasingly clearer picture of the actual size of the operation; if my sources were correct, essentially all of the school bullies had gotten together in rare cooperation, and planned to give their elementary school anti-mascot one last huge beating to remember them all by, as the next year they were going to different middle schools than I.

I began to plan my escape.

"Regard this fleeting world like this:
Like stars fading and vanishing at dawn,
like bubbles on a fast moving stream,
like morning dewdrops evaporating on blades of grass,
like a candle flickering in a strong wind,
echoes, mirages and phantoms, hallucinations,
and like a dream."
-The Eight Similes of Illusion, The Prajna Paramita

Escape Option 1: I ask my homeroom teacher for an early dismissal, which is promptly denied, as she is of the opinion that the day is ending early enough, and I do not need to leave any earlier.

"But I do really need to go home!" I insist.

"Why?", she inquires.

She knows why I have no doubt, and so I simply walk away and return to my desk.

Escape Option 2: I then decide to try to determine which door or doors the bullies will be waiting at. I excuse myself towards the end of the last class of the shortened day to go to the bathroom, and instead do a quick recon of all the normal exits to find which are uncovered.

Much to my chagrin, they are all covered.

By at least two boys each.

I begin to worry; it is becoming clear to me that the scale of this hunt will be larger than ever before.

Escape Option 3: Right there, I make the split-second decision to use the door on the other side of the teacher lounge, which is usually my fail-safe.

I double my pace to the teacher lounge and walk right in, planning, despite the refusal of my early departure request, to simply walk right out the door at 11:45 and go home, and damn whatever punishment I might receive if my mother ever catches wind that I played hooky on the last day of school.

I pass through the main part of the lounge and past the cookie jar that I had raided dozens of times over the years, payback you might say for turning their heads the entire seven years that I was terrorized by the worst of the worst in this place.

However, this is where this bad situation takes a turn for the worse.

This emergency exit is fed by two doors, one from the teacher lounge and the other from the gym, which is normally closed during school hours, but this day, the gym door is wide open and three boys are between me and the exit door when I arrive.

I hear them talking before I round the corner and I freeze, retreat out of the lounge slowly, and return to my homeroom.

The next fifteen minutes are agonizing as I do nothing but stare at the clock, watching the seconds tick by.

Final Escape Option: I know the hunters are waiting for me at the school exits, so I decide to wait for my homeroom teacher, and walk home with her. I had done this a number of times over that school year, and no bullies had ever bothered to follow past this point because, as everyone knows, a teacher would never let one of her students get beat up.

I wait for about an hour with her in my homeroom, cleaning the chalk boards and straightening up the desks, and abruptly she prepares to leave.

I have not been out of the room this whole time, fearing that one or more of my hunters may stick around in case I try to make a run for it or use the bathroom.

As my unknowing bodyguard and I exit the room and she turns around to lock the door, I rotate to my right and spy down the hall about 30 meters to the exit doors, and through them I can easily see two boys staring back at me from the other side.

My main provocateur and his trusty sidekick, a boy about my size.

My anxiety shoots sky high.

My homeroom teacher starts walking toward the exit, and I am unsure what to do. If I let her leave, I will be cornered with no support. I do not know if there are any other teachers still in the school, and I do not know if any other exits are still covered or not.

The halls are completely deserted.

I quickly calculate that the best choice is to follow her out the door, knowing that the boys are not likely to try anything directly in front of her.

As we emerge, the two boys immediately surge forward and join us as we walk the two and a half blocks to her house.

Mine is fifteen minutes past that.

I begin to panic.

For the duration of that seven minute walk that passes much too quickly for me, the boys chatted amiably with my teacher about their wonderful experiences this last year of elementary school, and when we arrive at the base of the driveway to her one story bungalow, they both hug her and wish her well.

I have said nothing for the entire walk. I'm hoping that my silence will alert her that something is very wrong.

It doesn't.

We all stand side by side at the base of the driveway and watch her slowly walk the twenty feet or so to the side door of the house, take out her keys, flip through them several times to find the correct one, insert that key in the lock, turn the knob, open the door, and disappear into the house.

As the outside door shut with a slam, all three of use turn to face one another, me on one side, the two boys on the other.

I'm almost out of options. I know that I will not be able to outrun the big guy; I am a long-distance runner, not a sprinter.

I back slowly onto the green lawn of the house, keeping them both in front of me, and then turn my head to the left to the large curtained bay window of my teacher's house, praying that the curtains flick aside and my teacher look out and see the predicament that I am in.

The boys advance menacingly, and I decide to do something that I had never, ever done before.

I stand my ground.

My homeroom teacher is in that house. I had walked her home many times to avoid getting beat up. She must surely know that. She certainly will not leave me to these jackals once she looks out the window and sees what is transpiring.

I turn and face the two boys, calmly get a good grip my metal-zippered jacket in my right hand, so that the heavy zipper is on the outer end, and drop into a defensive stance.

To my surprise, both boys falter. They turn their heads to stare at each other in disbelief, their mouths dropping open.

But my stomach is in my throat; bile is filing my mouth. My heart is racing, my breathing ragged.

My terror is plain to them.

They grin and attack.

I immediately swing my jacket at the big one, slashing the zipper square across his face.

They both falter again.

The brut raises his hand to the welt that is quickly forming and looks me square in the eye.

"You hadn't aughta done that." he growls.

And I know that he is right.

They rush me.

I drop to the ground immediately and into a fetal position, and cover all of the tender parts that I can.

They kick.

They punch.

One of them tries several WWE elbow-slams to my head. The last one connects hard.

I see stars.

This continues for I don't know for how long. And then, after one or two really good kicks each to my stomach and ribs, they stroll off back towards the school, laughing.

I lay there for about twenty minutes, sobbing, bleeding on the grass.

My teacher never came out of her house.

I limped all the way home.

Chapter 6

August – 1981
Brandon – Manitoba

"Childhood's over the moment you know you're gonna die." – Top Dollar, The Crow (1994)

I enjoyed that summer immensely.

Greg and I began fishing and would often head out for the day to our favorite, well-used fishing spot at a creek some ways off from where we lived. I don't think that we ever caught anything, we just enjoyed getting away.

Summer was always free of hunters.

On one particular day no different than any other, we headed out early to go fishing. I believe that the creek was about a forty-five-minute walk or so, though we were sure to dally considerably on the way, as during the summer break, our parents preferred that we disappear for the entire day.

I remember that I had a brand-new pair of glasses. The bullies had broken my last pair in front of my teacher's house. We were beyond poor, all of us living on social welfare while mother went to university, and I like to imagine that she couldn't replace my glasses for those first four weeks or so of summer for lack of funds.

I never told her how my glasses got broken of course; I had lost all faith in any adults in my life years before this, and at just shy of twelve years old, I already knew that I was all my own in this dark, bleak existence. I rarely saw my mother or her boyfriend these days anyhow, and they rarely if ever included my sister or me in their many adventures, which suited me just fine.

The day was a typical Manitoba summer day, sun shining, birds singing and not a cloud in the blue sky which stretched on as far as the eye could see.

Greg and I arrived at the creek around noon and sat for a while, enjoying each other's company, watching the fish give our hooks a very wide birth (the water was crystal clear), and simply enjoying the rare peace that we felt not being hunted by our school mates.

The creek was wide and fast moving at this spot; it was likely a drainage ditch of some kind, as the water poured here over a cement break of sorts, implemented ostensibly to slow the water at that particular juncture. The creek flowed about three inches deep over a cement break-wall that extended all the way across the fifteen-meter-wide creek. As a result, the normally slow-moving water gained significant momentum as it was tunneled here and went over the break, emptying into a large pond about eight feet deep or so.

Where the water poured over the break and into the pond, it dropped about two feet, resulting in a miniature waterfall which had a pressure far stronger than a boy not yet a teenager might expect.

After about forty-five minutes, the unthinkable happened; my hook got caught on some weeds on the bottom of the pond, which we could see clearly though.

Ten minutes later I lost my second and last wiggly worm, which consisted of a small metal hook partially covered with a florescent green or orange gummy material, likely silicone, which purpose my guess was to attract the fish.

The day was barely half over and I had nothing to fish with, and Greg was on his last lure as well. And what was even more frustrating to us at the time, was the fact that Greg and I could clearly see four or five of the same types of lure, snagged by weeds on the bottom of the pond, not feet from where we sat.

In fact, one lure in particular, a bright green one I recall, caught my attention, for the water seemed shallower where it lay, and I got the brilliant idea to retrieve it and keep fishing for the afternoon.

I hopped up, took off my shoes and, balancing carefully, took a step from the bank onto the cement wall running the width of the creek. The water flowed over my bare foot, but my grip held, and I cautiously took a further step onto the wall with my other foot.

And then another.

I was about two meters out from the bank, and only about two meters from my target. I took another step on the wall to where the flowing water was a touch deeper, and thus flowed with higher pressure.

I lost my footing only momentarily, but that was enough. The rushing water swept both feet right out from under me and flipped me head over heels into the pond smack under the waterfall.

Now, I could swim. My mother had made me take swimming lessons for years and I was up to gray, which at the time I believe was the second highest rank before life-guarding lessons began.

But I was not prepared for the falling water that kept on slamming my not yet adolescent body back down to the bottom of the pond each time I tried to swim up the surface. After three or four tries, I began to lose my sense of which direction was up, as the water frothed white from the waterfall at this point all the way down to the bottom, and I began to run out of air from my exertion.

Greg could not swim. I could hear him panicking on the bank, shouting something or other, but I wasn't listening, for I was fighting for my life.

As the falling water keeps slamming my small body down on to the bottom of the pond, my head strikes a rock and I see stars, and darkness closes in.

However, I am well used to pain at this point of my life, and my swimming lessons have given me a good set of lungs, and I am able to hold my breath and not pass out.

I quickly realize that fighting the pounding water is a losing battle, so I tuck myself into a ball and stop trying to reach

65

the surface, and simply let the water push me down and out along the bottom of the pond.

After about ten seconds, I feel the pounding of the water ease and I rise easily to the surface.

Greg is balling his eyes out by this point. When he sees me break the surface of the water, he screams out my name in relief. As I gasp for air, I swim to the bank and he helps to pull me out.

I lay there on my back on the bank, staring up at the tranquil blue sky for what seemed a very long time, my young mind grappling with the significance of what had just almost happened.

I had almost drowned.

I know it. I can feel it in my bones.

So distraught by this event am I that it is not until we are half-way home that I realize that I have lost my new glasses in that brief but harrowing struggle for my life.

And then I am terrified.

I know with certitude that my mother is not going believe, or even care if she did, that I believed that I had almost drowned. She will declare it a lie and most certainly a beating will be forth coming.

Greg and I hastily backtrack to the pond and peer into the water for about an hour, at which point I very reluctantly admit that the glasses are irretrievable.

I take my time returning home.

Shaking like a leaf, I inform my mother that my glasses dropped into the pond while fishing and that I had not been able to retrieve them.

She says not a word.

I send myself to my room and stay there the reminder of the evening without dinner.

From this point on in my life, I would take over the physical discipline that my mother left off, using the only disciplinary method that I knew of at this point in my life...physical pain.

Later that summer, mother suggested that I take up babysitting to earn some extra money. I was startled at the unspoken implication there; my mother believed that I could actually take care of a child. I mean, sure, I had been watching my sister for years when mom went out at night, but that was so easy because my sister and I were so fearful of our mother that we rarely, if ever, did anything to warrant punishment upon her return home.

Furthermore, mother rarely had ever shown any confidence in me prior to this point in my life, and so I jumped at the chance to prove to her that I was capable and responsible.

That Saturday evening, I headed to a nearby home to babysit two young children for a couple that I had never met before.

The kids were very shy at first, but they warmed up to my accents and goofiness, and I later put the kids to bed at the instructed time and went back to the living room to watch TV.

However, despite my best attempts, I failed to resist not poking around in their fridge and cupboards because they had so much delicious food that we didn't have at my home. I tried to be careful and help myself to only samples in varying amounts of whatever I found that appealed to my taste buds, and then returned to the sofa to enjoy my spoils.

The couple returned home some time later, paid me my five dollars, and I went home well pleased with myself.

I was not asked back to babysit again, and my mother never found me another babysitting gig.

Chapter 7

September – 1980
Brandon – Manitoba

I began grade seven at Vincent Massey in Brandon.

Greg did not go to that school, so I was once again on my own with not a single friendly face in the place. I was terrified for the first few weeks, as the kids there were way huge compared to elementary, and I didn't know how I was going to handle the increased damage once they figured out what I was and began laying into me.

Surprisingly though, months went by without a single confrontation of any sort. I began to realize that Vincent Massey was different; nobody in this school yet knew about my previous role as the school punching bag at Valleyview Elementary, so I did my best that semester to fly under radar and remain unknown.

Which went smashingly.

I talked to no other students the entire semester. I volunteered no answers in class. I never set one foot on the school playground the entire time I attended the school.

And no one ever said so much as "boo" to me there.

I couldn't believe my luck.

My mother and her Nigerian enforcer announced unceremoniously to me one day early that school year on my return home from a not completely unenjoyable day at school, that they had gotten married and that she was pregnant, and that we will soon be moving to Winnipeg.

I remember simply standing there in the front hallway where I had held a baseball to protect my mother from that man that I never did see some time back, just staring at my mother without any expression.

I mean, what did she expect from me upon this grand announcement? Congratulations?

Excitement that this guy was going to be around permanently?

After a few seconds, I simply asked if I had to call him dad.

The reply: "If you want to".

I simply turned and walked to my bedroom, where the largest percentage of the beatings had taken place to date, and closed the door behind me.

"But the fact that some geniuses were laughed at does not imply that all who are laughed at are geniuses. They laughed at Columbus, they laughed at Fulton, they laughed at the Wright Brothers. But they also laughed at Bozo the Clown." – Carl Sagan

I was inconsolable those last weeks in Brandon.

Greg and I hung out as much as we could.

On the last day that I was at his house, his sister Angela allowed me to kiss on her the lips for the first and last time. I was elated, and deeply saddened.

I'd failed at yet another chance to have someone love me.

We moved to Winnipeg towards the end of that year, and I began to attend what I've heard was one of the roughest schools ever to exist in our very fine city at that time, Churchill School.

Just how rough was this school you ask? Well let me elucidate.

At the time, Churchill had a very strong football program. In the second year that I attended this school, as one version of the story goes, the captain of the football team allegedly stole the girlfriend of the leader of the Main Street Rattlers, a well-known gang at the time, numbering in the hundreds if the whispers were to be believed. So it went that the Rattlers decided to pay the Churchill football team captain a visit at our school one day in early autumn, 1982.

All of them.

To be sure, once I caught wind of what was going on, I made myself very scarce and did not get the full story until the next day. Apparently, the Rattlers, about a hundred of them, gathered on the ample front lawn of the school and called the captain of the football team out.

And the captain went out, with the entire football team and pretty much every ruffian in the student body behind him, *and they drove the Main Street Rattlers off the property.*

It was a route, apparently. It was all the buzz for years.

So I get dumped into this school in January of 1981, halfway through the year, thus with zero chance of flying under the radar as I had at Vincent Massey. I did have considerable threat avoidance skills by this time though, and I began to develop a new tactic to reduce the frequency and damage level of violent encounters.

I quite accidently realized somehow, early in that school year, that if the bullies were laughing at you, they were not punching you in the head. I mean, laughing with genuine mirth, not with the sadistic glee I had grown up with in Brandon.

So, from the second half of grade seven, I began developing a sense of humor as a defensive mechanism, and became a class clown.

05:31 – 14 June – 2020
City of Manaus – State of Amazonas – Brazil

Its dark outside as I walk down the streets of a city I do not recognize. It is night, and the streets are deserted.

I am going somewhere, but I do not know where.

I see a younger man in the distance down the street, but I am unable to determine his exact age. He is somewhere between seventeen and twenty-five, I want to say.

I hear him saying something, to me, to somebody else that is there or not there, I can't recall.

I get the sudden distinct impression though that he can get me a job as a resident manager. I tell him that I have ten years of experience and that I would love a job out of the city, or out of the province, or out of the country, though I don't say this last one aloud.

He suddenly moves off down the dimly lit street ahead of me; two of his male charges are building some sort of fort made out of giant-sized furniture, and by the look on his face as he moves off, I can tell that they should not be doing that.

I turn slightly to my left and begin walking up the paved road, and about one hundred yards ahead of me, I see two people walking towards me in the night, dimly lit by 1880s-style streetlamps along both sides of the street. I can clearly tell that it is a man and a woman. They seem to be the same indeterminate age as the young man I had just talked with.

I don't know who they are.

But as they walk side-by-side purposefully in my direction, I get the feeling that they are together, and I feel in the back of my mind that they look familiar somehow. The man looks like my younger brother, my mother's third child, at the age he is now.

I do not recognize the woman.

Non-plussed, I continue walking towards them, and as they close the distance between the three of us to about thirty meters or so, the woman starts running directly toward me.

I am not alarmed by this, for I am still trying to figure out who they are and what they are doing here in this deserted darkness.

It is at this point that I notice steam rising off their skin into the cool, dark night air.

As I notice this, the woman, now sprinting full tilt towards me, launches herself into the air directly at me.

Her hair is of indeterminate color, long and tightly curled, shoulder length and flowing out behind her as she supermans through the air at me with arms outstretched, and as she draws alarmingly close, I am able to see that she has facial features, but that they are only shapes in her skin, which is pale and unbroken, like and old roman bust of Caesar, pupil-less eyes fully open.

She is fully horizontal in the air now and flying directly at me, face focused purposefully on mine, with her hands outstretched for my throat, when I wake with a hoarse scream, arms and legs flailing in the air to fend the demon off.

This is the first nightmare that I ever remember having in my life.

I do not sleep for the rest of the night, and I realize that telling this story is having a toll on me physically, mentally, emotionally and spiritually.

And I have thirty-seven years to go.

But I am consoled by the knowledge that the most terrifying parts of my story are done.

I begin my day of writing...

Second Semester of Grade 7 – Spring – 1981 Churchill School – Winnipeg

Even though I arrived halfway through the school year, I was still only second last on the totem pole in grade seven at Churchill for bully targeting.

The first was poor John.

We were both about the same size, though I presume that I was one year older than John for having been failed in grade five. But what really marked the difference between him and I to the bullies of our school was the simple, unfortunate fact the John had a skin condition of some sort, which left his face seemingly permanently packed and pocked with zits.

Big red ones. Often with white heads.

My skin was unremarkable. So, whenever John was present, he generally was the focus of the bullies.

When he was not present, I would still be punched in the arm, smacked in the back of the head and constantly targeted with spitballs and paperclips. However, these things hadn't bothered me for years. What the bullies at Churchill did not know was that I had run the gauntlet at Valleyview Elementary in Brandon for seven years, and this type pain I sneered at, inwardly of course, and outwardly would congratulate them on a good shot.

I never once defended myself. I had learned on the last day of elementary school that this was not the tactic for me.

Early that first semester, I was stabbed with a pencil in my upper left thigh at the beginning of math class.

Mr. DeJersey, our math teacher, was quite temperamental, if not completely batshit crazy, and would about once a class throw with impressive accuracy a piece of chalk, or a chalk brush, or anything else that was within reach at the chalkboard. And then he would turn back to the board and continue with the lesson unperturbed.

This was not an effective strategy though, as the boys in the class enjoyed the challenge of trying to piss him off enough to throw something, as a successful dodge meant that you were king for a day in class.

The boy to my left, I have no idea who it was, while Mr. DeJersey wrote on the board, simply, with no warning or provocation, leaned over towards me, and with a quick, short backhanded stab, he implanted his number two pencil in my leg.

It began to bleed immediately.

I recall laughing. Good naturedly.

I presume my reaction was not the one that had been hoped for, as this type of tactic was not used again. I took careful note of that, and whenever I got punched, tripped, spitballed or whatever over the remaining time at that school, I would simply give a toothy smile, sometimes give a thumbs-up, do a little dance or an extravagant circus tumble, and return to whatever I was doing.

I think the lead tip broke off in my leg.

I can easily see the lead mark there today.

Gym head never been my favorite class.

However, by that time I was growing bigger and gaining coordination, and the first sport that we took that semester at Churchill was floor hockey.

The very first class I was picked last as per normal, and since everyone wanted to score goals, but no one wanted to sit in the net for most of the scrimmage doing nothing, they stuck me in net.

Which frankly was perfectly fine by me because, 1) I got to play basically every minute of every single scrimmage that semester in gym class (I usually sat out most of the time in elementary), and 2) I was used to pain, so had no fear of the hard orange plastic ball that was normally substituted for a puck.

Over that year, I grew considerably in skill and confidence as a floor hockey goalie, and by the end of that semester, while I was not getting picked first all the time, I rarely if ever again was picked last.

"In a land of predators, the lion never fears the jackal." –
Dexter Morgan

Greg and I kept in touch by letter for about six months, and one weekend my mother allowed me to bus to Brandon to visit him, and we had a grand ol' time.

We were at a swimming pool when a girl that I had never seen before came over to me standing in the pool and kissed me on the lips.

I was elated, if mystified.

Several months later, Greg related to me in one of the last correspondences between us, that he was confronted again by our nemesis, and that Greg beat the tar out of him.

I remember smirking to myself at the table so much that night that my mother sent me to my room without dinner.

I didn't stop smiling until I fell asleep.

I have become hooked on arcade games and sugar, which have become my only escape from my bleak friendless life here in Winnipeg.

I'm delivering papers six days a week, and I invariably spend my meager earnings at the local corner store on small packs of cake icing and playing Galaga, a popular new arcade game.

My mood is increasingly dark and brooding these days, and I have spent all of my earnings already.

It is a Thursday, and I am walking down the back lane to the store, even though I don't have any money.

I just don't want to be at home.

I do a lot of praying to God these days. As soon as we moved to Winnipeg, my mother sent my sister and me to the Winnipeg Calvary Temple Sunday school on the church bus every Sunday, but it's not the same here. The congregation is way huger, and the buses are very well manned, so I have no use to this church as I did in Brandon.

On this particular day, I am praying for money.

I am so lonely, so sad, and I need a sugar and arcade fix badly. I'm praying so hard that my fists are clenched by my sides as I stand in the middle of my back lane, a few meters from the store.

I ask God to give me five dollars, and if he does so, I will love him forever. I express the plea about ten times and open my eyes and begin walking to the store.

Suddenly, about seven feet ahead of me, lying right in my path, I spot a five-dollar bill on the cement.

I freeze. My breath catches in my chest, and I struggle to fathom what has happened. Has God finally heard my prayers? I am dumbfounded.

And then I am horrified.

Most of the time I pray to be saved, for the miracle of tongues and to be accepted for what I am. I realize that I really don't want God to answer this particular prayer for money.

What a waste of an answered prayer!

So, my young mind comes to a simplistic solution; just give the money back to God, and my other prayers may yet be answered.

Brilliant. Absolutely brilliant, I think to myself.

I pick up the crisp blue five-dollar bill, put it in my pocket, and head right home so that I am not tempted to spend it at the store. Sunday and church are only three days away, and returning the money should be a piece of cake.

Not so.

Sunday comes, and we are not sent to Sunday School as per usual. Instead, my father begins taking my sister and me for visitations on weekends.

I leave the money at home for safe keeping.

The next weekend I am sick, and my mother does not let me go to Sunday school on Sunday morning.

The following Sunday we go out of town to visit some family friends, and I'm not able to go to church.

The money starts to call to me.

Spend me, it says. Think of all the icing you can have, it says. Maybe you will finally get that high score in Galaga. God didn't give this money to you. Don't be so stupid. Why would he answer your prayers now? That does not make sense and you know it.

Spend me.

But I don't spend the money. I desperately want to be saved by God, and though day by day it is getting harder and harder to resist the call of the cash burning a hole in my mind, I resist.

Another number of weeks pass, and I have not been able to get to church because of parental visitation, or any other number of reasons. On this particular day, I need a fix so badly that my remaining will simply evaporates, and I spend the money.

I feel terrible afterward, and I cry myself to sleep that night.

The very next Sunday comes and wouldn't you know it, but off to church we go.

I am listless during the bus ride and simply stare out the window the entire way there. I am dreading church today, but the more that I think about it, the less I know why.

It was all a stupid fantasy anyway. What am I so worried about? God is not going to punish me for spending that money. What an absolutely ridiculous thought.

We arrive at the church and I head off to my class, as my sister heads off to hers. Since I am not so comfortable with the people at this church, I sit more towards the back of the semi-circle.

The lesson concludes and, as was the tradition in that church, the teacher hands the closest student the collection plate. It is passed around, some students putting money in, others not.

When it comes to me, I simply pass the heave metal plate on to the person sitting next to me.

The teacher suddenly speaks up;

"Micheal, where is that five dollars?"

My face completely drains of blood.

It suddenly becomes crystal clear to me that this whole thing was a test by God, and I have not measured up.

My heart shatters into a million pieces and I know that I have, yet again, failed, utterly and completely, someone that wanted to love me.

I never attended that church again.

Three girls took me under their collective-wing that year; Lisa, Sabrina and Jackie, who was the prettiest of them all. I was, and still am, a sucker for pretty girls, and they were not cruel to me. They teased me not unkindly, and then laughed at my silly banter as my sense of humor was developing quickly, and the accents that I developed in elementary had grown in accuracy and number.

Saturday Night Live was a favorite show of mine at that time and still is to this very day, and often I pretended that I was an actor in a live skit, and that people were laughing with me, and not at me.

That was the only thing that got me through most days at that school.

One day I am standing at my locker and without any warning whatsoever, my sweatpants are pulled down around my ankles.

I freeze in horror. I am eight years old again and my mother is punishing me in front of whomever might be present.

I look down. I do not know whether they intended to, but they pulled my underwear down as well. My little willy is hanging out humiliatingly for all to see.

Tears immediately start streaming down my face.

I say nothing though as I bend down and pull up my pants as my mother would instruct me to do after a licking, close my locker, and simply walk away from them.

I don't hear any laughter.

To their credit, they never did anything like that again.

Now that we lived in the city, my sister and I were allowed visitation with our father on a much more frequent basis. Times with him were always fun, as we often went to my grandparents' house in Charleswood, where we picked crabapples and played hide and seek with our cousins, out back of the house and around the old rundown garage that held tons of mysterious old things to play with.

I was quite the long-distance runner by this time, a skill acquired through necessity early in my elementary school years.

And this is how I met my second friend, Chris.

Chris was also quite the capable long-distance runner, and in the spring of that year, once the snows melted, gym classes began to take place mostly outside, which was perfectly fine by me as I was never hunted with the intensity in that schoolyard as I had been daily in Brandon.

Gym classes always began with a mile run around the school grounds, and right from the very beginning, Chris and I were always first and second. We began to hang out that spring, and to this day I consider him to be a life-friend. I also became good friends with his friend Mel, and the three of us would spend most of our free-time together over the next couple years playing football and extreme hide-and-seek over a four-block area, which included the Osborne and Kylemore Safeway across the street from Chris's house, and the entire grounds of the Fort Rouge Leisure Centre next to Fred Tipping Place.

Chris was picked on now and then as well, but he was so non-plussed about it that the bullies rarely bothered him as they did John and I, to my best recollection anyhow.

One day, John and I were in Mr. LaBelle's French class and we are getting on each other's nerves for some reason; perhaps it was the stress we both constantly felt at being targets in the school, but for whatever reason that it was, John and I decided to fight each other.

Right there in class.

Now, in case you are getting worried that we hurt each other or some other nonsense like that, please remember that we were both string beans at that time and would be for years. What we considered a fight was, to everybody else, simply two angry chickens flapping their wings furiously at each other, clucking up a storm, but not really doing any damage of any kind.

We were solemnly escorted to the principal's office by our none-too-impressed teacher, where we were instructed to sit and wait to be spoken to. And with that, Mr. Labelle departed the office.

John and I sat, looked at each other, and laughed and laughed until the principal told us to go back to class.

Years later, I heard that poor John had decided to stand up to Robbie, one of the biggest bullies in the school, and was promptly punched in the face, shattering his nose and jaw.

I have often wondered what became of him.

The next spring, my mother got the brilliant idea to register me with the Fort Rouge Community Centre for football.

I was easily the smallest guy on the team, but as this was a coached football team and not Valleyview Elementary, I was encouraged to persevere, and by the end of the summer before the season started, I was able to remain standing when I practiced blocking even the bigger boys.

The last game of the season, and the coach decided to put me in with only a few minutes left in the game, as we are up a couple touchdowns.

I was nervous but excited. I was a defensive end, as I had not yet developed any significant skill at catching the ball.

The ball was snapped, and I began back-peddling fast as I had been taught. Predictably though, my entrance to the field during the last minutes of the game was quickly noticed by the opposing team, and I was covering the quarterback's target, though I didn't know that quite yet.

The receiver that I was covering does a short down and out. I don't react in time to prevent the catch, but, as trained, I moved up quickly as the receiver jumped into the air and caught the ball, and I made the tackle successfully.

I was promptly pulled, but it didn't matter, because for the first time ever, I had been fearless in a physical confrontation.

I made careful mental note of that.

I didn't join the team the next year.

When Chris and I were alone, we played a lot of video games, as that year he had received a Commodore 64 at some point from his parents, who always treated me with great kindness, and for whom I still bear a lot of love for to this very day.

Chris and I decided to get into programming our own video game, as I believe that we were learning computer language in school at the time. Our first and only game was DeJersey Manor, where you had to solve a puzzle to escape a crazy math teacher who would throw chalk at your head and kill you, if you did not make the correct sequential decisions that the game prompted you for.

Time passed and computers improved quickly, and since both of us were huge hockey fans, Chris and I got into a particular hockey game which I will simply call NHL Hockey. We started playing this game sometime towards the end of high school I want to say, and in the beginning, we were pretty evenly matched. However, since the game was his, Chris played it far more than I could and, as one would naturally expect, he became far better than I.

And Chris was particularly competitive.

As was I.

It was during these years that I developed a distinct hate for losing, which began to happen after not too long on a regular basis. Yes, I could win a game or two here and there, but as time went by, Chris had to try harder and harder to let me win, which I know he did, much to his credit, but which he always denied, much more to his credit.

As the days, then weeks, and then months passed and I was unable to consistently put together any significant number of wins, I began to punish myself for my poor performance.

At first, I began ridiculing myself, calling myself a "stupid idiot" and a "fucking loser", but soon I graduated to punishing myself physically, as I used to be punished by my mother.

It started with a slap to the knee, a stomp to the cement floor, a rap to the head, but soon I began to lose control as I become angrier and angrier with myself at dismal failure after dismal failure at this game that a monkey could play, and then over the space of months and then years, that escalated into to dozens of violent punches at a time to my thighs or my head, as all I saw was red from the furious rage blazing like a supernova in my chest, as loss after loss built up over the years that we played that game.

I don't think that Chris ever knew why I did that. And to his credit, he never asked, and he never ever thought me odd for it.

I worshipped him simply for that.

And this was how I punished myself for almost the next three decades, whenever I felt that I had failed at something, no matter how inconsequential it was.

Years later, Chris and I are best of friends and we are out tossing the old pig skin around after dark in the Safeway parking lot, because we can mostly see the ball in the bright parking lot lights here.

Two figures approach us from the dark; two neighborhood boys who have played on the school football team, and they challenge us to a two-on-two.

We look at each other and simultaneously say "Ok".

We play for about twenty minutes and hold our own against these skilled players, and in fact are one touchdown up, if I recall correctly.

Last play of the game, though none of the four of us knows it at the time. Rob is receiver (he was quite the wide receiver in his day) and I am covering him, while Chris rushes the quarterback, whose identity I cannot recall.

Being pressured by Chris, the quarterback lobs the ball up in a wild Hail Mary (since they need to score).

Immediately, I peg the ball as uncatchable and stop covering Rob, who, clearly not in agreement with my assessment of the ball's trajectory and his running and catching ability, doubles his speed and leaps quite impressively through the air, with a hang-time several seconds in fact, and promptly smashes right through one of the huge Safeway storefront windows.

He is uninjured, and after thirty minutes of the four of us waiting for the police to show up, we realize that the store is not alarmed, and we call the police ourselves.

Nothing comes of it.

Chris and I considered this a significant victory.

"Your time is limited, so don't waste it living someone else's life. Don't be trapped by dogma — which is living with the results of other people's thinking. Don't let the noise of others' opinions drown out your own inner voice. And most important, have the courage to follow your heart and intuition. They somehow already know what you truly want to become.
Everything else is secondary." – Steve Jobs

When Mel hung out with Chris and me, we often played

hide and seek after school a lot of that really enjoyable year for me. I could hide decently well, but I was not so good at finding these guys, and that was just fine by me.

I'd realized that the beatings had ended in Brandon, and now my mother's go to disciplinary method for my sister and I was grounding.

A week here. Two weeks there.

I was amused by it.

For a while.

My curfew at thirteen years old was 22:00 sharp, and I presume much like any other teenage boy without a watch and who gets so absolutely lost in playing with two friends that he has never had before at the same time, I just simply was not too very concerned with any punishment that I might receive anymore for being tardy, and would often come in a few minutes late.

We were good boys; we never drank; we never smoked; we never caused any trouble.

And I just wanted to have fun.

It was my new addiction.

One night much like any other, I came home late by about half an hour, I want to say. No more.

My mother was not impressed, and she warned me that if I was late the next night, I would be grounded.

Predictably, I lost track of time running all over the community playing hide and seek that next evening, and I arrived home twenty minutes tardy.

I was promptly informed that I was grounded by my mother, who was waiting by the front door when I arrived.

I asked for how long.

The answer: "We'll see."

My fourteenth birthday passed with no gifts or celebration for me.

Then the same with Christmas (I got an orange in my stocking).

Then New Year's.

Then Valentine's Day.

Then Easter.

Six months in total passed. The entire time I was not allowed to leave the yard, and I was not allowed to have any friends visit.

I was an avid reader of fantasy novels by this time, and I remember passing away the intensely lonely months reading about dragons, knights in shining armor and magic. And perhaps it was one of these many tales about young heroes that escaped evil masters and accomplished seemingly impossible feats for, as the months stretched on, for the first time in my intensely abused life, I began to ponder on the cruelty of this woman who was my mother.

What had I done to earn this horrendous punishment?

Yet a young teenager, I began to sense the state of my own social under-development. I had only two good friends. I was not interested in girls. And I now I been cruelly denied any social contact with anyone outside of my immediate family for half of an entire year, simply because I had arrived home twenty minutes late.

My inner voice speaks to me in my head and chest equally, for what I remember to be only the second time in my life.

"Micheal, we are not growing up living with this woman. If we want to live our life, we must leave."

Sometime later in the spring, I am informed that my punishment is over, but I have already formed a plan, that unbeknownst to me, would change my life forever.

Some years ago, my father had told me that if I ever wanted to come and live with him, I simply had to ask. I thought nothing of it at the time of course. Leaving my mother was unfathomable to me prior to this time.

A form of suicide, if you will.

But after sixth months of traumatic isolation, I have decided that I will never again allow this woman to impose her will on me.

As soon as I am released from bondage, I call my father and tell him I need to speak with him.

Later that same day, I climb into his truck in the Robin's Donut parking lot down the street from my home at

Brandon Avenue and Osborne Street. Pausing not a second, I remind him of his promise to me years ago, and I ask him point blank if I can come and live with him.

Right now.

This very second.

He looks at me blankly for a moment, and then simply says "Absolutely".

I am elated.

I run back to the house, run up to my room and grab the single pre-packed gym bag hidden in my closet containing all my worldly possessions that I dare to take with me, go back down the stairs to the kitchen, and stop at the door to the basement for several minutes.

My mother is downstairs ironing clothes. With a clothes iron. That has an ironing cord. I am terrified. But, still being a complete momma's boy, I desperately want to tell her of my plan of action, and give her the chance to do something that she has never done in her life up to this point; allow me to voice displeasure at her parenting, and ask me to stay with her, and my family.

She does not look up from her ironing as I descend the stairs slowly, one at a time, terror growing with each step that brings me closer to her grasp.

I stop on the bottom stair purposely; if she tries to grab me, I plan to bolt right up the stairs and out the back kitchen door which I have already unlocked in preparation of my escape, then out the back gate and down the backlane to my father's waiting vehicle, and to freedom.

To life.

I clear my throat. She does not look up or acknowledge my presence.

I launch into my much-rehearsed speech.

"Mom. I feel like I am not being allowed to grow up here living with you." Her husband, my sister, my little brother, my grandmother and one of my mother's four bothers all live in this two story, three bedroom house, and we had just been informed that there was another baby on the way.

She does not look up from her ironing.

I continue.

"I've decided to go and live with my dad. He is waiting outside."

Nothing.

She does not speak the words I desperately want to hear. The words I desperately need to hear.

I look at my mother for a long moment. I feel that I still somehow love this woman that destroyed any chance for me and my sister of an enjoyable childhood, yet I desperately need to hear that I have some value to her, some value to this household.

She remains silent.

She doesn't look up from her ironing.

She does not speak the words I desperately want to hear. The words I desperately need to hear.

I turn and walk up the stairs, out the <u>front</u> door, and calmly walk the one hundred or so meters to my father's waiting vehicle, and get in.

I would not see or talk to my mother again for almost four years.

Second Semester of Grade 8 – Spring – 1983
Winnipeg – Manitoba

I presume that since I had started the year at Churchill, I had to finish the year at Churchill. I took the city bus every day to that area of the city, though I never walked past my house on Brandon avenue, but rather took a parallel street.

I didn't ever want to run into my mother, or her husband.

Life with Dad and his new wife was simply amazing. He trusted me. He talked to me about what I wanted. He let me play outside with my friends until any hour of the day or night. He did not hound me about my schoolwork. He did not strike me, threaten me, or ever make me feel small in any way.

As one's head must inevitably feel better when one stops banging that head against a cement wall, my life took on a sense of normalcy for the next seven years that I lived with him. I raved to my sister so much about that when she came for visitations, that one year later, she moved in with us too, however she maintained her relationship with our mother.

I, contrastingly, never made any attempt to contact my mother.

To me, she was dead.

Late May – 1983
Winnipeg – Manitoba

I had recently discovered my father's black leather jacket, hanging in the basement of our new house on Trent Avenue, that he had kept since he was quite young.

I was thrilled.

"Dad, can I have this?" I doubtfully inquired.

He looked at me blankly for a moment, and simply said, "Absolutely".

I was elated.

I wore the jacket to school.

A couple days later, I lost the jacket. Well, more accurately, someone stole it, but I just considered it one more failure as a son on my part.

I was distraught. I searched and searched high and low for it all over the school until I got a tip; Jim had it.

Over the next two weeks, I would pester Jim as much as I dared, for he was one of my frequent aggressors over the short time that I had spent at that school. He confirmed readily enough the first time that I asked him if he had the jacket, but clearly he had by this age developed quite the poor memory, for he kept forgetting to bring it to school for me.

I am desperate.

I am not afraid of my father; he has never lost his temper with either my sister or me, nor has he ever given me any reason to fear him, and likely never will, which is precisely why I am so upset with myself.

I am enamored with the jacket; it's my father's and it made me feel connected to him. He showed me a kindness that frankly I did not expect, and here I go and lose his treasure on him within days of receiving it, after he has kept it for decades.

I am such a selfish, careless child.

I decide to take matters into my own hands.

I find out where Jim lives, and on the weekend, I go over to his house, planning to ask him point blank for the jacket, not caring one iota if it earns me a pounding.

I have to get that jacket back.

I find the house and without pausing, open the gate and go directly up the door and knock.

No answer.

I knock again louder. Ditto.

The screen door is shut but the main door is open, and I can see into the house. I cup my hands on either side of my head to shade the sun shining in from behind me to see if anyone is around, when I spy my father's jacket partially covered by another piece of clothing on the stair bannister, not fifteen feet from me.

I stare at it for a short moment, then reach up and take hold of the doorknob and pull. Its unlocked, and it opens quietly.

Without a moment's hesitation, I step softly into the house and close the screen door gently behind me.

The house is silent.

I take three quick strides and pull the jacket off the bannister and out from under another jacket, and I freeze. The jacket has been absolutely destroyed. It's basically ripped in half, held together by only a few threads.

Bile rises from my stomach.

"Well, that's that." I say under my breath, leave the jacket on the bannister, and I turn around and head to the door.

Just as I reach out to push the screen door open, I hear a voice behind me.

"Can I help you?" says a woman.

Surprisingly, I turn around without any fear and see who I assume to be Jim's mother, looking at me through highly suspicious eyes.

"Yes," I respond calmly. "Is Jim home?"

"No, he isn't" is the curt answer.

"Oh, ok." I reply. "I'll just see him at school then."

And with that, I turn around smartly, push open the screen door, and go home and tell my father that I have lost what likely is one of his favorite keepsakes.

He looks at me blankly for a moment, and simply says, "Oh well".

Of course he wouldn't be upset with me.

I feel like crying.

End of June – 1983
Winnipeg – Manitoba

The end of the grade eight school year at Churchill School brought a completely unexpected humanity that I will never forget, and will always be grateful for.

I was asked by a schoolmate named Gretchen to the grade eight prom. Dumbfounded, I accepted, and that night of wild dancing and fearless fun at that school was the first and last such time in my life.

Afterwards, she let me kiss her goodnight.

I never understood why she extended that kindness to me.

That was the last time that I ever set foot in that school again.

Chapter 8

September – 1983
Winnipeg – Manitoba

"You live on the corner of Trent and what street?"
"That's correct." – Harry Harding

The school that was the closest to my father's one-bedroom apartment and where I was to start the grade nine schoolyear was Kildonan East (KE). I recall that the rumors about the school were that it was fairly rough as well, and so I did not know what to expect.

Would it be like Brandon all over again, or would it be like Churchill?

Or would it be something completely new?

As it turned out, I was never to find out.

Right as the school year started, my father and his wife purchased a house on Trent Avenue, and as a result of the different school zone, I only attended KE for about a week, and was then transferred to Miles Macdonell Collegiate (MMC), which was grades nine through twelve.

This being the third time in as many years that I had changed schools, I had clued into the fact that this was an opportunity for me to recreate my image from school anti-mascot and into something far less sufferable.

However, I still had a huge problem; my eyesight had worsened to minus nine for each eye, which was near legally blind I believe.

Certainly, I couldn't t see squat without them.

A few days into this new school year at this new school, and I find myself in the main gym, trying very hard to look normal and not stick out.

MMC, at that time at least, is tops in volleyball in the city, and they have a formidable men's team that year, and they are practicing in the gym when I enter.

I walk about seven feet inside the gym doors and look about for any of the few classmates that I might recognize so early in the year. I am standing with my hands in my pockets, gazing into the crowd of students on the stage, who are mostly chatting and watching the practice, when suddenly I'm nailed right in the head by a spiked volleyball.

My glasses fly off and, half blind, I crawl around on the gym floor desperately searching for them for twenty seconds or so, all the while knowing that I am being zeroed in on by someone, as that hit had to have been intentional.

But I know that at minimum, half the gym must be watching and laughing at me.

I find my glasses and quickly stand up, not sure what to find in front of me when I open my eyes, expecting the normal hideous laugher to burst forth any moment from my antagonist and/or the majority of the students watching, who surely had seen what had just occurred.

My face is burning hot with humiliation, and expecting the worst, I put on my glasses and open my eyes.

To my surprise, no one is approaching me.

Not a single person in the gym is laughing.

The tall athletes continue their practice as if nothing had happened.

I peer about the gym suspiciously, for I know that these types of occurrences for me are never "accidents". Rather, they are intentional, repeated and systematic aggressions which will gradually increase over time, until mute terror is my daily companion in this school.

As I look around, I'm nailed a second time right in the head and my glasses flying off, again.

I drop to the ground, find them quickly, put them on, and without another look around I scramble from the gym, fearing to look behind me.

No one follows.

Sick to the stomach, I go straight home and ask my father if he will purchase contact lenses for me.

He looks at me blankly for a moment, and simply says "Absolutely".

I am elated.

That year passed without violence for me, but definitely not uneventfully.

For example, I got my first girlfriend, Bonnie.

About a foot shorter than me, she had gorgeous long flowing black hair and she was sweeter to me than any girl had been before.

However, she dumped me after about three months together to pursue a new amor, and that very first rejection by a girlfriend stung, as it normally would for any typical teenager, I largely suspect.

I didn't let that slow me down at all though. I was encouraged to try harder with girls, who seemed, to my great delight, to enjoy talking to the new and improved contact lens, brown corduroy pants, bright red short-sleeved button-down shirt, and grey leather zip tie wearing Micheal.

I also was adopted into an already formed group of friends who had known each other for years.

I was speechless at first when Craig, a man-boy on a huge Scottish frame, but with gentle blue eyes and a kind smile, out of seemingly nowhere asked me if I was interested in joining him and his friends in the library after school to play Dungeons & Dragons, a popular role playing game at the time.

I had no idea what D&D was or how to play, but Momma didn't raise no fool, and I eagerly accepted.

I instantly had an entire group of friends, and life was grand. My new circle at first extended only to those friends of Craig at the school; Chris, Craig's sister Christine, Pam, Maurice, Ted, Jason, the other Christine, and later Albert and his girlfriend Tamara, Alex and Darren.

Every one of them I still love with all my heart to this day. I don't think that they knew at that time what their acceptance meant to me, for I would never ever tell anyone of them what had transpired in my previous schools.

I didn't want them to think any less of me.

I grew in confidence and social skill over that year, feeling like I finally belonged somewhere.

I acted in the student play the next year, playing the part of the uncle in the school production of Lizzie Borden.

I also began dating a new beauty that second year at MMC, Allyson, with whom I had fallen in love on first sight very early on the previous school year, but hadn't been able to get up the nerve to ask her out.

I also gained the nickname Hextall, after my hockey hero Ron Hextall, who hailed from Brandon Manitoba and was the first-string goalie at the time for the Philadelphia Flyers, a rough and tumble hockey club of the National Hockey League (NHL). The Winnipeg Jets were always my first love of course, but Hextall was my first and only sports hero, for like me, he had an absolutely massive temper. His frequent two-handed backhands with his redwood of a goalie stick were renowned over the entire league, while his ability to handle the puck was unmatched.

I still have his autograph.

Thanks for waiting with me, Allyson.

"All meditative techniques, including concentration and visualization, are simply ways to connect to the source and to awaken gradually to the Buddha within - your original nature, your natural mind. This is what people in the theistic traditions sometimes call the Godhead, or Self with a capital S: the true Self, the natural state. We come to our true state only by the practice of purifying and mastering the heart and mind. If we master the mind by training it and bringing it back to the source, we arrive at and reconnect with our true state, which was there all the time." – Lama Surya Das

I memorized a sizeable passage from Shakespeare's Macbeth for English 100 my first year, presenting it nervously to the entire class.

I actually got a couple claps.

I was greatly encouraged.

The next year I would memorize an even longer passage from Romeo and Juliet, and my memory improved greatly over high school. Years later, quite for fun, I would memorize all one-hundred-and-eight lines of Edgar Allan Poe's "The Raven", and would be able to recite it at will for years, inspired by, what else, but the TV show, The Simpsons.

Before long in that second year, Allyson and I were high school sweethearts and one could rarely ever see us apart. We hung out with our circle of friends in the cafeteria pretty much every day playing Oli, a card game more well known as Asshole. We were a decent bunch of kids and were not particularly keen on the original game name, so we opted for another, after Oliver North, a US general and National Security Council staff member during the Iran-Contra affair, a political scandal of the late 1980s. He was on TV all the time, and we felt his name would fit more than suitably for our purposes.

Those friends were Mark, Jim, Murray, Gordon (Hoodaa!), Pam and others whose names escape me many years later.

Some years after high school, Mark would succumb to a medical condition that he courageously suffered through since childhood I believe, and I grieved for him deeply.

While writing this book, I would learn that my sweet friend Murray passed away from a stroke.

I miss him.

Sometime during that year though, for a reason that I cannot remember, I decided that I would like to try meditation, and the first place that I located in the yellow pages was an organization for transcendental meditation.

It was a two-week course, and I not-infrequently used that meditation from time to time to ease the intense headaches that I had felt periodically for years.

I was only threatened with violence twice in all those years of high school at MMC.

The first time was by a shifty character well known in the school for hanging out at the back doors of the school and smoking pot, whom I will call Bill. Very early on the first year in the school cafeteria, for some offence that I cannot remember, perhaps he demanded that I give up my seat to him and I refused, I cannot recall, but he was quick to challenge me.

"Meet me by the back doors after school."

The second threat was from Bonnie's new boyfriend. He had been the star that first year in the school's production of Dracula, which had been an absolutely massive success. His role as Dracula was simply spectacular, and one could easily see why Bonnie was drawn to him.

I saw them in the cafeteria sometime after they got together, and I spitefully gave him the evil-eye. When Bonnie left, he walked over to me and said: "If you have any problems with me going out with Bonnie, we can meet after school by the back doors."

Now, I would not blame a soul for thinking that these encounters must have chilled me to the bone, given my life experience with aggression thus far. And to be sure, I was incredulous, though not for the reason that one might expect.

For you see, both of these boys had given me the <u>option</u> of getting the tar beat out of me, or not. And, as I have previously iterated, Momma didn't raise no fool. I was a coward, through and through, I had absolutely no doubt about that, and I simply didn't show.

And that, as they say somewhere in the South Sudan, or so I've heard, was that.

September – 1988
Winnipeg – Manitoba

In my first year of grade twelve, Maurice and I became the best of buds.

We hung out together all the time, our senses of humor being highly compatible. Our dance moves were killer on the Norma Jeans dancefloor, a very popular hotspot in Winnipeg at the time. We would go so often that we had VIP cards, the primary function of these cards ostensibly being to avoid the busy wait line out front, by allowing card holders to use the VIP designated entrance at the rear of the building. However, the bar was so popular that more people had VIP cards than did not, and it would not be unusual for us to use the front door anyway.

Good-bye one-hundred and twenty-five bucks.

I highly valued Maurice's friendship during those years, and I missed him terribly when he moved away to pursue a career in a branch of the Canadian military. He went on to have a highly successful and respectable career.

About that time, Craig and Pam began dating and would eventually go on to marry and have three beautiful girls. She is Polish and at the time danced with a professional dance group, The Sokol Polish Folk Ensemble, which consisted of a choir and a dance group. They performed many years during Folklorama at the Krakow Polish Pavilion, and the festival was a highly successful international cultural event for many years, and I believe it still continues to this very day.

Pam danced at Folklorama that year, and she "dragged" her boyfriend Craig along. Given his size, he was tasked with pavilion security, and he invited me along to keep him company.

And I am so glad that he did, as I had an absolute blast.

The people were friendly, the food was awesome, but what really intrigued me was the dancing. The dance group consisted of about ten to twelve dancers at the time, ranging in age from about sixteen to, I want to say, thirty or so. They did about four dances a show and about four shows a day, and the pavilion operated for seven days.

Right from the first show that I saw, I was highly enamored of the dancing. Every chance that I got, I would sit upstairs in the cultural exhibit area which had a window overlooking the stage downstairs, and pay close attention to every single dance that they did. As the reader may recall, I was exposed to music and dancing at the parties on Westaway Bay as a child, and so presumedly had a modicum of rhythm.

I would return with Craig to the pavilion the next year.

All of my friends graduated high school on time in the summer of 1988, but I did not. And this was my doing, I readily admit.

Over the years at MMC, I had gained quite the reputation as a floor hockey goalie, which I hugely enjoyed, and during grades elven and twelve, I would skip any class in order to participate in any floor hockey block that came available. As a result, I failed English 300 three times. I was doing well in school when I attended classes, but I loved the game and being popular so much that I could not pass up a chance to play.

I stayed for an additional year at MMC and did graduate in 1989, but by then, things had changed for me and Allyson.

After graduation, she immediately went into nursing school, from which she would graduate four years later and then go on to have a spectacular nursing career in the US.

I, on the other hand, spent one more year in high school, and then took a year off because I had absolutely no idea what I wanted to do.

Life up that point had been basically about survival, and while the years at MMC were the best years of my entire schooling to be sure, my mental and social development was still deficient in many ways, and thus at that time in my life, I just could not fathom how I might contribute to society in terms of vocation.

Over those years, Allyson and I drifted apart and would break up and get back together a handful of times. Our interests had grown apart though, and I was more interested in playing NHL Hockey with Chris than doing anything productive with my life, and she and I ended our relationship during the summer of 1990.

Chapter 9

Early Spring – 1990
Winnipeg, Manitoba, Canada

*"If you depend on others to make you happy, you'll be
endlessly disappointed." – Unknown*

Some early that year, a friend would set me up with very
nice girl, and we would date for a few months that year.

I have named in this book some of those that I feel hurt
me significantly in my life, but I will not identify this
person, because simply, shortly after we started dating,
she explained some of her own demons to me, and while
this particular life event for me would be highly damaging
to my, unbeknownst to me at the time, already
destabilizing state of mind, I knew, even at the time, that
she was just doing the best she could to move on in her
own life.

My girlfriend and I are driving in her sportscar down
Lagimodière Boulevard on a dark and cloudy summer day.

We are arguing.

Again.

Suddenly, her face changes, and I clearly see that she has
had enough of this conversation. She pulls over to the side
of the road and tells me to get out of her car.

I comply, and she drives off.

I stare baffled after her departing vehicle, confused as to what has just happened. Surely she would not leave me here. She is just angry and will come back when she cools off.

She doesn't.

And the heavens open

It is at this point that I suffer my first partial mental collapse.

I am drenched in seconds, but I make no effort to get out of the downpour. Instead, I simply start walking towards Regent Avenue.

Raging in my head is the painful acknowledgement that yet again, many years after I have moved out of my mother's house, despite all the improvements that I have made to this excuse of an existence, I continue to fail the prominent female figure in my life, and yet again, I'm being punished by her for simply existing.

Tears are unnoticeably merging with the rain drenching me, and by both freely run through every piece of clothing that I have on.

I am unable to make any decision about any facet of my current circumstance.

Should I go back and wait for her more?

How do I get home?

Will she be angry if she goes back for me and I am not there?

Taking the bus does not occur to me, nor does calling someone for help.

My thoughts are foggy and slow as I plod along in the pouring rain. For the entire two-hour walk home, I ball my eyes out like a nine-year-old child and punish myself physically for my horrible failure with this woman, by violently and repeatedly punching myself in the head and thighs, and by biting my arms and hands.

The darkness growing in me deepens considerably.

Last day of the Krakow Polish Pavilion, Folklorama – August – 1990
Winnipeg – Manitoba

Folklorama time came around again, and Craig and I eagerly headed off to the Krakow Polish pavilion with visions of Pierogis and Kiełbasas dancing in our heads.

However, things would go quite unexpectedly this year.

As in previous years, I paid avid attention to every single dance during that week that the pavilion was operational. I grew quite familiar with the choreography for several of the dances, including in particular, a super-goofy and lively dance called Polka Baciarska.

This dance required between four and six couples to dress in outlandishly styled and mismatched color suits for the men, and dresses and blouses for the women. It was a fairly long dance, and the basic story told was one of the love of dance, drink, fatigue and hilarity.

And I absolutely loved it.

I had grown to know most of the dancers, and I hung out with them every chance that I got.

Typically, the very last show of the very last night at this pavilion was the night that the choir and dancers relaxed and engaged in pranks of various kinds, on either the choir conductor or the dance choreographer, but most usually both.

For example, the choir might change the order of the songs without informing the conductor, or the dancers might switch costumes, the men wearing the women's dresses, and the women wearing the men's suits.

It was always in good fun, and this particular year the dance crew approached me with an idea; they knew that I had been paying particularly close attention to the choreography for Polka Baciarska, and they asked me to take the place of one of the dancers to see if the choreographer noticed.

I eagerly agreed, for I was very sweet on the beauty that was to be my partner, else I likely would have been too shy.

The ploy went off spectacularly; my steps were nowhere near perfect, but the very unique nature of that dance was that it was all in good fun, so I had been relaxed ahead of time that no one would even notice, much less care.

As soon as it was over, all us dancers ran back to the change room, laughing and clapping each other on the back, as it appeared that the choreographer didn't notice the doppelganger amongst her crew.

I was removing my borrowed costume when suddenly everyone stopped talking. I turned around slowly, and the choreographer was standing right in front of me.

She gave me the cool measure of her eye and simply said, "Dance practice is Tuesdays at 7:00 PM. I expect to see you there next week."

She then turned around sharply and walked back through the crowd of dancers and singers, many of whom were smiling at me from ear to ear.

And just like that, I was a member of the Sokol Polish Folk Ensemble dance troop.

I first dated one gorgeous girl in the group, and after a short while, moved to a second.

However, as the second relationship wore on, I began to inexplicably become unhappy, both in the relationship and in my life in general.

Dancing was great and I had thrown myself into it, heart and soul. I had finished my first year of computer sciences at Red River College, having promised my father when I finished high school that if I could not think of something that I wanted to pursue in terms of vocation by the time one year had passed, I would go to college and gain some work skills.

On no Sunday in particular, my girlfriend and I were attending their family church for a reason that I cannot now remember. It had been many years since I was in a church, and as the sermon was given and the congregation sat, prayed, stood, sang, sat, listened, sang, prayed and so forth, I dismally contemplated the sequence of events that led me to leave the church many years earlier.

Suddenly, I remembered that I had a five-dollar bill in my pocket.

My heart quickened.

"Is it too late?" I asked myself.

Maybe not.

When the collection plate arrived at our row, I reached into my pants pocket and pull out the bill and cupped it in my hand. As the plate came to me on my right, I took the plate with my right hand, and moved the left to drop the money in.

At that very moment, my girlfriend sitting on my left, reaches over with her left hand and covers my hand holding the money, looks me square in the eye, and shakes her head.

Momentarily baffled, I didn't drop the money in, and the collection plate quickly moved off.

I had no idea why she did that, and I further had absolutely no idea why I let her stop me, yet again, from giving back to God that five dollars that I had foolishly spent on sugar and arcade games so many years previous.

Immediately, I became very upset with myself once again.

"Why did I let her stop me?" I lamented.

Again, I'd failed at paying back a long overdue debt, and I held my girlfriend at least partially responsible, and I broke up with her shortly thereafter.

Neither my mother nor I had made any attempt at communication with each other over the few years after I so abruptly left her home.

However, sometime after my eighteenth birthday in 1988 and during the Christmas holidays, I was feeling particularly depressed, and I allowed my sister to convince me to come with her and visit with that side of the family.

Mother and her husband had had a second child, a beautiful baby girl with down syndrome, and they were living at the time in a decent area of the city, somewhere in the northwest corner, just past Keewatin.

They had begun investing in rental properties in the city, and during these next few years my mother and I were able to restore our relationship to something actually nice. She was very mentally stable through these years, and we grew close.

We didn't though ever talk about my exit from her household or <u>any</u> of the previous events prior to my departure.

I helped her manage her properties until she and her family move up north, for her husband had graduated university and had accepted a principal position in a school up there, as the northern location bonuses were very good.

They would live up there for a number of years, and I would have virtually no contact with her during that time.

My sister and I had moved out of my father's home, as he and his second wife had had a child, a boy, and would soon have a girl as well. My sister and I decided that it was now time to give our father space. Afterall, he had been newly married when we suddenly took over the household some eight years previous, and we knew that we had to give him space to raise his new family.

My sister and I rented the lower level of nearby townhouse.

Early Spring – 1992
A Robin's Donuts Shop – Winnipeg

*"To recognize that you are the source of your own
loneliness is not a cure for it. But it is a step toward seeing
that it is not inevitable, and that such a choice is not
irrevocable."*
- Robin Hobb, Golden Fool

It had been over a year now since I'd had a date, much less a girlfriend, and this girlfriend-less stretch was really the first significant one that I had experienced since I began dating in grade ten.

As the weeks and then months without a prominent trusted female figure in my life to provide me with constant emotional support wore on, the world around me began to gradually lose its brightness. It got harder and harder to get out of bed in the morning, and when I did, the world just didn't seem as interesting.

I was all too familiar with the feeling of course, for it had permeated my being for as long as I could remember; depression.

I was working. I had gotten my first job as a fry guy when I was sixteen, and soon graduated to line cook, and as soon as I turned eighteen, I began waiting tables which, by far, was the best bang for your buck.

At this particular juncture, I was waiting tables at a family restaurant on Leila and had been there for a while. I continued to dance with Sokol, and I had started taking private lessons with fellow dancer and the daughter of the choreographer, who was somewhat older than I. Her previous partner had been South American, and so she was quite accomplished with South American dance steps, not the least of which was Lambada.

By this time, we had already been dancing privately together for some time. She and I were great friends; she was pretty, really funny, super smart, and when our bodies rubbed together on the dance floor...Hubba Hubba!!

But this was the first real friendship I had had in my life with a woman. Up till then, I had only dated them. And I begin to confuse our deepening friendship, combined with the sexual excitement that can normally come up during dancing and the loneliness that had slowly been increasing in intensity, and I decided that I wanted to be a hero to her, a knight in shining armor, if you will.

She was divorced at this point from a very abusive husband and had a child, a young boy of about six or so. The scenario reminded me of my own all but fatherless childhood, and I remember not wanting her boy growing up without a consistent ethical male presence in his life, and in my young foolishness, I thought that maybe I could prevent that.

So on no particular day, I called my dance partner and asked her to meet me for coffee, to which she readily agreed.

Sometime later, she arrived, got a coffee and sat down across from me at the table I had been holding for some time.

I delivered my offer.

She listened calmly to what I had to say, and then sat silently for a time.

My heart was in my mouth, but I waited patiently.

Being far wiser than I, and knowing me as she did, she told me that, tempting as it was, I was not ready for this kind of commitment, and besides, she had just begun dating an old flame.

I knew that she was right, but it smarted badly, and my world became just a little bit darker.

I would come to label this desire to save my partners as my Knight in Shining Armor Syndrome, and it would have an indelible impact on many future relationships.

Chapter 10

Summer – 1992
Treherne – Manitoba

The dance troop was there to participate in a cultural festival that takes place in this quiet rural area each year. The event is always well attended by the public and other Polish and Ukrainian dance troops, from all over the province.

Some months had passed since the donut shop denial, and my mood was constantly dark. The red-hot fury that now seemed to permanently reside within my chest meant that my temper has returned in full force, and I constantly lost it at the simplest things that do not go the way that I want.

But dancing and hanging out with my friends in the troop was keeping me going somehow. I was also starting university in the fall, and those two things kept me moving forward, if all but grudgingly.

While I had absolutely no interest in dating anyone at this time, during the weekend, I spotted and then kept my eye on a young, dark-eyed, dark-haired Ukrainian dancer from Dauphin.

I never approached her though, and the weekend passed, and I returned to the city.

First Half of 1993
Winnipeg – Manitoba

"Find joy in everything you choose to do. Every job, relationship, home... it's your responsibility to love it, or change it." – Chuck Palahniuk

After finishing one year of community college just over a year ago, I had decided that computer programming was not the path for me, and spent the next year trying to figure out what I wanted to do with my life. Not having taken to that science, I wracked my brain for something that I really enjoyed doing, having received that advice from multiple sources.

The reader will hopefully recall that I was particularly skilled at accents, and my repertoire had grown to some thirty-four different accents and voices by this age.

Additionally, having been hanging with the Polish dance troop for some years, I had absorbed some of the language quite readily, and was constantly complimented on my pronunciation and accent by the Polish community.

I realized that learning languages was what I really enjoyed doing at this time in my life.

I thus decided to go to the University of Manitoba to study languages, with an eye to working for the Canadian Foreign Service in the future as a diplomat, and then maybe later for the United Nations.

That first year I studied Russian, German, Polish and Spanish, and topped it all off with a single course in International Relations. The professor who taught that course was British, much to my delight, and had the storytelling ability of a bard, and I was completely enamored of his stories of international diplomatic crises over the last few decades, rounded out nicely with considerable information about his expertise, anti-terrorism.

Now, writing things by hand was never my forte. The reader will hopefully non-judgmentally recall that I had failed English 300 at MMC three times, and I had finally only earned the necessary credit in English to graduate by taking and passing the lower level 301 class.

I was highly dreading having to write university essays by hand, which I had been forewarned was unescapable in this type of course.

However, fate would be exceptionally kind to me, for the university had several newish large computer labs, which meant that I could type up my papers electronically, and I actually was a pretty decent typist by this time, having been provided many such classes through high school, and I had also owned a personal computer for a number of years.

My first university paper was on the Vietnam War, and my first submission came in at roughly one hundred pages.

I got a B-plus.

I was flabbergasted.

I went to graduate student that had graded the paper, and she advised me that it was far too long, other students having only written about twenty or thirty pages.

I asked if I could rewrite it, and this was graciously allowed, and I ended up with an A-minus.

I would receive only one paper marked lower than an A for the remainder of the years that I studied at this exceptionally fine institute of higher learning. However, by graduation, my GPA was quite low, not having attended the student orientation that was offered each year for new students, and I did not learn until the middle of my second year when and how to drop classes that I was not doing well in.

Laziness and beer may also have had something to do with it.

The very next year I would declare political studies my major and would go on to write up to four major papers a year.

During that summer though, I moved in with Chris, a friend of mine that the reader may recall from my D&D days at high school, and a couple of his roommates on Nassau Street North. He and I would become the best of friends over the next couple decades, and the course of his life would eventually change the course of my life, as later that same year he would leave on the adventure of a lifetime though South America.

Long before this eventuality though, we had a number of well attended parties in that tall three-story brick house, in addition to several Hat Nights. Chris and I drank a lot of beer together, and I really came to admire him deeply for his happy-go-lucky approach to life.

Summer of 1993
Treherne – Manitoba

The dance troop was again in Treherne to participate in the annual cultural festival in the area, and very early on in the festival I spotted that same dark-eyed, dark-haired beauty from last summer.

But that past year, having been especially lonely, gave me the impetus that I needed to talk to her, and we hit it off instantly. We continued to date through the summer, and I would drive up to Dauphin whenever I could. Work was good and I had purchased a new sporty black Chevy Cavalier without needing a cosigner.

We fell in love.

As time went on, we began to talk about moving in together when she turned eighteen, myself being twenty-three at the time, but she was scared that her parents would never allow her to move out of her family home, so she being young and innocent, and I being older biologically yet immature mentally, we concocted a highly inadvisable plan.

When her family went on a trip and left her home to tend the farm with her younger brother, I drove up and picked her up with a couple suitcases and took her to live with me in Winnipeg.

Now, I knew at the time that there were many better ways to continue our relationship without putting her family through this terrible ordeal, but so enamored of her was I, that I refused to even consider them.

We lived together for considerably less than a year as I recall. As soon as she had moved in though, my darkness returned. I felt terrible guilt for the pain that I had caused her family by not being more mature about the whole circumstance, but what was done could not be undone.

We broke up less than a year later.

Some weeks after, she asked me for one of the chairs that we had bought together, a wicker rocking chair.

She came and picked it up herself, noted to me that I looked sad, and I never saw or heard from her again.

I slipped deeper and deeper into a depression over the next three years or so, dating sporadically from time to time but having no meaningful romantic relationships. My darkness had been my constant companion since childhood, and so I didn't realize anything was wrong with me.

I forged on ahead at university and made some great friends at the steakhouse that I worked at, primary of which were Tony and Heather, he hailing from the UK, and she from the US, I believe.

Tony and I became great friends, and we would hang out together after most shifts and put back a couple pitchers of dark ale, and eat at least fifty chicken wings absolutely lathered in Head Cook Davian's incredibly hot, yet superbly delicious, suicide sauce.

Rumor had it that he let it age for two weeks prior to serving it.

And this was when I began to drink heavily.

Prior to this, I would estimate that I drank pretty much like my friends, but I absolutely abhorred people who got drunk and did the most ridiculous of things. I found that lack of control and judgment in others when inebriated to be anathema to me, and I scorned those who drank too much. I had seen so much of it in my family growing up that I swore I would be better than that.

I would fail.

Summer – 1995
A Small Town on the Western Border – Alberta

"We're the middle children of history, man. No purpose or place. We have no Great War. No Great Depression. Our great war is a spiritual war. Our great depression is our

lives."
- Tyler Durden, Fight Club (1999)

I bussed to this small town to pick up my new car, a 1995, 275-horespower Black Chevy Camaro Z28.

It cost me just over $40,000.

How did I get it?

My mother co-signed the loan.

I had picked up a second job and was now making too much money to qualify for a student loan to help pay my university tuition, so I decided to take a year off, pick up a third job, and bank some serious cash with which to finish my Bachelor of Arts degree.

I hadn't had any romantic prospects for some years now, and my loneliness was all-encompassing. When I did not have a woman in my life providing me with acceptance and love, there was nothing to hold my darkness at bay.

I moved through those days, weeks, months and then years on automatic pilot; study, work, drink...study, work, drink, and so on, and so forth.

With more money pouring in than I'd ever had before, I got the brilliant idea that buying a nice new sportscar might give me the confidence boost I needed to meet that special someone. But my credit was shite...I had never learned any budgeting skills, and so always paid pretty much every bill late.

I asked my dad to co-sign, and he sagely thought for a moment, and simply said, "No".

Desperate to change the energy level in my life, I decided to do something that I had never done before.

I asked my mom for help.

Now I am not blaming this on her. I bought the car, and I did end up paying it off completely, after a fashion, but this was an incredibly stupid decision that I made.

And why she said yes, I will never know. She had recently left her second husband up north and brought my brother and sister back with her to Winnipeg. We reconnected upon her return and spent some time together.

January – 1996
My Third Job

"As the moon bows before the brilliance of the sun, so must this rose yield to your beauty." – Unknown

I started working in an upper-class restaurant at the beginning of that year serving tables to pay for my horribly expense car.

I was drinking more and more to medicate my darkness, though of course I don't know that this was what I was doing. All I knew was that when I drank alcohol, I felt a lot less terrible. Up to that point I had been primarily a beer drinker, but after a wine sampling upon my hire at this high-class restaurant, I gained an intense appreciation for quality red.

Early that year, I was horribly enamoured of one of the hostesses there. She was the perfect woman for me; gorgeous, flirtatious and feisty, with a constantly brilliant, happy smile.

And I fell madly in love.

That Valentine's Day, I secretly sent her a dozen yellow roses with a poem that I had specially created for her.

That was all that I had the courage to do.

She was way out of my league.

Shortly after, that luminous being that I thought the universe rotated around suddenly died by suicide.

I wondered if my anonymous Valentine's Day gift played any part.

And I think that perhaps I should have been braver.

Maybe I could have saved her.

I began to drink more often, and more intensely.

January – 1997
The Same Restaurant

"The human heart was built to break." – Stephen Jenkinson, Die Wise, 2015

I was back in university now, taking just a few classes to move my degree along while continuing to work three jobs. I now wouldn't graduate by April, and so planned to take some courses in the summer, though I likely would still need to take a half-credit course or two in the fall to complete my degree.

My plans for my future were still basically the same, but I had decided by this point that it might be helpful to gain some international experience after completing my degree, while at the same time banking a decent amount of cash to pay off my growing debt, by taking an ESL teaching position somewhere in Southeast Asia. I had calculated that after one year of working overseas, I should have enough money to live and work in Europe for some time. With my language and political studies progressing nicely, I had become obsessed with the idea of traveling to Germany, Russia, France and Spain before submitting an application to the Canadian Foreign Service.

I was folding linens in the basement when she descended the stairs, and as I looked up and saw this newly hired waitress and our eyes connected for the first time, such was the existential shock that I swear our souls recognize each other.

We instantly connected on the deepest level that I have ever connected with anyone up till that point in my life, and we fell madly in love.

About four months later, I moved out of the house that my sister and I were renting on Fifth Avenue (no, not that 5th Avenue), and into my new girlfriend's apartment right across from Churchill School.

She was so smart, and our senses of humor were a dead ringer for each other.

Life was great.

For an all too short while.

Late March – 1997
A Country Bar in Winnipeg

"Take your shot, Funboy. You got me, dead bang." – Eric Draven, The Crow (1994)

My girlfriend and I had an argument of some sort much earlier in the day, and I've shown up unannounced to try to talk with her. This is her favorite hangout and has been for years. She knows everyone here. Her ex-boyfriend is a bouncer here.

I haven't yet clued in that I struggle to deal emotionally when the primary female figure in my life is angry with me; disharmony in love sends me crashing into darkness.

I find her easy enough on the dancefloor and wait for the song to finish.

As all songs do, it does, and she walks directly away from me.

I slip quickly through the crowd and reach out after her and grab her arm.

She knows that it's me, and spins instantly around.

"If you don't leave right now, I am going to have the bouncers remove you." she spits menacingly.

The universe itself seems to stop moving.

The other patrons inside the bar fade from my vision, and all I can see is the violent anger in her face directed at me, the woman that professes to me every morning that we wake up together in our bed, that she loves me with her whole heart and soul.

This is the woman that I have chosen to give my love to, and she is distinctly threatening to have the shit beat out of me.

I feel instantly betrayed by the woman that I love and trust the most in the world.

Again.

Red fury bursts forth in my chest, and I snap.

I lose it.

"WHO THE FUCK DO YOU THINK YOU ARE?" I scream in her face.

Without thinking, I reach out with both hands and shove her roughly backward.

Her mouth drops open in complete astonishment.

"FUCK YOU!" I yell in her face with all the force that I can muster, turn and stalk from the bar.

As I'm clearing the front doors, I realize what I've done. I have physically assaulted another human being again, and I am instantly ashamed.

And then, as I am walking the thirty feet or so to my car, I hear the heavy wooden doors open and close behind me, and I hear booted feet following at a steady pace behind me.

Momma didn't raise no fool, and I instantly comprehend my situation. One or more of her male friends, having witnessed my furious act of aggression on their female friend, have decided to even the score.

The steps are steady and slow, so I unhurriedly finish the brief walk to my car, unlock it with the remote, open the door, throw in my keys, close and lock the door, and turn to face the music.

Approaching and then stopping about ten feet in front of me is one of her many friends here, who I instantly recognize. He is about the same size as me, is wearing dark blue jeans and a black long sleeve shirt, a cowboy hat and shit-kicker boots, and I have absolutely no doubt that he is going to mop the parking lot with me.

I resign myself to my fate.

"Look," I calmly say. "I know why you are here, and frankly I don't give a fuck. You are right, and I deserve to have the shit beat out of me for what I did. I regretted it instantly, if that makes any difference. I won't fight back. Do what you think you need to do."

And then I simply stand there, my arms hanging limp by my sides.

I know that he is quite drunk, and I look directly into his eyes as he stands there, staring right back at me.

I cannot read his dark expression.

After about twenty seconds, he turns around and walks back into the bar.

I key in the remote code on the keyless entry pad on my vehicle door, get in and go home, alone.

Early April – 1997
Our Apartment – Winnipeg

My girlfriend and I made up and I had recently moved into her place across from Churchill School.

Things were going smoothly, and she wanted me to meet a couple of her male friends, and so we agreed to host them in our apartment. By this time, I had quite the taste for red wine, as did she, and so we picked up five or six bottles of various types.

The evening went smashingly. I really liked these guys, and they seemed to really like me.

As the late hour approached, my girlfriend, quite sleepy from the red wine, retired to the bedroom and left the three of us to finish the open bottle of wine, which we did all too quickly.

But we were having a lot of fun talking together, and so we opened another.

And then another.

And then the last one.

We said our goodnights and I crawled into bed beside my girlfriend, very pleased with the whole affair.

Early the next morning, I was roughly woken from my drunken stupor to find my girlfriend hovering over my head. I could easily tell though that she was furious.

"You drank all the red wine?" she yells. "That was for you and me to share!"

I rubbed my eyes, trying to figure out where the hell I was. And then memory of the pleasant evening previous came flooding back.

"What's the problem?" I mumbled as I sat up in bed, rubbing the sleep out of my eyes.

"I'll go buy some more later." I said, figuring that should solve the program.

Silly rabbit. Trix are for kids, for she then screamed in my face;

"And those are MY friends, not YOURS!"

I remember blinking several times.

"Sorry" I mumbled. "I won't hang out with them anymore."

With one last murderous look, she turned and stalked from the room.

Mid-April – 1997
On my Way Home

I've just finished my shift and am heading home down Pembina in my speedy black Camaro Z28.

I've distinctly noticed that it has not improved my mood at all, and the thing is costing me an arm and a leg.

As I pass Jubilee on my right, a vehicle comes through the yield right behind me and comes right up on my rear bumper.

Peering into the rearview mirror, I see a non-descript fiftyish male in a white t-shirt and jean jacket glaring at me. He is driving a 1972-ish boat of some kind, and I'm mildly surprised that it is still running.

Anywho, the old gaffer ain't too happy with me for some reason; I never did find out why.

I take my foot off the gas so that I slow down enough to let him pass, but instead, he stays in my lane right on my ass, and as I simply let my vehicle roll to a stop, he inches the front bumper of his vehicle until it is snug up to my rear bumper,.

And then floors the gas pedal.

As my sportscar is jolted forward by the force of the vehicle behind me, I quickly hammer the brakes, and our vehicles basically stop moving, though the aggressor keeps his foot on the gas and his almost-bald times simply spin in place.

I pull out my shoebox-size mobile phone and call 911.

As soon and the guy behind me easily spies my huge monstrosity of a wireless communication device, he takes his foot off the gas, throws his car into reverse, squeals the tires backing up about four feet, and then hammers the gear and floors it.

As I watch in astonishment, his vehicle pulls even with mine, he turns his head towards me and gives me the finger as he passes by.

Just Prior to Final Exams – Late April – 1997

"The things you own end up owning you." – Tyler Durden, Fight Club (1999)

For the first time ever, I decided to take a very close look at my finances, and very quickly realized that I was far too in debt to be able to climb out any decade soon. One of the jobs that I had been working ended unexpectedly sometime back, and I had been without warning, yet unsurprisingly, fired from that second restaurant job that I had picked up to help pay for that insanely expensive purchase.

What I reluctantly concluded was that I was financially boned.

After talking my situation over with my dad, I decided to declare bankruptcy.

It was a sound financial decision.

A couple days later, I sold the Camaro to a dealer and got shite for it, and as mother had co-signed the loan, I still had some twelve thousand plus dollars of it to pay off, or her credit would take a massive hit.

Things between my girlfriend and I had been getting better and better, and I was beginning to second-guess my decision to go overseas. I loved this woman with a fiery passion that I had never felt before, and so based on that love, I made a fateful decision.

At the end of a long and particularly profitable week of tips at the original and only job I had left, I bought a very inexpensive, but quite sparkly, diamond engagement ring.

The next Friday night, I waited for my amora nervously in our home. She was serving tables, so I didn't expect that she would be home until around 10:00 PM or so.

By midnight she hadn't returned home, so I went to bed.

She came home around noon the next day, advising that she had stayed at her mother's.

I accepted this answer, but my spidey-sense started to tingle, and so I decided not to say anything about what was burning a hole in my pocket.

The same thing happened the next night; she did not return home after work.

My spidey-sense went on tilt.

I have absolutely no idea why, but right about the witching hour, I pulled out my girlfriend's address book from under the phone in the living room, and flipped to the page where her ex-boyfriend's address and phone number were listed.

I noted the address and sped across town on my twelve-speed bike, as I no longer had wheels.

I arrived at the address and low and behold, parked directly in front of his house was my girlfriend's white car.

Again, I instantly realised that this woman that I am so in love with, and that I've changed my dreams for, has again betrayed my trust, this time though, the betrayal was penultimate; my love for her was not good enough, just as it never was for my mother.

My sanity began to waver.

I went home, and to bed.

The next morning, she arrived home and I met her at the door and greeted her with a smile.

"Where were you last night?" I politely inquired.

"I spent the night at my mom's again."

"Really?" I followed up. "Then why was your car parked outside of your ex-boyfriend's house?"

She was facing away from me and so I saw the instant tension in her shoulders. She did not turn around though, but simply said, "Yes, his truck broke down and so I lent him my car."

"Well that was a very nice thing to do." I stated matter-of-factly and dropped the issue.

She did not come home that night, so bright and early in the wee hours of the morning, I again hopped on my bike and rode the half hour or so back to her ex-boyfriend's place.

Her car was nowhere to be seen out front of the house, but Momma didn't raise no fool, and I circled around the block to the backlane that ran behind his house, and rode up to his garage.

I dismounted my vehicle and fearlessly opened the unlocked gate, entered the property and peered through the dirty garage window, and low-and-behold, guess whose car was in there.

Well, to be sure, I was in full denial.

"Maybe its true," I deluded myself.

"Maybe he just parked it in there overnight to protect it."

It was a rough area after all.

But deep down, even though part of my mind crumbling mind was actively trying to delude itself into believing that she might not be in that house, I knew that regardless of the facts, if I waited until later to confront her at her apartment, she would just deny it yet again.

On this realization, I walked my bike down the backlane a few houses and placed it out of sight behind another garage. I then peered out from behind that garage and back down towards his house, his yard, his garage, and my girlfriend's car.

And I waited.

I didn't have to wait long.

After about twenty minutes, the garage door suddenly opened, her car backed out, the garage door began closing automatically, and the vehicle promptly started driving down the back lane, directly away from me.

As it pulled away, I saw the back of her ponytail poking out over the driver seat headrest, through the back window.

It was at that point that I believe that I suffered my second partial mental collapse.

"I strove to find and examine the pieces and forces that had determined why my life had gone as it had. Yet the more I studied...the more the truth eluded me. What life showed me, in my years apart from the world, was that no man ever gets to know the whole of a truth."
- Robin Hobb, Fool's Errand

As my girlfriend is driving in her car down the back lane and away from her ex-boyfriend's house and me, I jump on my bike and start peddling furiously after her.

I know that I need to confront her now. If she gets away, she will just lie to me again, and I want to put this to bed right now (pun intended).

Her car turns right out of the backlane and onto the street, and five long seconds later I round the corner sharply after her on my bike and hop the curb to conserve speed.

Her vehicle is at the end of the block, stopped at the red light, waiting to turn left towards her apartment.

I panic.

If she gets onto Burrows Avenue, I will never catch her, and I realize that I must stop her vehicle at any cost.

I double my speed.

The traffic light turns green, but her car does not move.

Now, the reader will hopefully recall that by this time I have been Polish dancing for seven years, and so my legs were quite strong; in my furious determination to catch the vehicle and confront this betrayal once and for all, I triple my speed.

My mental state has completely fragmented, and I really have no idea what I am going to do when I catch up to the car to get her attention.

As I pull up alongside the left side of her still unmoving vehicle, I simply cock my right arm back towards my left shoulder and slap her driver-side window with my right palm.

As I do so however, my shift in weight on the bike causes my handlebars to dip slightly to the right, and the right handlebar catches on her driver-side rear view mirror, wrenching the front tire of my bike sharply to the right, and I somersault right off the bike and none to gracefully through the air.

As I am airborne, this is the thought that goes though my head;

"Years later, I am going to look back on this and laugh."

And right I was.

But I am not laughing this day, and gravity takes over and I land flat on my back some six feet ahead of her vehicle, and then slide for an additional three or four feet. Ignoring the pain as I decades ago had learned to do, I pick myself up off the ground and limp back to her vehicle.

She is sitting in her car with her hands on the wheel at ten and two, simply staring at me though her closed driver-side window, mouth hanging open so widely that I probably could have parked a semi in it.

Instead, I simply pick up my bike, jump on and peddle though the intersection, the traffic light still being green.

She immediately follows me in her car, shouting at me to stop through her now open passenger window.

I stop.

We have words, hers pleading, mine sharp.

"Please, lets talk about this Micheal. I can explain."

"Explanation is not necessary" I say simply.

I ride to her apartment, call my friend Albert, and he and I move my things out in less than an hour.

I would not speak with her again for over a decade.

Summer – 1997

"There's a difference between knowing the path, and walking the path."
– Morpheus, The Matrix (1999)

I applied myself to my university final exams like an escaping prisoner digging a tunnel to freedom, for I finally knew where I was going if I could graduate; out of this country and far away from her, to South Korea.

But I was eighteen full credit hours shy of qualifying to graduate, and so, desperate to escape the city where I might run into her one day, I registered for all eighteen credit hours over the six weeks of summer. Which was insane. But I felt quite insane. Perhaps I was insane. I don't really recall, to be honest.

Every day and night for those many weeks, my mind was numb; It was all I could do to concentrate on my studies, and perhaps it was those very studies that kept my mind off of my broken heart, and thus held my fragile state of mind somewhat together.

I planted myself for the entire summer in the Student Building computer lab and turned out paper after paper, even posting an A in my *United Nations in World Politics* course.

In my *Comparative World Religions* course, I dove especially deep into the questions of religion and the existence of a higher being, and when people would ask me about my religion over the next many years, I would advise them that I was not a religious person whatsoever, but that I did identify very closely with Buddhism, though I did not practice it at all.

While completing my studies that summer, I posted my application to a recruiter in South Korea and accepted the first job that I was offered.

As soon as I finished my last exam, I got the fuck outta Dodge.

"I will miss the sea. But a person needs new experiences. They jar something deep inside, allowing them to grow. Without change, something sleeps inside us, and seldom awakens.
The sleeper must awaken." – Dune (1984)

My friend Chris had returned from South America by that time with a Brazilian girlfriend, and they would marry late that summer up at Elkhorn Resort where he was managing the dining room.

The ceremony took place by the lake up there on an absolutely perfect late summer day, and both bride and groom were glowingly beautiful in their simple attire. The ceremony was short and attended by only a select few friends, myself included.

My state of mind was very fragile when I arrived there, and so I mostly kept to myself. I really don't know what I would have done if I had not found Hannah.

We met about two weeks after I arrived, and again for the just second time in my life, I felt that existential electric shock when our eyes first met in the dining room, where Chris had given me a job to make some cash before I left the country.

After that, we were together for the entire number of weeks that I was there while waiting for my work visa to South Korea to be processed. She told me that she would wait for me if I wanted, but my plans were again as they had been before meeting Ms. Liar-liar-pants-on-fire, and I honestly did not expect to be returning to Canada any year soon.

On October 27th of 1997, I left Canada, and except for brief visits, would not return for just over a decade.

PART II: South Korea

Chapter 11

End of October – 1997
Kyungsan City – Kyoungi Province – Republic of Korea (South Korea)

"If you wait until all conditions are perfect before you act, you'll never act." – Unknown

I arrived in Kyungsan City on October 28, 1997.

The flight was long, but that was good, for it seemed the farther I got away from Winnipeg, the better I felt. By the time the roughly twenty-four hours of travelling was complete and I was deposited at my dorm by my new employers, a husband and wife team, I thought very little of the strange turn of events in Winnipeg over the first half of this year that led me here.

My free dorm room was little more than a large closet, a rectangular maybe eight square meters. From where I was standing at the door looking into the room, there was a twin mattress on the floor in the far left-hand corner of the room. Opposite that was a small bookshelf in the back-right corner against the right-side wall, followed by a small kitchen table with a single chair. On the right side of that was a kitchen of sorts containing a small counter, a sink, a gas burner and a single set of cupboards that end at a wall separating the rest of the room from the toilet and shower, which were immediately on your right as you entered the room.

I was exhausted. I slept deeply.

Early the next day, I was picked up by the team in their eight-person family/school van.

The husband traditionally is the family head in eastern culture, and thus the husband there held the position of Director of the school, and his wife was the head teacher. As her husband drove the little van, she gave me the run-down of the city, and I eagerly stared out the window at that strange new world and drank in all the unfamiliar sights.

Kyungsan was a small city of just over a million people, and I had never seen anything so jam-packed in my entire life, both in terms of buildings and people. To this point, I had only been out of Canada once on a two-week trip to Puerta Vallarta, Mexico with my dad, his wife and my sister when I was seventeen.

Kyungsan was far more interesting.

We arrived at the school and I got the grand tour of all three classrooms. As it turned out, there was only me, the head teacher, an English grammar teacher and a math teacher.

Kool.

Once the tour was over, the head teacher took me back to the first class that we had visited, which was now full grade one students, about twenty in all.

She handed me a small English language workbook and said, "Okay. You teach now."

Then she promptly exited the room and shut the door.

Every single last student turned to look at me.

Now, the reader may recall that my formal education was in politics and not education, and I had never provided any type of classroom or group instruction prior to that date, and so I just stood there for some time, at a complete loss as to what to do.

I'd always admired how Chris was with everyone that he met, so I thought to myself, "What would Chris do?".

Since that first year at MMC when I first met Chris, he was always an extremely gregarious and well-liked fellow. He had a way with people that just made everyone want to hang around him. If he had been there, I largely suspected that he would have simply taken a seat cross-legged on one of the desks, opened the book to no page in particular, and just started asking simple questions of the students.

So that is exactly what I did.

And it went swimmingly.

Thanks, Chris. ▢

I had been in Korea for about ten days by this point.

Moving half-across the world is quite effective at wiping your memory clean, if at minimum for a time.

Earlier in the week, I had located an internet café at a very well-known university about a ten-minute walk from my tiny dorm room, and I am there again, writing an email to my dad. Grandpa Harding had fallen ill right before I left, diagnosed with terminal cancer.

He would not live long.

Suddenly, I was tapped on the shoulder.

I turned around to find a young Korean man standing there smiling at me. He extended his hand and said in somewhat accented English, "Hi. Are you American?"

"No", I replied. "I'm Canadian."

We chatted for a bit, and it turned out that he owned a pool hall right across the street from the university. I told him that I loved playing pool, and he invited me to visit him sometime.

I told him that I would.

I left the café shortly after and started walking back to my dorm. One had to walk over a four-lane wide bridge that spanned a very long gorge that was used by the university for agricultural research, and the hour was late and it was dark as I enjoyed the quiet yet energized Korean night.

The bridge was very-well lit, and as I walked along the left side of the bridge to where I would turn left to go to my dorm, up ahead on the opposite side of the of the bridge, I could see two city busses with their lights on, parked one behind the other with about four feet separating them.

The two bus drivers were standing face-to-face between the two busses, talking intently.

As I drew parallel to them, they suddenly began to fight, fists flying faster than a Bruce Lee movie.

I was freaked right out by this. I had never witnessed a real live fight before in adulthood that I could recall, and didn't want to see how this turned out, and I really didn't want to become involved, so I hurried on past and on to my dorm for the night.

"Everybody has a plan until they get punched in the mouth." – Mike Tyson

The next week I was at the same internet café.

I sent off a few emails and then thought about heading home, but it was Friday and I was feeling antsy. I had not yet seen any other foreigners here in Kyungsan, and I had the whole weekend to kill.

Then I remembered the invitation that I received last week, and I easily found the pool hall across the street and went up to the second-floor entrance.

The place was huge; it had about ten snooker tables, about four bar tables, a bar, fifty-two-inch Samsung televisions mounted all around the outside walls, and a bright set of stained-glass lights over each table.

As soon as I entered the hall, I was greeted in English from behind the bar on the right side. The Korean chap I met last week was there and he welcomed me over. We grabbed a couple beers and moved off the play some pool. The hall was empty, so we had the run of the place.

After about and hour, my new friend offered me some soju.

"What is soju?" I asked, and was promptly informed that soju was basically the same as sake from Japan; it was a clear, colorless, distilled beverage, typically made from rice, wheat, or barley, and could range from 40% to 70% alcohol by volume.

While soju could be bought in Canada at this time, I had never tried it before, and the distilling process was quite unlike that of beer, and soju was of course nothing like red wine, both of which I mainly drank those days, so my body was not going to be able to process that drink very well, but I had no idea of that at the time.

We toasted to friends well-met and downed a shot each. As he set down his shot glass, he looked up at me and asked, "How was it?"

To be honest, it tasted tinny, but it was otherwise tasteless.

We had another.

And then another.

Some time passed and I was having a blast.

I was drinking beer, I was drinking Korean soju, I was playing pool (which I've always loved) and one of my favorite episodes of The Simpsons was playing on the huge TV mounted on the wall across from us.

And I was a world away from her.

Life was smashing.

For a time.

As my perception began to fog from the strange distillate and my thinking slowed, three men entered the hall and were immediately greeted by the owner and waved over.

We five were all about the same age. My host introduced the new arrivals to me, and we all set about chatting, drinking and playing pool.

Shortly after that, my vision faded completely, and I wouldn't recall the following events for several days.

I'm limping across the bridge towards my dorm past where I had seen the bus drivers fighting last week.

I don't recall how I got here.

Stabbing pain is shooting out from my bottom right-side ribs, making it hard to breathe. My left wrist hurts badly. My head is pounding.

I know something has happened to me, but my head is just too foggy to remember what.

I limp on and pass the end of the bridge, turn left and head up the incline between the single-story rows of basically shanty shacks and towards where I think that my dorm is.

I can't think clearly, and I am limping very slowly to ease the pain in both my ankle and my head, when up ahead, a group of high school kids rounds the corner, walking towards me. They are wearing typical Korean school uniforms; navy blue pants and white and short-sleeved collared shirts.

I pay no notice to them as they approach.

As I pull even with I want to say the six of them, they suddenly surround me very quickly.

I stop. I don't know what is going on because my brain is processing at one-tenth of its normal speed.

One of them speaks in Korean and I only recognize one word; money.

I'm being robbed.

I have been studying Korean since I got on the plane some time back, and I respond in Korean;

"Don't have."

Because I don't. I haven't been paid yet.

"MONEY!" he yells in Korean.

I say nothing.

The circle draws tighter.

Now I am not a very happy camper at this particular juncture; my whole body hurts but red hot fury is burning in my chest and adrenaline is racing through my veins, and I decide that I am not going to cooperate with these young punks.

I play stupid, letting my arms hang loosely down the sides of my body, feet shoulder-width apart, knees slightly bent (I took Kungfu for about six months when I was sixteen...thanks Gramps!).

As the kid that spoke earlier, I presume the leader, takes another step towards me, I suddenly send out a massive roundhouse and clock him right upside the head. He goes down and the others immediately jump on me, kicking, punching, wax on, wax off, and in no time I am on my knees, both of my arms twisted by the wrists behind my back.

I'm helpless.

They kick me a few more times, take my Swatch, my nice grey sweater with the leather patches on the elbows that my mother had given me last Christmas, and fumble though my pockets and remove my Swiss Army knife.

Finding nothing else of value, they drop me on the ground right there and walk away.

I lay unmoving for several minutes. Then I heave myself up, crawl all fours for about fifty meters, and finally climb very slowly and painfully to my feet.

I then proceed to stumble the two-hundred or so remaining meters to my dorm, get inside and lock the door, and promptly pass out on my twin mattress on the floor.

The next thing I knew, I was awoken by a pounding on my dorm room door.

I opened the door, without asking who it was, and was immediately greeted by two rather large gasps.

It turned out that it was Monday and, not having shown up for work, my employers had fully expected not to find me there. Rather, they had expected to find the unit empty, me having done what was commonly referred to amongst the ESL teacher community as *The Midnight Run*.

The midnight run was what newly-arrived-to-Korea teachers, upon arriving in that strange new Southeast Asian country with its strange language, food, customs and culture, and finding that they had bit off just a little more than they could in fact chew, did to get out of the one-year contracts that we all had to sign.

They would simply wish their boss a great weekend on Friday, go back to their flat, pick up their already-packed suitcase, and head out to Incheon International Airport for their midnight flight back home.

Monday would come, and the school would be out a teacher and the several thousand dollars in visa processing fees and travel costs required to bring that teacher out in the first place.

And they would have to start the hiring process all over again.

My current-but-I'm-not-sure-for-how-much-longer employers entered the tiny dorm room and closed the door behind them as I collapsed back on the mattress.

"What happened?" the head teacher then asked.

I have no doubt that it was plain to them that I was in a great deal of pain, and I imagine that I had quite a few bruises and such, and the dorm room must have stank horridly. I had slept right through Saturday and Sunday apparently.

"I really can't remember much...", I mumbled. "I do remember that I was robbed by a bunch of high school kids. They took my watch and my sweater."

They looked at each other suspiciously.

"Where did you go?" she then asked.

I remembered the name of the pool hall and relayed it to them, and my director picked up the small local phonebook near my phone on the small kitchen table against the wall. He quickly flipped through the book, located what he was searching for, picked up the phone and placed it on the floor in front of him as he sat down on the only chair in the room.

He dialed a number, and the call was quickly answered.

The conversation seemed to start off friendly enough, but soon my director became very heated and yelled into the phone. I didn't know what was being said at either end of the line really, but the tone was clear: my director was very angry.

He hung up the phone and then spoke with his wife for some time. She then relayed to me that her husband spoke to owner of the club, who claimed that I came in to the hall, got drunk and became very violent, fighting with him and his friends and smashing lights and causing other damage.

I remembered none of this.

I could see that my director was thinking deeply about what had occurred here. I could easily imagine things from his perspective; he had many students that had already paid for English lessons with a native speaker, and he and his wife had already invested significantly to bring me out there and house me in that dorm.

He clearly was trying to come to a decision.

I waited silently, prepared to accept whatever came.

He looked me thoughtfully up and down one last time, perhaps assessing the degree of my injuries and what he felt so far of my character, compared with the story that he had heard from the pool hall owner.

After a few minutes, he made a decision.

He chose to trust me.

He told me to take the rest of the day off and rest up, and he would be by first thing in the morning to take me to work.

I thanked him and faded out into oblivion.

A number of days later, my memory of the events of that evening slowly returned, and I would relate the story to many people over the years, which I called of course my "Soju Experience".

Most foreign teachers who have worked in Korea will have one, though mine always seemed to be the wildest that anyone had ever heard.

After the other three men enter the pool hall and they all ply me with free beer and soju, one of them asks if I've served in the military.

In Korea, all males must serve around twenty-one months in the Korean military once they reach an age between eighteen and twenty-eight. I would also later learn that during this tenure, each member of the military is trained in authentic Korean Taekwondo to at least the level of first-degree black belt. Koreans typically choose to begin their military service at around the age of twenty-one or so, and so essentially what this means is that basically most every male in the country of my age (I'm currently just shy of twenty-eight) has lethal weapons for hands and feet and various other appendages.

Anywho, back to the hall.

I explain that Canada has no such military service requirement, but they clearly are very sceptical about this.

And then it hits me; it is not my claim that Canada has no mandatory military service that they are skeptical about; they think that I am American.

Since the Korean War, the United States has kept a strong military presence in South Korea. At that time in 1997, some 33,000 US troops were in the country, most on temporary assignment. Some years later that number would drop to about 26,000.

The majority of these troops were young, eighteen to twenty, serving the first of a number of required overseas posting. So these youngsters, fresh out of high school, joined the military and were sent overseas to the be a buttress against North Korea and other nations that the US considered to be a military threat in the region.

The training was excruciating, and the threat of military conflict hung constantly over their heads. The US had military bases in a significant number of cities and regions throughout Korea, and on weekends, these boys were given passes to leave the base and relieve stress.

So, as one might imagine, on weekends, the nightlife in any city that housed or was close to a US military base exploded with US military personnel seeking to blow off a considerable amount of steam.

Over the decades that the US had military troops in the country, which was basically since the armistice was signed, GIs had earned quite the bad reputation with Korean nationals, for the Korean news was a constant source of allegations against US troops including assault, rape and murder of Korean citizens.

I remember hearing one such news story very early on in my tenure in Korea.

A GI had allegedly murdered a Korean sex worker, and then had set fire to the hotel room that they had rented to cover up the crime. In accordance with the legal agreement between the South Korean and US governments, the GI was removed from service, and rather than the GI being subjected to Korean law, he was sent back the US to stand before a US military tribunal.

As a result, I surmise mostly unfairly, American ESL teachers were assumed to be of the exact same temperament as American GIs by Korean nationals, and not infrequently experienced varying degrees of discrimination and sometimes even outright hostility, if Korean nationals even suspected they were American.

Please understand that I am not saying that the entire nation's population held this view of foreigners in general and of Americans specifically, because the overwhelming majority of Korean citizens that I met treated me with great politeness and respect, and I eagerly absorbed and still use to this day many facets of their wonderfully rich and ancient culture.

The reason that I am explaining about this now, is that I want the reader to understand why many American ESL teachers claimed to be from Canada instead, and why a good number would even go so far as to wear a Canadian pin or other similar symbol of the nation.

I considered that a very sage threat reduction strategy.

Now, I'm not saying that this was the reason that these four gentlemen decided to ambush me this night, and I never did find out. But clearly, they had some strong reason to dislike Americans, and they had convinced themselves that I was one.

One of them abruptly tangents the current conversation topic and asks me if I would like to learn some Taekwondo holds.

I am very skeptical about this, but they have been plying me with alcohol and my spidey-sense is significantly muted, and I am a trusting sort of fellow, and my host has given me no reason to suspect that anything is amiss, and so I grudgingly agree.

One approaches me from behind and I let him put me in a *Full Nelson*, which means that my arms are locked behind my head and I am effectively defenceless.

I'm told to try to break out of the hold, which of course I fail miserably to do. I relax and laugh, expecting to be released.

But this does not happen.

Instead, my now-captor tightens his hold.

I being to struggle, much to the mirth of his three companions. Then, as the three begin to approach, my captor, still holding me in that Full Nelson and standing directly behind me, hooks his right leg around the front of my right leg, trapping it, and slams me face first down on to the floor.

Now, I am no weakling, and many years of dancing has left my legs quite strong, and I am very flexible, and so somehow, I manage to regain my feet.

But my captor still has me in this hold and is clearly quite well-versed in marital arts, for he effortlessly flips me heels over head backwards.

I fly through the air with the greatest of ease and come crashing down on a pool table, a billiard ball crunching into my ribs and my left foot smashing the light fixture overhead.

My captor losses his grip, and even though pain fills my senses, I manage to roll off the other side of the table and further have enough wherewithal to grab a pool cue that is lying on the table.

I leap to my feet and hold the four-foot pool cue out before me like a buck-and-a-quarter quarterstaff.

After that, everything is quite a blur.

At some point I started flailing around with the pool cue, trying to keep them all back.

The pool cue caught another nearby light fixture over another pool table and smashed it.

This caused all four of them to back off just enough that I made a desperate dash for the door.

I don't know if I got away clean, or they just decided that things were not going as they had planned and let me go.

Either way, the police were not called, and so that strongly suggested to me and my employer that they were not confident enough in their innocence to involve local law enforcement.

You know the rest of the story.

Chapter 12

The End of 1997
Kyungsan City – Kyoungi Province

When my first payday came (Korean companies paid their workers only once a month), all of the teachers were called in to meet with the director.

He informed us that, because of the financial crash that was taking place in the country at that time (the country's economy had to be temporarily propped up with a sixty billion dollar loan from the International Monetary Fund), the Korean teachers would be taking a one-third pay cut to keep their jobs, or else the school would have to release someone.

Not me though. They would continue to pay me according to my contract, which the Korean teachers did not have with the school.

I remember being quite relieved with this at first. I had a specific amount of money that I needed to send back to Canada each month to pay off that brilliant vehicle purchase to protect my mother's credit, else I would not have enough saved by the end of my one-year contract to continue my travels through Europe as I had planned.

However, as the meeting wore on and the director moved to other school issues that needed to be addressed, the innate sense of justice that my life to this point had instilled in me nagged at my conscience, and I quickly came to a decision.

"If my colleagues have to take a pay cut so that the school could continue to pay us all, then it was only fair that I do my part to help, and take the same pay cut."

The director very graciously accepted.

Now I fully realized that the cut in pay would mean that I would not have enough money by the end of my contract to continue with my travels, so I asked the director to find me additional work, which he quickly did.

I worked first for a local school, teaching a number of classes in addition to the thirty hours a week that I was teaching for my employers, but a few weeks later I myself was able to locate a twenty-five hour per week job early in the mornings at an adult language institute in the nearby major city of Daegu (of which Kyungsan is basically a satellite city). All my classes at my main job are for students and take place after school, so there was no schedule conflict.

For the next nine months I got up crisply at 04:45 and took the 05:00 intercity bus into Daegu. The ride was about forty-five minutes each way, and I used the time to continue my Korean language studies.

At some point I decided to invest in a motorbike and taught myself to ride in one of the busiest cities in the world.

I'm still tempted to ride to this day.

After about three months, I finally met another foreign teacher who gave me the low-down on where all the expat hangouts were, and I very quickly made a good group of friends, and life was grand. To my great pleasure, I also seemed to be popular with Korean women, which I simply put down to their interest in Westerners.

My new favorite hangout teemed with other teachers from many different English-speaking countries, and the house band, *The Drunken Lazy Bastards*, was entirely comprised of expats.

The guys that I became friends with at that time were the wildest bunch that I had ever hung around with, and they accepted me like I was a normal person. To this day I still highly value those friendships; Harold, Greg, Cody, Brian, Ted Shaw (host of *The Ted Shaw Show*), Chip, Todd and Mike.

Thanks for simply accepting me.

As my one year contract with my school drew to a close, despite the many hours that I had put in teaching extra classes, I still did not have the money that I needed to continue the dream of travelling through Europe, so I made the decision to stay one more additional year and move up to Seoul, where one could make real money.

I would never realize that dream.

Chapter 13

Early 1999
Seoul – Kyoungi Province

I moved about quite a bit for those first few months in the Korean capital city, first staying with one friend, and then another.

Very early on in Seoul, I met an independent recruiter in Seoul named Jiyeon. She was Buddhist and a proud lesbian, and we become fast friends. I still consider her a life-friend to this day. She and I would work together in various capacities the rest of the time that I lived in Korea, and whenever I needed more work, she always came though.

I dated a few Korean women, but the romantic interest for me was really not there, and so I basically swore off dating them by March.

And so of course, this was when I met her.

I'd made friends with a young chap in US military intelligence, and he had a date one Friday evening and asked me to come along, as she was bringing a friend with her. I had no interest in meeting any Korean women, but I agreed because, well, that's what friends do.

We were to meet our dates in a very popular dance club called Hollywood, in Itaewon, which was the foreign sector in Seoul. It was great for shopping and many different ethnic food restaurants, had many bars and taverns and was always packed with people, both Korean and foreigners from many other countries alike.

The girls were already there when we arrived and I was introduced to my "date". She was very pretty, but I had zero interest, so much so that when she politely asked me my name, I told her that I did not have one.

She was taken aback somewhat by this response, but in the Korean way, she remained very polite. The four of us danced the evening away and all went our separate ways at the end of the evening, which, in Itaewon, was likely 05:00 or 06:00, as certain clubs did not open until around 02:00 to catch the crowds that exit the late evening dance clubs which closed at 04:00 .

If one so desired, it was completely possible to party twenty-four hours around the clock in that area of the city.

Kool.

I ran into my "date" a couple more times over the next couple weeks or so, and slowly we began to chat and get to know each other.

And then we fell madly in love.

She was from a south-coast port city and spoke English very well, having studied for one year in Australia, and we both loved to dance, and we made each other laugh.

I proposed to her the following Valentine's Day, and we were married on September 4, 2000 in her hometown.

This is an appropriate point to relate two stories from two of my many visa-runs to Japan.

Both trips occurred about two years apart, the first about one year prior to my marriage, the first time that I ever set foot on Japanese soil in my life, and the second trip exactly one year after my marriage, which was the last time that I have set foot on Japanese soil to date.

For both of the experiences that I relate in these stories, drugs played a prominent role, and both experiences would have an equally profound affect on the course of my life.

Early Summer – 1999

That second year in Korea, I was not on a one-year teaching visa, but rather on a six-month tourist visa; Americans only got three months. As a result, every six months for the next few years at least, I needed to leave Korean soil and return to receive a new six-month visa stamp in my passport. That was the system at the time.

I remember one particular turnaround flight during those early years was only thirty minutes or so after my arrival, so I deplaned the inbound flight to Fukuoka, Japan, and boarded the return flight back to Incheon without setting foot on Japanese soil, technically speaking.

Up to this point, I was still a very quiet person. Yes, I had a great group of very outgoing friends in my life, and when I grew over time to be very comfortable with them, I let the real weirdo in me out. But I still very much was, as I had always been, socially awkward around people that I did not know well. It would not be until years later that my psychiatrist would advise me that this was likely social anxiety left over from my childhood.

Basically, it worked like this; because I was bullied so much in school, I naturally began to remain as inconspicuous as possible in any new group of people until I could get the lay of the land, so to speak. I would not so much as say a peep until I knew exactly who was a threat, who may turn into a threat, what potential threat level they could represent, who in the group might help, who might remain indifferent, and who I may be able to use as a decoy if I need to get out.

Anywho, along came the time for me to need to leave South Korea for a new tourist visa, and I had already well-researched the options, and had decided on a course of action; I would fly to Fukuoka, the nearest international airport, accompanied by Lee, a new friend of mine who had made the trip a number of times up till then.

Lee and I had met in Itaewon a short time after my arrival there and hung around together a fair bit. He was American, and as we quickly learned, I am less than one day older than he is.

He would later marry a Korean national as well, and we would commiserate from time to time over the next few years.

13:12 – Date Unknown
Downtown Fukuoka – Japan

We arrived early afternoon in Fukuoka, and the plan was that we would check out the downtown area for a couple of hours, then grab something to eat, then party all night and take the first flight back to Incheon in the morning. To help with the "party all night" part, Lee and I were able to "procure" some LSD and our new favorite party drug, ecstasy.

So, check out the downtown area we did, and we stopped after a couple hours and got some authentic Japanese ramen at a local convenience store, and then headed to a nearby park to enjoy.

Afterwards, we decided now was the time to begin, and we each dropped a hit of acid, and lay back in the long grass to gaze up at the sky and wait for the acid to kick in, which it invariably did.

I was laying back, almost asleep, if I recall correctly, and suddenly, I heard laughter.

I panicked because, even in the middle of a crowded city of roughly a million and a half inhabitants, I did not hear a single vehicle horn, no screeching of tires, no loud groups of people, and certainly, no one laughing like a little school-person loud to break the tranquility of that perfect moment...

It was at this point that I realized that I was high and completely off in Lalaland.

But then I heard the laughter again, and louder, right beside me in fact.

I blinked and looked over at Lee sitting right next to me in this little urban park, and he was giggling and pointing out along the foot-high green grass. My gaze followed the direction that he was pointing, but I didn't see anything for the hundred feet or so of waving grass that looked not the least bit humorous, much less worthy of bales of laughter.

And then I saw it; an adolescent cat was jumping after butterflies in the grass, and while the grass was tall enough to completely cover the little thing when it was on the ground, when it jumped after a flitting butterfly, its cute teeny head popped up just over the horizon of the grass for as split second; you had to be watching carefully to see.

But Lee had seen, and each time the cat made a leap after a butterfly, its head popped out of the grass, and Lee pointed and at first giggled, and then howled with laughter.

I quickly realized that we really didn't want to attract the wrong type of attention, so we decided that it was time to head over to the place where we had decided to spend the evening, night and the wee hours of the next morning, a nightclub called *The Happy Cock*.

18:23 – Date Unknown – 1999
The Happy Cock – Downtown Fukuoka – Japan

The Happy Cock was a surprisingly decent-sized bar/nightclub located on the ninth floor of a stick-of-a ten-story building in downtown Fukuoka.

When Lee and I emerged from the miniature three-person elevator and stood at the door to enter the barely half-packed club, I spotted what passed for a stairwell to the bottom floor; nothing.

There were no stairs.

I thought to myself that if there was a fire here tonight of all nights, Lee and I were as good as dead.

21:24
The Happy Cock

"When you feel happy, really happy, it somehow seems that you've always been happy and that you'll always be happy. The same is often true when you feel sad, or lonely, or depressed, or broke, or sick, or scared. Something, perhaps, to remember." – Mike Dooley

A few hours later that evening, Lee and I had taken our second and last hits of acid, and we had also taken one and a quarter hits of ecstasy each.

I was on the dance floor, dancing with a couple acquaintances that we had met along the way earlier in the afternoon and invited to join us here, and while I was feeling pretty good physically, my mind was racing from the acid, which was how it typically had affected me the few times that I had taken it prior to that point.

The way that acid worked on my mind was thus: Each time that I had tried LSD before, I had become intensively self-critical; I would question anything and everything about my life. Why do I fail at so many things? Why do all the women in my life hurt me? What am I doing here in Asia? Hiding from life?

Acid typically affected me for about four hours, so the two or three times that I had tried it previous ended up being more mentally exhausting than fun, and as a result, I never pursued LSD for it's mental/psychological state-altering properties hence or since.

That evening though, the ecstasy had me dancing, and the unusual addition of the acid had me predictably intensively critical over my inability to just walk up to people and talk, much less ask them to dance. This was an evolution of the social anxiety that I had suffered from since childhood and it had caused me so many lonely nights as to be one of a seemingly constant cycle of subjects that my brain examined on a rotating basis most waking moments.

Autumn – 1990
Winnipeg – Manitoba – Canada

"This is your life, and it's ending one minute at a time." –
Fight Club (1999)

I'm twenty years old and Maurice and I are at our usual weekend haunt, Norma Jeans, in an area of downtown Winnipeg called The Market.

We've entered the nightclub proper through the kitchen door (that's where those with VIP cards entered from…this sufficed nicely as a poor man's red-carpet entrance), and are already cruising the dancefloor for cute girls.

As always, I'm Maurice's wingman. I don't have the self-confidence to do any of the talking at this point in my life, but Maurice has it in spades…he's French after all.

We are dressed in the typical Miami Vice style of the times, we each have a drink in one hand, and are suavely moving through the throng of nightclubbers.

And that's when I see her.

I see her most nights that we are here, and we have been coming here about a year now, and tonight, as ever, she does not disappoint.

She's dressed in a number that I have seen her in before and always love; a skin-tight, intense blue (or is it aqua-green?) one-piece fabric dress that covers her from her shoulders down to her upper-mid thigh.

Any areas in between that do not need to be covered, are not covered.

She is about the same height as me, 6'0", 6'2" in heels...through I am only 6'1" in heels. She has gorgeous blue eyes and Farrah Fawcett-type blonde flowing hair to her shoulders, and on the dancefloor, she moves so gracefully that I long ago convinced myself that she is a ballet dancer; I have an eye for dancers by this time, as the reader will hopefully recall.

And she is drop-dead gorgeous.

Now, I have seen her here so many times that I have lost count by this time. Maurice and I basically start here every Friday and Saturday evening, and top the night off at Marble Club just up the block.

Ever since the first time that I saw her, I've wanted to ask her to dance, but that is a very hard thing for me to do. I am simply terrified of rejection. I have, at infrequent times throughout my young adult life to this point, summoned up the courage to ask someone to dance, or out on a date for example, but it has to be very clear to me in advance that she is interested and not going to say no, which would shame me immensely.

Each time that I have seen her here, I have tried and tried and tried, to no avail, to summon the courage to ask her to dance. And I know that she recognizes me each night, because she always gives me this cute little Marilyn Munroe-like shy wave of her fingers, as she smiles at me through thinly slit, almost closed almond-shaped eyelids.

Nothing after that, mind you.

But she does always give me that wave.

Every time.

But this has been nowhere near enough for me to be able to sufficiently delude myself into believing that she won't say no to me for even once of the likely scores of times that I had seen her here previous.

It has happened many times in the past, to be sure, with other women previous to her; sometimes I had been able to summon sufficient courage, more often not though. Sometimes they said yes, but mostly they said no, and rather than getting used to it, it just kept on getting more and more painful each time that it happened.

But tonight, I had already decided long before the time that Maurice and I arrived that I was going to ask her to dance, and damn sitting on the outside anymore.

We waited at the "VIP" door for what seemed like the longest time ever, and by the time we get in to the club, I'm so anxious that I have already mostly-convinced myself that even if she had come tonight, she was most likely already gone.

My eyes dart out over the dance floor first.

She's not there.

Clenching my jaw as I move off and deeper into the mass of bodies, she suddenly steps out from behind the person directly in front of me, perhaps coming around a corner, or out from the ladies' room.

185

Regardless, there she is, and I go right up to her.

She smiles.

Dimly, as I recall.

My spidey-sense immediately goes off, but its too late.

I follow her gaze just over my left shoulder and behind me, and as I turn, I see that she is not alone tonight, of all nights, and as my body finishes the pivot that my head has already started, I come face to face with her date for tonight.

He is my exact double.

"My life is passing me by.", I say silently to myself.

Date Unknown – Early Spring – 2000
A Basement Techno Bar – Osaka – Japan

This event occurred after Fukuoka, but it gives some insight into the events of that night and I believe that it would benefit the reader to hear about it, if only to help set the correct cultural context for the upcoming previous events. A very particular facet of Japanese culture would have an immense factor in the epiphany that my alcohol and drug-addled mind were trying very hard to come to at The Happy Cock.

My best friend Don and I went there that night, both to Osaka and to the bar, on one of what would be a number of such visa runs together. But that was the first time that I had been there, both in Osaka and the bar; it wasn't the first for Don as a Korean/Japanese friend of his, and thus a friend of mine, owned the bar, which was pretty dope.

We'd been there for an hour or so and were on our third drink or so, Don with his CC and coke, and me with beer. It was just myself, Don, the bartender, an employee and nice enough fellow, if my memory does not deceive me.

There were no patrons on this business late afternoon to that point that I had seen, but that, conveniently enough for our story, was where things changed.

Don and I were sitting at the bar when we heard a heavy wooden door open, and we both looked up and to our right as first one, then two skirted sets of attractive female legs descended the steps into the bar.

They were promptly followed by two suits.

I gathered that these are local white-collar workers, and that they have come in here for a Friday post-workday beverage or three.

I would be both very right, and very wrong.

Don and I returned to what you would find us doing for the vast majority of the times that we would be seen together over the many years that I was privileged to call him my friend; playing Cribbage.

After a few hands, the bartender, whose name I cannot recall, put a tray up on the counter containing fifty shots of some alcohol. Having served tables for about ten years, I turned to the bartender and whispered, "Dude, now's not the time for free shots; there's no one here.", nodding to the only exceptions in the place, the table of four business types.

He winked comically at me and advised, "These no free. These for guest." And he nodded towards the table of four that I had just myself nodded to.

I was sure that I was miscomprehending the situation. I quickly glanced over at the four and confirmed that yes, they were sitting at a table comfortable for only four, so I thought to myself that they were not likely to be expecting anyone else to join them.

As the bartender picked up his tray and proceeded to the table of four, Don and I watched entranced as he removed each and every shot from his tray and placed it on their table, and once all shots had been transferred, he bowed very low to the entire table and held it for a three count at least, then returned upright and retreated smartly back behind his bar.

Don and I were still staring at the table of four. Unnoticed of me earlier, but which I could clearly see by that time, the bartender had also dropped off a deck of regular, western-style, fifty-two-card playing cards.

And thus, these four began to play some game of that, it quickly became clear to me, they all knew the rules to, which seemingly were many.

Some time passed and the fifty shots were finished, by the winners or by the losers, I couldn't yet tell.

One of the men spoke then loudly to the bartender, who shouted "Hai!" immediately in response and then began to set out another tray of fifty shots.

I was dumbfounded. I had absolutely no idea what was going on, nor what was about to occur.

This time I was watching very carefully when the shots were dropped off, and I noticed the bartender also set a single black marker on the table.

It struck me at that point that he seemed quite non-plussed by the entire situation, and so I assumed it be to a regular occurrence there, or at least not so outside the realm of acceptable as to warrant any reaction from him.

From that point the game clearly intensified, the stakes seemingly doubled if you will, and now you could tell who the losers were; they were the ones that drank, but in that second and more exciting round, each time the loser drank, they also removed a piece of clothing.

It was not a private event, as far as I was aware.

As the round progressed, cards were played, shot glasses were deftly emptied and then slammed down on the table, pieces of clothing were removed, and the four participants became louder, and louder, and louder.

It was not that any were becoming angry at losing (they were in fact all laughing their asses off), or that they were becoming quite drunk (which they were, but that was not the most interesting part); the only way that I can put it to you that makes any sense is that each and every one of them was focussing all of their energy very purposely and intently on...having fun.

In my admittedly limited exposure to true Japanese culture up to that point in my life, my sense of it was that it could be quite intense. Consider simply these three well-known products of the Japanese culture; Bushido, Kamikaze pilots, and a sense of honor so deep that they will slit their bowels from stem to stern if their lord requires it. That's intense, no two ways about it. And so the Japanese are a highly energized people, reserved in public, but shrouding a vast undercurrent of intense emotion just beneath the surface, and that emotion fuels everything that they do, every moment of every day. When its time to work, they work as hard as they can, with all of their energy and emotion; and when its time to play, they do <u>exactly</u> the same.

The beginning of round three clearly commenced with the arrival of a third tray of shots. And, thankfully, the four did stop just short of nudity; they were all down to their skivvies.

But the stakes did in fact increase again, for the black marker that had earlier been placed upon their table and ignored, now entered the fray.

In that final round, the losers drank as per usual, but instead of also removing a piece of clothing, the winners now wrote things written in Japanese script right on the bodies of the "losers", in, what other than, black marker.

And, honestly, I couldn't tell which they seem to enjoy more, winning, or losing.

The last shots are drunk, and the game clearly ends.

The four became very quiet and reserved again, put back on most of their clothing, paid the tab, stumbled back up the stairs and left the bar.

Don and I looked at each other.

You could have heard a pin drop.

01:33 – Date Unknown – 1999
The Happy Cock – Downtown Fukuoka – Japan

"My vision is much sharper through the eyes of my shadowed self." – Dexter Morgan

Some time had passed, and I was still high yet intensively inquisitive about why I could not just talk to people.

And the reason I was lamenting this particular as of yet under-developed social skill of mine? Because Lee had that skill in spades. He was a natural-born gabber. And he had great energy when he was high.

And for the last two hours, I had been winding my neck tighter and tighter, following Lee as he made lap after lap around the club, talking to anyone that he felt like.

And they all loved him.

Contrastingly, I was on the dance floor, dancing in the neighborhood of my two acquaintances, but entirely occupied inside my own mind where I was deeply ensnared in the critique de jour, compliments of the LSD; my fear of rejection.

A few hours earlier Lee, and I had looked on with genuine awe as first one set of GIs, then another set, busted clearly choreographed and well-practiced moves out on the dance floor. Back in Winnipeg, while not completely unheard of, something like this would have been considered pretty audacious, at least in my time.

Anywho, the GIs; sure, their moves were decent, but what had really spelled me was the reaction that their moves got from the primarily Japanese crowd; they absolutely drank it all in.

I mean, all of it.

Over the next three hours, I watched mystified as sets of dancers would, one by one, as if per some pre-established schedule that I was not privy to, bust out a set of moves for thirty seconds or so, and it was as if the crowd itself was a single, fluid, living being, for it would flow in waves of moving people until the new source of energy was complete surrounded on the dance floor.

Then, the crowd as a whole would feed off of the energy of the dancers, and would then feed that energy right back to the dancers, in the form of cheering, yelling, shrieking, shaking, dancing, jumping up and down, laughing, crying, you name it. The two energies would feed each other, intensifying the cheering, intensifying the dancing, until it all reached a frenzied crescendo, like an orgasm, if truth be told, and the crowd then dissolved into individuals again, returning to simply dancing where they were, until the next energy wave began.

I suddenly become aware of myself, and I open my eyes.

Myself and my two acquaintances, a young and very reserved couple, are completely alone on entirely half of the club dancefloor.

The rest of the crowd of some two hundred people, including Lee, is on the other end of the dance floor, having an absolute blast, giving and taking each other's energy in true symbiotic fashion.

Suddenly, I hear a click in my head, and instantly and thoroughly it all makes perfect sense; I don't get any energy <u>from</u> people because I don't give any energy <u>to</u> people. I hoard it all like a child saving a five-dollar bill in his pocket for Sunday school, because he's afraid to get called out.

I stop dancing and turn to the couple near me, and simply say, "I don't want to be on this side anymore."

And with that, I turn and walk off the dancefloor to the table nearest containing two young Japanese gentlemen, who watch me quite baffled as I approach.

I lean over to the nearest one, who smiles, and I say, "My name is Micheal. What's your name?"

For the next two hours until the bar closed, as that couple would later relate to me on the flight back to Incheon, each of them wound their neck tighter and tighter, following me as I made lap after lap around the bar, talking to anyone that I felt like.

And they all love me.

The next two years were undoubtably the best of my life to that point.

With my epiphany in Japan, I began to pour out my seemingly boundless energy whenever I was drunk or high and there were people around, and with my partner's natural beauty and charm, we were quickly a very popular couple, were invited to all the afterparties, and even became the unofficial king and queen of Hollywood, where we had originally met.

We lived together in Seoul at first for a while, and then her parents lent us the key money that we needed to lease at first a basement apartment in Guri City, another satellite city of Seoul just to the north, and later a much larger fourteenth-floor apartment a short ways away in the same city.

Essentially, key money is a large amount of cash that one provides to the owner of a residence that they wish to lease, which can be anywhere from a couple thousand dollars for a small unit, to hundreds of thousands or even millions of dollars in the more affluent areas of the city. For the term of the lease, the residence owner puts the key money in a high-interest bank account, and returns it in full once the lease conditions are complete.

During these years, I was in high demand as both a private and a business English tutor and made a decent amount of money, but such was our social life that the money was spent as fast as it came in.

Which was fine by me, because I had never been so popular in my life.

Ecstasy was on the menu pretty much any night out, which was still necessary for me at that time, for unless I was either high or drunk, I still could not act on my new-found social realization.

Most of my buddies from Daegu had moved up to Seoul, and we all become quickly absorbed into the city's vibrant techno scene. Brian was already by this time an excellent rock-and-roll DJ, and Todd would eventually break onto the scene as a techno DJ, and would gain quite a following in some of the most popular clubs in the country.

I further met other great friends in Seoul such as Tim, The Timmie, Mic and Holidayz.

And then there was Don.

Don and I met early on in my tenure in Seoul, and we quickly became the best of friends. Hailing from rural Ontario, he was highly intelligent and hard-working, quite the networker, and was the only person that could and can, to this day, beat me at Cribbage on a regular basis.

I don't think that I could ever explain just how, but Don's friendship kept me alive many times over those dark years.

I consider him a life-friend to this very day.

Afterall, he did throw me the Best. Bachelor. Party. Ever.

Of the many return trips that I made to Japan during these years, one early one stands out.

I am at a friend's apartment in Osaka, and we are just getting ready to head to buy some magic mushrooms for me, but first he wants a hit of this great new drug that he's into called Meth.

I ask him what it does, and he tells me, after which I hear my inner voice speak clearly within my head and chest equally.

"Micheal, we do not want to become involved with this substance."

I can't say that these were the exact works that I heard, but it certainly was the crystal-clear meaning that I got (pardon the pun).

My friend sticks a piece of something whiteish into the tip of the hollow casing of a plastic pen that he is utilizing as a form of pipe, takes out his lighter and heats the end of the hollow pen casing with the substance, takes a long draw, and then offers the pen and lighter to me.

I politely decline, and we depart.

The next time that I would hear from my inner voice, it would tell me that I was going to die.

Chapter 14

Mid-August – 2001
Osaka – Japan

The second Japan story takes place two years later.

It was the fourth time or so that I had needed to leave the country to renew my tourist visa since that first time two years ago that I had first set foot on Japanese soil and had that very real epiphany.

Over the intervening twenty-four months, I became more and more popular, and was partying harder and harder than ever before.

Being popular had become my newest addiction, but it was beginning to take a tole.

For example, my wife and I constantly had no money. It was spent by me on "lifestyle necessities" faster than it came in.

And no amount of partying was ever enough for me.

I started Friday after work, and went all night with the boys through Saturday and then all day, afternoon, evening and night Sunday, until 02:00 Monday rolled around, and I had to resign myself to the fact that the weekend was over, and I crawled into bed.

Life went on like this for week after week after week, until sometime right before my wedding, my darkness reappeared.

Intensely.

Partying was not quite doing it for me anymore, and the long four days in between were increasingly not sufficient to fully recharge at first my physical, but soon mental and emotional energy, for the weekend.

However, counterintuitively, I didn't slow down but rather intensified the partying, figuring that I simply had to try harder.

I recall that it was Thursday that I arrived in Osaka, and had planned to have an absolute wild time all the way through to Monday, and had scheduled a Tuesday return flight so that I would have time to sleep and recover.

Partying seemed to be the only thing that relieved my darkness in the slightest those days, and I had planned to redefine the word that trip.

I had hoarded money for some weeks to build my spending fund. Magic mushrooms were legal there in Japan, and my ability to sniff out ecstasy in any club was becoming quite legendary.

And besides, I was in Osaka; I was connected there.

Thus I found myself at my friend's basement techno bar, anxiously waiting for him to show up, as he would be able to get ecstasy.

Right at that moment however, I was on my third beer, and the trusty bartender was checking on a potential mushroom source for me at another table.

He returned to the bar where I was sitting and nodded, and I pulled out some yen from my pocket and handed it to him.

Seconds later, I had my magic mushrooms, however, much to my disappointment, they were significantly smaller than usual.

"Oh well" I said to no one in particular. "I'll just have to take double then."

And I did.

"Stop me if you've heard this one. Jesus Christ walks into a hotel. He hands the innkeeper three nails and he asks, "Can you put me up for the night?"" – Eric Draven, The Crow (1994)

About an hour later, I still cannot feel any effect from the mushrooms, and brilliantly I take another two or three.

FLASH

I'm tired of waiting for my friend to arrive, and I head out on my own to find a busier place, leaving rough directions with the bartender on how to find me.

I quickly encounter a busy tavern that is serving, of all things, Labatt Blue, a staple Canadian beer at the time.

I order two.

FLASH

My friend is moving through the crowd ahead of me. I ask him if he has any E, and he shakes his head no.

He begins to move towards the exit and looks back at me, and beckons for me to follow.

I follow.

FLASH

I'm waiting on a street corner while my friend goes into the now second motel to see if they have any rooms for the night.

They don't.

FLASH

I'm standing right in front of our two-story apartment building. My wife is likely pissed at me as usual, and not undeservedly so. I'm always coming in at all hours of the day and night.

Exhausted, I head up the single flight of open-air stairs to the top floor and try the door to our apartment.

Its predictably locked.

I begin searching all my pockets for my keys, but I've misplaced them again.

I knock on the door a few times, knowing that she is likely fast asleep, or at least pretending to be fast asleep, and I quickly accept that she is not going to open the door.

My failsafe: I've always been pretty athletic, at least post-elementary school, and having done this a few times now, I step back out onto the open-air stairwell, reach out and up through the large opening in the cement wall, and grab the top of the upper lip of the two-story apartment building.

I then pull myself onto the roof.

Knowing the rough layout of our one-room unit, I immediately head to the other side of the building where our bedroom is.

Without looking, I lay flat on the building roof and, as I have done so many times before, I deftly reach out over the ledge of the building with my right arm to feel whether or not my wife has left the window open with my hand; she has, so I slide the window open and Spiderman-like, easily lower myself onto the window ledge and into my one-room apartment.

FLASH

I am instantly wide awake.

I remember all the events leading up to this very moment, and I am one hundred percent aware that I have just broken into someone's apartment here in Osaka.

And I panic.

Instead of simply climbing back out the window, I rush through the tiny bedroom that is definitely not mine in Seoul, and yank open the door.

I quite literally feel like I'm in a nightmare and I need to get out of this place no matter what. I didn't mean to do this. I've really fucked up this time.

I could get killed right now.

Every single individual facet of my brain and personality are all screaming at the top of their imaginary lungs inside my head; "GET THE FUCK OUT OF THIS BUILDING!"

I'm in a hallway. I reach for the nearest doorknob with my right hand and turn it.

Its locked. I try the next one to the left.

Its open.

I open the door and step into the room quickly, shutting the door behind me.

I see a large window in the opposite wall. Without thinking, I walk over to the window, open it, poke my head outside quickly to check the ledge room, and deftly exit the building through the second-tory window and step out on a three-inch wide ledge overhanging the sidewalk, which is about fifteen feet down.

I glance first quickly left and then right, and spying a landing about ten feet away on the next roof, and I shimmy the ten feet to the right with my arms outstretched on either side of my body to center my weight towards the brick wall, and easily pull myself onto the property.

The investigating detective would later tell me that, as drunk and high as I was, he had no idea how I safely made that climb without falling.

Now I'm fully aware that I am at minimum trespassing on a second property in Japan and I am simply terrified; I do not have the heart of a criminal, quite the opposite in fact, I would argue.

Despite all of my temper tantrums over the many decades and many girlfriends of my adult life, I had never ever struck a single person in anger or in drunkenness. I've fumed, I've raged, I've yelled, I've punched doors, walls, myself, anything really.

Pushed, yes. Once. And I immediately regretted it. But intentionally struck, never.

I don't have a violent bone in my body.

Angry bones, many. But of violent ones, none.

As I am frantically searching for a way off of this roof, I move past a slightly open door, at which point a boney, ninety-year-old hand, if it was a day, reaches out and simply clamps onto my wrist.

Startled, I look at my wrist in this surprisingly youthful grip, I look up into this old man's cataract-filled eyes, and I hang my head.

Busted again. I do not resist.

Mid-August – 1981
Brandon – Manitoba – Canada

"You can get by on charm for about fifteen minutes. After that, you'd better know something."
- Roger Knapp

I was about eleven years old.

My mother had put me in scouts some seasons back, and while I'm sure she intended that I make some friends, I was simply too scared of new boys and I kept solely to myself, and besides, Brandon was really just a large village, and the boys there already knew what I was.

But there was one boy that took me under his wing, and I will never forget his name; Todd Cunningham. Or something to that effect. Anyways, he always made sure that I was left alone, especially during that trip one year to The Calgary Stampede.

Now, I didn't make any friends at scouts, but I liked it because I could do interesting things, I could earn badges, and of course, it got me out of the house and away from my mother. In fact, I enjoyed getting out of the house so much that I took a shine to their main fundraiser at the time, called *Trees for Canada*.

Essentially, what us scouts did for a few-week period over the spring and early summer, was go out into the community knocking on doors and asking for donations.

205

One dollar a tree I believe. I was both a dedicated and diligent worker, and for the first couple summers I sold the most in my troop, if I recall correctly.

So here I was out collecting for Trees for Canada, or at least that was what I was telling the people whose doors I knocked on, asking for, and getting some donations. I had a great spiel because I'd been doing this for a while now.

But on this particular occasion, as the reader may have already sensed by now, things were not quite on the up and up, for I had crossed a line in the sand; the line of the law.

I had two addictions at this point in my life; sugar and video games. Sugar helped my brain to produce dopamine, and video games distracted me from the hollow pit that was my lonely life, helping to pass the endless hours that I was alone.

When I was absolutely desperate for money for a fix, I feigned collection for Trees for Canada. I think that this was about the third time. Despite my current endeavor though, I did have a sense of fairness and had successfully rationalized the whole situation; I was collecting money for Trees for Canada, I was just putting it to a much more direly needed use. Come the summertime and Trees for Canada is officially underway, I would be sure to plant the extra trees.

I had my scout colors around my neck, but was not wearing the rest of the uniform, as that would have been too difficult to sneak past mother and out of the house.

As I walked up the driveway of a non-descript single-story bungalow, I could see that the inner door to the house was open, which meant that there was a good chance that I was going to score, especially if it was a grandmotherly type, as they always seemed to take an instant liking to me.

I knocked on the door, and it was quickly answered by a middle-aged man with a bit of a potbelly, in a t-shirt and shorts.

"Okay...so I'm not likely to score now..." I think to myself, but never having been one to give up easily on anything, I launched into my spiel anyways, and surprisingly, after only a moment's pause, the not-unkindly gentleman spoke.

"Sure. Hold on. I need to grab my wallet."

He then held open the screen door with one out-stretched arm and beckoned me with the other.

"Come on in."

I peered through the gloomy doorway, into what I could make out was a kitchen.

It seemed harmless enough.

And I needed that fix.

I stepped into the house, and then first the screen door, and then the heavy wooden inner door, were shut and locked behind me.

I slowly walked the ten feet or so down the brief entranceway of that house and came to a stop on the last of three steps up to the kitchen.

This was as far as I felt comfortable going into the house.

The man shuffled past me and through the kitchen, and off to where I hoped to be wherever his wallet was.

After about a minute he returned holding the wallet, or some money, I can't be sure. All I remember is that my heartbeat quickened, for I was going to get a hit soon.

"So, do I have to sign anything?" he asked.

Normally he would have to, but of course I didn't have any genuine supplies at that time, but momma didn't raise no fool, and I did have a pad of paper upon which I had created a chart for collecting some basic information, to give my little charade a guise of authenticity.

"Yes, just fill this out please." and I handed him the pad.

He looked briefly at it, then muttered, "I need to get my reading glasses." and disappeared again.

It was during this roughly one-hundred and twenty seconds that my spidey-sense began to tingle. I can distinctly recall looking back down the ten-foot hallway to the at least double-locked doors there, and feeling that not-unfamiliar urgent tugging equally in my mind and my chest.

"He knows. Get out. Get out now."

And I probably could have made it. But my survival instincts were at war with my addiction, and even at that young age, addiction always won.

I waited.

He soon returned and said, "Son, do you have anyone that I can call, just to confirm your purpose here today?"

One of few questions I knew that I never wanted to hear while doing that. No one had ever asked me that question before during a genuine collection, but I always knew it could happen.

I knew at this point that I was busted; it was only a matter of time. Then sheer stark terror filled my entire chest cavity, because I suddenly knew deep in my soul that this could now only end one way.

With my mother being called.

And the reader should know by now what follows.

But I do not run, for I believe that I still have one more play; I desperately bluff. I never give up. Until I need to.

As cool as a cucumber, I respond.

"Yes. Why, did you want to call her?"

My inquisitor pauses at this. Briefly. Then nods.

My mouth goes instantly dry. But I never give up. Until I need to.

I give him my phone number, off by one digit at the very end. Suddenly, his hands darts toward my head, and I involuntarily take a step back in fear, thinking that he is going to strike me.

Instead, he calmly picks a phone up off its wall-mounted cradle and hands it to me.

I blink, take the phone, and dial the number that I had just given him.

A woman answers.

"Hi, Mom?" I inquire into the mouthpiece innocently.

"No, Sweety. I think you must have the wrong number" is the kind reply.

"Oh, sorry." I say and press the hang-up button. I look the gentleman in the eye and explain.

"Its not her".

He looks at me sternly and says, "Try again."

I do.

"Hi, Mom?" I inquire into the mouthpiece questioningly after dialing the exact same number.

"No, Sweety. You still have the wrong number".

I hang up the phone without a word. I hand it back to the man and hang my head. I have no more plays to make. I've made my last bluff.

He takes the phone from my outstretched hand with one sturdy hand, and with the other firmly takes hold of my wrist.

I'm busted. I do not resist.

Mid-August – 2001
On a Rooftop in Osaka – Japan

The Japanese elder called the police from his kitchen, and then he silently stood there next to me for the next seven minutes or so, firmly holding my wrist, while I simply stood with my head hung in shame.

The police soon arrived and bustled me out very gently.

I cooperated fully.

I was escorted to the very local police station where I was processed and then put in a cell with three other men, all Japanese as far as I could tell, or cared for that matter.

I was exhausted and heartbroken at my disastrous failure of a life.

What had I done?

As this was the weekend, I was left alone completely for the next three days.

I made no effort to talk to my cellmates, and they did not bother with me in the least.

I slept.

10: 12 – Monday – 20 August – 2001
Day 4 in a Japanese Jail – Osaka

I awoke.

A male was speaking in Japanese, loudly and curtly.

"Hadding!"

I groggily lifted my head off of the small black Styrofoam block that served there as a pillow, or at least that was what I was using it for at that particular moment, and turned towards the sound.

A guard was standing at the door to the cell, looking directly at me.

And then it hits me, like a bright red brick right in the fucking head; that wasn't a nightmare.

I sat up quickly and my cellmates indicated to me that I should step forward, which I did.

I was not scared at all, just resigned to my fate, whatever that may turn out to be.

The big metal door was unlocked and opened, and I was escorted out my cell, down the hall and into an interview room. Cuffs were placed on my wrists and then affixed to the table that is on one side of the very small closet-like room, and my escort then exited the room and closed the door firmly.

Time passed. I frankly don't recall how long, when entered two individuals: first a woman, and then a man. The woman was about 5'0", boney but not emaciated, with black short hair to the nape of her neck and typical Japanese features. He was just shy of my height, somewhat portly, with a kind face.

I pegged them both as police detectives assigned to my case.

I briefly wondered which of them would be the bad cop.

As it turned out, it was neither of them.

They both sat, and as I was already sitting, the man spoke politely at me in Japanese and dipped his head slightly. He then turned to the woman, who then turned to me.

"Good morning," she said in accented English, and bowed somewhat at the waist in her chair in my direction.

My mouth was hanging open, and I believe a fly may have landed in my throat.

I quickly shut it.

"Good morning" I responded quickly, bowing my head and eyes in what I hoped was a respectful amount.

She then quickly introduced first her colleague and then herself, and then asked me to state my full name, which I did. A few more identifying questions were asked, which I answered accurately.

Then the gentleman spoke for only the second time, as he had been writing in his coil notepad, and his colleague translated.

"Do you know why you are here?"

And to be quite honest, I had no fucking clue. Seriously. I knew that I would not be here without cause, but I could not imagine what I may have done wrong.

Since the RCMP picked me up at that unbeknownst to me at the time retired cub scout leader's bungalow so many years ago in Brandon, I had walked the straight and narrow with the law (for the most part), so the only thing that I could think of was that I had been arrested on a drug charge, though I did not remember obtaining any ecstasy.

And so I simply told them the truth; I didn't know.

The "translator", as my mind was now referring to her as, and I didn't mean that in any diminutive sense, it just seemed to me to be primarily her function, translated this, I trusted, back to the detective, who considered silently for a moment.

He then spoke gruffly to the translator, who asked me, "What do you remember?"

And so I told them everything that I did remember, up to and including that second helping of magic mushrooms that fateful Thursday evening four nights ago, which took a few minutes.

During this time, she stopped me now and then to presumedly translate whatever I had said up to that point to the detective, who may or may not have had any further questions about the information provided.

Then I was asked what happened after that second helping of magic mushroom, to which I simply replied: "Excellent question."

I considered deeply for several minutes, and all that I was able to relate back was that I had been at some sort of bar or party, having a good time, and that I decided for some unfathomable reason to scale from a second story patio at this location, down to the ground.

I rubbed my temples at this point and advised them that I could not be any clearer on anything that I had related to them.

The memories were just too hazy.

They considered that for a moment or two, and then the detective spoke sharply, they both stood up, one knocked sharply on the door and called out, and the room guard opened the door.

I was thanked by my interviewers and then escorted back to my cell.

Wednesday – 22 August – 2001
Day 6 in a Japanese Jail

I was left alone for the next two days which, I spent mostly sleeping.

On the occasions that I was awake, whatever time of day or night that may have been, I simply lay staring at the ceiling, or if the door to the two-foot by three-foot closet that served quite nicely as a bathroom was open, out the mesh hole in the outer wall that helped the air to circulate.

For either daylight or stars could usually be seen.

I was advised one morning that my Korean/Japanese friend had deposited some money for me, so that I could eat extra food.

I was always very grateful for that.

I began waking earlier in the mornings, simply because my body was starting to recover from that night.

My memory though, not so much.

So I was awake, laying on my mattress, staring up at the ceiling, when the guard stepped up to the bars and said my name.

I lifted my head and turned, and the guard politely motioned me out of the cell.

I stepped into the plastic sandals that I had been allotted, and followed my escort down the hall and outside the police station and into a waiting sedan. I squeezed in the backseat next to the person that was already there and was unceremoniously bumped over by a third person getting in behind me, the detective on my case.

As the vehicle pulled away, the translator, who was the person that was already in the vehicle when I climbed in, explained briefly that we were going to see the public prosecutor.

On the drive there through downtown Osaka, I caught myself looking out the window in interest at the passing city.

Until, that was, I remembered what I was doing there, and where I was going.

I hadn't ever imagined I would be viewing that beautiful city through that particular lens.

I lowered my eyes so that I could not see where I longed to be.

The prosecutor, as it turns out was the Japanese version of me; we were of similar height and weight, similar in build and similar in demeanor, and he was a snappy dresser.

He, however, was getting paid to be there, I assume. And he was sitting on the business-side of the desk.

I, contrastingly, was clearly on the business-end of the desk, and on my immediate right was an early middle-aged woman that I did not recognize, dressed smartly in a long skirt and blouse, and she softly informed me that she was my translator, appointed to translate for me by the courts, and that she did not work for the prosecutor.

I smiled gratefully.

The prosecutor reviewed my file for some time, and then asked through my translator a number of questions of me that I answered to the best of my ability.

The meeting was over seemingly before it began, and I was collected by my escorts and we returned to the vehicle.

Once I had climbed in and the vehicle pulled away, the translator, again sitting on my right, said to me, "The prosecutor has decided that you will remain in Japan custody until your memory of that night returns."

Swell.

07:57 – Wednesday – 24 June – 2020
My Hostel Bunk – São Paulo – Brazil

My sleep has been improving night by night as I get into this part of my life.

Despite four decades having passed since I really last thought of many of the events in Part I, my terror came back very readily. It was palpable; I could feel it in my chest. Not fury, but terror. That was what I remember feeling most during those childhood years. It was my only constant companion.

Fury would come much later, and remains to this very day in that child within me.

I suspect that it will always be so.

Contrary to what I expected then when I started writing Part II, I do not feel that deep, existential sadness now that I know that I felt then. Now that I feel that I understand everything that has ever happened to me in my life and exactly why it happened, I find that I can easily spot the various mental illnesses that either influenced or drove much of my day to day actions during that time of existential darkness.

I hope this is helpful to the reader.

Else, writing this book is easily the easiest thing that I have ever written thus far in my life. Its as if the book itself has already been written in my head and I am merely finding and putting down the correct words, in the correct order. I am easily writing eight to twelve hours a day, and in fact the words are wanting to get out so badly this morning that I feel them pressuring my ribs out from the inside of my chest around my Solar Plexus at this very moment.

09:05 – Sunday – 26 August – 2001
Day 10 in a Japanese Jail

"A yakuza, a chef, a jewel thief and a Canadian ESL teacher are sharing the same cell in jail...stop me if you've heard this one..." – Micheal Harding

I was removed from my cell every two or three days and asked whether I remembered any more details of the night in question. Invariably, I had to answer in the negative. What happened that fateful night still remained a complete mystery to even me.

The detective had been adding in other questions slowly over the course of our many interviews, but these I presumed had been simply to establish my state of mind that night, as most of the questions centered around the massive amount of magic mushrooms that I had ingested; how much, how big they were, what color, how did they make me feel, did they cause sexual arousal, etcetera.

A number of days later, after it sank in that I would likely be remaining there for a not-insignificant amount of time, I started to look around to get the lay of the land, as it were.

At some point soon after I arrived at the jail, someone, likely the larger younger gentleman whose mattress was to my immediate right and who was super chatty all of the time (he reminded me of a little Buddha), made an attempt at introductions, but as I spoke no Japanese at all, and really did not care to, nor had the mental faculty to, talk with anyone at all that I didn't have to, the introductions were blessedly left off rather quickly.

Then one particular morning, when the weight of my darkness on my soul was seemingly slightly less crushing, I sat up on my twin mattress, crossed my legs under me, and turned and faced my three cellmates.

They all immediately did exactly the same.

After an awkward moment, the larger gentleman to my immediate right said something in Japanese, presumedly checking to see if I had by chance picked up Japanese since I had first arrived, during the few short times that I had been removed from my cell.

I didn't say that of course. That would have been rude. I simply sat and looked at him blankly.

He then waved both of his hands in front of himself and said, verbatim, "No English".

Great.

And then out of nowhere I suddenly say, "Kannst du Deutsch sprechen?"

13:02 – A Spring Day – 2001
Itaewon – Seoul – ROK

It was a lovely spring day there in the bustling national capital city, and I was slowly backing up my 250 CC black Honda motorbike into a narrow space right ahead of the next parked vehicle.

In Korea, you parked wherever you could. At least that had been my experience thus far.

Until this day.

I'd turned off the engine, but I hadn't even dismounted the bike yet and a young police officer walked up to me, ticket book in hand.

He said something to me in Korean, which I didn't understand. My spoken Korean was decent at that point, certainly better than most of my expat friends, to my memory anyhow, but the young officer spoke so quickly that I caught nothing.

Not that I was really trying, to be honest. I had been stopped on the bike a number of times prior to then, but as soon as I raised my visor, which was darkened and fully mirrored so as to reduce glare, and the Korean police officer recognized that I was a foreigner, the response had been every time to simply wave me through.

Most Koreans can speak English decently to varying degrees, but they are extremely shy in using it. That had been my experience thus far anyhow.

So I simply raised my head and flipped up my visor with my left hand, and looked the officer squarely in the eye. At that time, I had pale westerner skin, skyish-blue eyes, a bit of a Harding nose, and I had completely bleached my short hair in techno style.

One couldn't mistake me for Korean.

To my pleasant shock, the young officer said in perfect English, "Your Driver's License, please."

Now, I hadn't spoken any Korean thus far, and my mind assessed the situation in quantum time, and my counter to the officer was immediate.

"Kannst du Deutsch sprechen?"

The officer looked up from writing the ticket, peered at me intently directly in the eyes, paused for a moment, smartly snapped his ticket book closed, and simply turned and strolled away.

I went about my business, quite pleased with myself.

Sunday – 26 August – 2001
Day 10 in a Japanese Jail

Clearly my new friend did not speak German as he laughed so hard that he very nearly toppled over on his mattress.

I then asked, "говорите по русски?"

He simply shook his head no.

"Parlez-vous en Français?"

Negative.

"한국말 하세요??"

He blinked in what I assumed to be surprise, and then launched into some decent Korean.

Winner winner, chicken dinner.

My new friend, now speaking Korean that I would later learn he had picked up from his Korean wife, introduced himself and suddenly we could communicate.

Roughly.

But more than before.

My friend first introduced the gentleman to my immediate left and taking up the top left-side corner of the metal-bar cell, and who was simply covered in tattoos. My friend advised me simply, "He is yakuza.", and stared me directly in the eye until I acknowledged to him that I understand what that meant.

And that's all he ever said about that gentleman.

Next, he introduced the old man who was, I want to say, around seventy-two. Respectfully of course. This was, among other things, a highly age-stratified society.

The old man, he explained, was here because he stole a diamond ring.

"A jewel thief?", I asked in Korean, with interest.

He giggled.

"No," he explained, "he was released from jail last week, and having nowhere to go or any family or friends to depend on, he ran into the first jewelry store that he could find and grabbed the first thing of value that he saw. He then dashed from the store, and turned himself over to the first police officer that he could find."

Cleary, my surprise was readily apparent on my face, for he leaned in and added, "Its warm here, the food is free, and he is respected by both the other prisoners and the guards."

I nodded slowly in understanding, and then he dropped one last detail.

"This is his third offence. He is going to prison for a long time."

That slowly settled in my mind.

I felt great compassion for the poor old man in that moment.

Finally, my friend then told me of himself. He was a chef hailing from Hong Kong, and had overstayed his visa there in Japan, and so was arrested and would remain there until he could pay the fine.

"How long have you overstayed your visa?", I inquired.

"Thirteen years."

I blinked.

"You're going to be here for a while." I advised quietly.

He nodded and hung his head.

The next number of days slowly crept by without notable event.

I spent most of my time darkly brooding over the situation that I had gotten myself into out of sheer stupidity, my mother's words echoing constantly in my head.

I lamented how my wife must feel. Did she even know what had happened to me?

When I could summon any mental energy, I tried to make sense of whatever particular memories of that night were clearest, or seemed to be the most real, on that particular day of my detention. I had been able to recall by that time that when I had landed on the roof from the ledge that I had shimmied over, and right before the old man made his brave citizen's arrest on me, in my sheer panic of being potentially arrested, I had attempted to empty out all my pockets over the edge of the roof, just in case, contrary to my memory, I had managed to obtain some ecstasy. The mushrooms were not a problem, for the reader will recall that they were legal in Japan at this time. However, I full well knew that if I had any ecstasy on me at the time of my arrest, I, like my Hong Kong cellmate, could be there for a while.

In one particular interview during that time, I lamented petulantly to the detective that none of this would have happened if my Korean/Japanese friend had not left me by myself on the street in the first place, while he checked on a room for me; if he'd simply taken me into the motel with him, all of this could have been avoided.

Suddenly, the room darkened and filled with thunder.

Then I realized that it was just the detective slowly standing up and pushing his chair back at the same time. I twisted my head to stare up at him as my handcuffs are always clamped to the table, and he glowered down on me like an angry Samurai god.

I assume that his next words were translated, whether at the time or maybe later, but I sincerely believe that I picked up the sense of his words merely from the angry tone and gestures alone.

"This whole situation is not his doing, but your doing. You are at fault. You got drunk. You ate too many mushrooms. You broke Japanese law. You got arrested. What has he done? Bring you money so that you can eat."

I hung my head in shame, and was promptly returned to my cell.

Otherwise, I was treated by the other prisoners and guards alike as a mild celebrity of sorts.

There were no walls in my area of the jail, only bars, so no one had any privacy, with the exception of the small toilets, which I'm not complaining about in the least.

I was let out every couple of days or so to wash in private, which was not afforded to the other prisoners, with the exception of my yakuza cellmate. I could have used what served as the exercise yard, a small, open-aired, ten-foot by ten-foot area at any time, but I had neither the physical nor mental energy for such an endeavor.

To help pass the time as my memory slowly returned, I was very kindly permitted by the guards to fashion a complete deck of western-style, fifty-two-card-deck playing cards, which I utilized equally to both play solitaire by myself and a form of a popular card game from my youth, known as "Go Fish", or simply "Fish", with my cellmates.

The yakuza always won.

04:09 – Thursday – 30 August – 2001
Day 14 in a Japanese Jail

I suddenly sit bolt upright and wide awake in bed. I've remembered exactly what happened that night.

A pinprick of sun begins to inch up the wall next to me through the airhole in the bathroom outer wall.

It is the longest sunrise of my life.

11:09 – Day 14 in a Japanese Jail
Police Interview Room

"Oh lord, please don't let me be misunderstood." – The Animals, 1965

I'd explained what exactly happened that fateful night almost two weeks previous and the detective had taken many notes, and we three were sitting in silence, each pondering whatever each may have been pondering at exactly that moment in time and space.

I remember exactly what I was thinking: this should clear everything up.

It didn't.

The detective then asked me to relate the entire story one more time. I took a deep breath and began again, at the beginning.

I had arrived in Osaka, ready to party hard. My friend did not show at the pre-agreed upon time, and thus I set out on my own to find adventure. I obtained some mushrooms, took far too many, and drank way too many Blues. I recalled my friend finding me somewhere, who knows where, and he, seeing my completely incomprehensible state, wisely and compassionately tried to help me find lodging for the night.

We tried several places I further recalled, and it was while he was inside the third motel I want to say, checking on availability, that I suffered what I assume to be a psilocybin-fueled hallucination; my mind told me that the building directly across the street was my apartment building in Seoul that I shared with my wife.

In my hallucination, I had just stumbled up the side street from getting out of a taxi, half in the bag from partying all night, and so I crossed the street and took the open-air flight of stairs up to the second floor of the building before me in Japan. I tried what I thought was my door in Korea, which was predictably locked, so I scaled the roof and dropped into some poor complete stranger's bedroom window on the other side of the building at 06:20 in the morning.

The detective was broodingly silent again for a few minutes. He then turned and spoke to the translator, who then turned and spoke to me.

"Tell us, one more time please, what you feel when you eat these magic mushrooms."

My spidey-sense started tingling; what an odd thing to have asked me next.

I provided the same basic answer as I had provided any previous times that this question had been asked, which I then realize had been more than once.

I then politely asked, "Why do you wish to know this?"

The detective looked at me over the glasses that he wore when reading, as if he was assessing my very worth, and then spoke to the translator, who then turned to me.

"The building that you broke into is a kindergarten schoolteacher residence. He wants to know what these mushrooms cause you to feel, because he needs to decide whether or not to advise the prosecutor that at least one of your motives for breaking into the residence could have been to commit rape."

I stared at her, absolutely dumbfounded.

"That's not what they do!" I argued heatedly. "That's not what I intended...I didn't...that wasn't...". My voice trailed off at this point.

They had both already stood up and were preparing to exit, when the translator turned back to me and added, quite sadly, "I don't think that they will be letting you go today."

"No shit, Sherlock." I thought to myself. Was that even an option?

I didn't say that of course. That would have been rude.

I simply sat and looked at her blankly as she closed the door behind her.

09:31 – Wednesday – 29 August – 2001
The Public Prosecutor's Office

I had repeated the entire events of the night in question to the prosecutor twice. The same court-appointed translator was again sitting on my immediate right, and I was very grateful for that continuity of service by her and by the government of Japan.

After a few minutes, the prosecutor spoke to me and my translator relayed.

"He says that he is finishing up your case now for submission to the court. He says that he will give you a few minutes if you need, and then he will permit a final statement from you."

I was somewhat flabbergasted, but as Chris had taught me so many years ago, when you gotta do something unpleasant, best just get on with it.

And with that, I put together not my best heartfelt plea to date or since, but as I was wrapping up, I suddenly broke off.

My translator waited for a moment, then asked, "Is that all you want to say?"

I looked from her up to the prosecutor and asked him directly in English, forgetting for the moment that he would not understand me.

"Was there anyone in the bedroom when I climbed in that first window?"

My translator relayed my inquiry, and I sat back in my chair and relaxed. The response: No.

And then I suddenly followed-up.

"What about the room to my right where I yanked the doorknob in my desperate panic to get out of the building? Was anyone in there?"

This time, after the question is posed in Japanese, the prosecutor simply nodded once, and his dark eyes seemed to bore into the very back of my skull.

But I didn't see him anymore. My vision had completely faded to black, and what filled the inside of my head and chest with such sudden intense pressure as to cause me to feel that my skull and ribcage are about to spontaneously explode, was grief. Grief for the suffering that I unknowingly caused some poor girl or woman, in my inebriated and intoxicated state, out of sheer stupidity.

I hung my head in shame.

I then spoke quietly to my translator.

"Could you please ask the prosecutor to relay my sincerest apologies to this person that has experienced great concern for their physical safety because of my thoughtless actions. Please believe me when I say that I am completely horrified by what I have done."

She translated, and with no response, the meeting was over.

I was returned to the jail, and to my cell.

The next number of days passed very, very slowly.

I was grief-stricken that I had caused suffering in another human being.

I no longer had the energy to play cards with my cellmates, and even my friend gave off trying to engage me in any discussion.

My thoughts were all dark, and the hate of what I was intensified.

Chapter 16

11:37 – Tuesday – 4 September – 2001
Day 19 in a Japanese Jail

"Hadding."

I somehow managed to lift my head and peer towards the cell door.

A guard stood there and spoke crisply in Japanese.

Suddenly, all heads in the cell and the neighboring cells turned to stare at me.

My buddha buddy looked at me sternly, "You go!" he hisses.

Alarmed, I leapt to my feet. I looked inquiringly at my friend as my heart pounded its way up my esophagus.

And then he smiled. "You go. Now."

Comprehension slowly dawned on me. I was being released.

I glanced at the guard inquiringly and he motioned me forward.

I took a step, and then reached down and grabbed what I could of my deck of paper-and-tape playing cards.

I was escorted out past the interview rooms and out to a main office area that I vaguely recalled being processed in when I had first arrived in the jail nineteen day previous. My meager belongings were returned to me and as I turned to walk out the front door, the detective stepped out around a corner, saw me, and stopped, facing me.

I bowed stiffly at the waist for about ten seconds, and then spoke a single word.

"Arigato."

He smiled kindly and nodded his head in return.

I left.

As it turned out, the person that I had to thank for my sudden freedom from that Japanese jail, where I was not ill-treated in anyway, was my wife.

When my friend there in Osaka discovered that I had been arrested, his peeps informed my peeps in Seoul, who notified my wife, who was, as one would expect, absolutely beside herself.

She tried countless times to call the police station in Osaka, and on the rare occasions where she was able to speak with someone, they advised her that they could not discuss my case.

She quickly grew frustrated and conscripted a Korean/Japanese friend of her own, and they flew to Osaka to beseech the detective investigating my case in person.

As my wife would later relate to me, the detective was very apologetic to my wife and her companion, advising that it just was not possible to provide any details about the case while it was being investigated.

Heart-broken, she rose to leave.

Suddenly, the detective motions for her to wait, departs through a closed door behind the secure area, and returned a few minutes later bearing three photos, which he carefully placed on the low shelf in front of her.

"Can you please point which, if any, resemble your current or former residence in Seoul?", her friend interprets.

Baffled as to why he might ask her this, of all things, she spied one which was a dead ringer for our last apartment building, if the shading was slightly off.

The detective simply picked up the three photos, bid her farewell in the Japanese fashion, and disappeared into the secure office area.

Sobbing, she left the building with nothing.

12:32 – Tuesday – 4 September – 2001
Downtown Osaka – Japan

This, unbeknownst to me at the time and up until I called my wife minutes after my sudden and very welcome release, occurred sometime between where the prosecutor advised me that he was considering charging me with attempted rape, in addition to break and entering, criminal trespassing, and so forth, and my sudden release.

If my devoted wife had not come to Japan, even though she was clearly advised not to, I have no doubt that this particular story, and likely many or all of the stories after it, would have ended somewhat, quite, or completely differently.

I stopped at the first payphone that I saw after leaving the police station and called my wife in Korea. She cried. I cried. I promised her that I was coming home and that I would be a better husband.

And the last thing that I said to my wife before I hung up the phone was, "Happy Anniversary."

We had been married exactly one year previous.

I would keep the first of those two promises to her, but I never was quite able to keep, to my eternal sadness, the second.

"Sticking feathers up your butt does not make you a chicken." – Fight Club (1999)

Everything that has a beginning, has an end, and the good times in Korea very slowly ground to a halt.

My wife and I both knew that we wanted children, but of course, living that party lifestyle was not conducive to parenthood.

I was trying to be a better husband however, though self-admittedly I had absolutely no idea what that really meant.

However, what I <u>did</u> know was that I would have been very content to continue partying ad infinitum, not ever wanting those good times to end, of which I had had so few of in my life.

But end they did.

18:11 – 1 July – 2020
My Hostel Bunk – São Paulo – Brazil

The next story that I tell has been bouncing around in my skull for a few days now, likely more. I have resisted telling it because, simply, it was one of my most shameful moments that I experienced in the throws of substance abuse during those years.

I neither <u>do</u> want to tell it nor <u>don't</u> want to tell it because it is shameful; rather, I tell it for these three reasons:

One: I have learned, after many decades of self-imposed ignorance of the inner-workings of my own mind, to trust my sub-conscience and look closely at, rather than to try the utmost to ignore, these kinds of thoughts when they arise.

As I examine this particular memory, sitting in my bunk with my USB fan, black light and glowing blue and white striped bedsheet strewn with carbs (a trick that I have use for decades to get the creative juices flowing), I see the following two benefits of sharing the story with you;

Two: It sets what I believe to be very important ethical context for the reader; it is an example of how far from my moral base I transgressed under the influence of alcohol and drugs during those years.

And this is important for the reader to be able to understand the depth of my self-hate that developed in me over those years for the often-tragic judgement I consistently exercised. When I was twenty-one and going to Norma Jeans with Maurice, I looked down with considerable haughtiness upon those compatriots of mine that lacked sufficient control and imbibed too much, and as a result, did stupid and often dangerous things.

Clearly, I had things to learn.

Three: This beautiful inside-and-out woman, this saint, who married a foreign man with all the best of intentions, against the preferences to be sure of her family, deserves for the world to know what she endured for the honor of that family, for in those early years, I am sure that was the only reason that she did not leave me.

And then once there were children, it was too late.

Shame, after all, is only an emotion.

Chapter 18

03:41 – Late 2002
Hollywood Nightclub in Itaewon – Seoul – ROK

I didn't slow down at all after my sobering experience in Japan, but rather I sped up considerably. The post-epiphany Micheal could talk to anyone, anywhere, at any time, about pretty much anything. He was bold, charming, funny and witty.

And he never, never went home before the partying was all done.

A typical Friday evening of getting ready for the weekend of fun with the boys out on the town, but things had gone very badly between my wife and I since I arrived home from work in the late afternoon. She was tired of all the partying and wanted to cool it.

And it was not the first time that we had had <u>that</u> conversation.

"Feel free to stay home an relax tonight if you prefer." I said to her flippantly as I laced up my boots. "Don's already waiting for me."

She glowered at me for a moment, an early attempt at looking imposing, but she knew that I would be out all-the-more longer if she did not tag along to drag me home at a relatively decent early-morning hour, and predictably, she relented.

However, once we arrived at the nightclub, she did not join in my attempts at having a good time as she usually would have, and the petulant child in me came out immediately.

"Be that way..." I muttered and grabbed another beer at the bar before heading back to the pool table to wait my turn. Don and I played here every weekend; we were the local sharks if you will. People with real talent didn't waste it playing bar tables in Itaewon, but as far as competition went at this primarily 00:00 – 06:00 popular dance club in Itaewon at the time, we were it.

I didn't see my wife for the rest of the night.

At about 03:45, as several guys and I started hashing plans to head up "The Hill", the next normal destination for most people in Itaewon at this hour, I felt a tap on my shoulder.

It was the bar bouncer, a jolly-looking portly fellow that stood only about 5'6", but nevertheless commanded impressive stature. He, like most people in Hollywood, had taken a keen liking to me and my wife, and we sorely loved him back.

"Your wife is passed out drunk in the booth at the far end of the dancefloor...", he told me in Korean. "You need to take her home, now."

that was not the first time that she had done that. Whenever she became extremely angry with my behavior, she resorted to the one thing that had always worked. She intentionally drank so much so quickly and got so far past intoxicated that she couldn't walk, forcing me to take her home.

But just last month I had finally figured out how to turn off the switch in my head that felt an eternal pit of sadness when any woman in my life cried. She was using it every day now it seemed. Girlfriends as far back as I could remember had used that tactic on me to colossal success, but suddenly she could ball her eyes out now and I would not blink an eye.

So I did something that even at the time absolutely shocked that highly alcohol and drug-muted sense of justice buried somewhere deep within me. I reached into my jeans pocket, pulled out the equivalent of twenty USD, handed it to one of the kindest men that I had ever known and said, "Please give this her when she wakes up so that she can take a taxi home."

I thought that I saw tears in his eyes as I turned and walked out of the club.

05:53
The Hill – Itaewon

I was with the boys in between clubs and I felt my cell phone vibrate against my leg. Inside the clubs, the music was too loud to feel that.

I pulled out my phone and see that it was my wife, and that she had already called fifty-nine times. I had not yet completely stopped taking her calls yet as I would in the coming years, so I answered.

"What?!" I all but yell into the microphone.

We were walking down the hill and its always very loud at this hour, and I strained to make out what was being said, but I couldn't hear anything over the din of mostly-hammered early-morning cavorters.

At least not at first.

Then I began to hear what I figured was sobbing. She was crying, again. Then she mumbled something into the phone, but I didn't even try to hear what it might have been.

I simply hung up the phone.

Crying women did not have any affect on me anymore.

08:22

We didn't have our jackets on, and the morning wind was a bit brisk.

Don and I had stepped outside to have a cigarette. I would not start smoking on a regular basis yet for several years, but I had always smoked the occasional one when I was hammered, right since the first time that occurred at the age of seventeen (Sorry, Stepmom!).

My phone vibrated against my leg again.

I was high and drunk at the same time, so without looking to see who it was, I answered it.

It was my wife.

I could only make out a single word.

"Keys..."

I hung up the phone, figuring that she'd eventually get the message.

11:19

I was in the bathroom at Gecko's, the most kickass restaurant/pool lounge ever to grace Itaewon while I lived there. I was half-sober, so I was taking another half of a pill of ecstasy, when I felt my phone vibrate again against my leg.

Frankly, I'm surprised that it has any battery left.

I take the phone out of my jeans pocket and look at the smaller outside screen; 29 messages. I sighed in consternation and flipped the phone open, and pressed the button that began message playback.

It was from my wife; she was waiting outside of our one-room apartment door, and she can't get inside. She did not bring her keys.

I instantly flagged down a cab and got to our apartment in about twenty-five minutes. I took the open-aired stairs two at a time to the second story of the building and immediately stopped. My wife was huddled on the floor, back to the wall next to our door, wearing only her light down jacket.

She lifted her head slightly at the sound of my arrival.

I took the keys from my jacket pocket and threw them on the ground in her general direction.

They hit the floor, slid about eight feet, and came to a stop by her leg.

Without a word, I turned and went back to the life I wished at that time that I could have forever.

10:58 – A Few Week Later
Outside of a Club in Itaewon – Seoul

A typical Saturday morning for us in Itaewon, or rather, should I say a typical continuation of the partying that started the night before on Friday.

The sun was shining brightly overhead. My wife and I, Don, and several others that I do not recall, were outside on the sidewalk discussing where to go next.

However, my wife was tired; not exhausted tired, though she was surely that as well, but she was tired mainly of all the partying. She had asked about dialing it back some a couple times, but I would hear nothing of it.

We began to argue. We broke off from the main group by a couple meters, ostensibly for some privacy, though surely they could still hear most everything that was being said.

She was standing directly in front of me, begging me to hail a taxi, when I told her if she wanted to, she could go home and I would come later.

With no warning, she slapped me across the face, hard.

I saw stars. And before I could react, she slapped me again. Harder.

When my vision cleared, I saw Don looking at me from about ten feet away, expressionless, and I was deeply ashamed. I was nine again, getting slapped across the face by my mother with no warning, merely for asking for more dinner.

I hung my head. We went home.

Chapter 19

The Remainder of 2002 to the End of 2003
Guri City – Kyoungi Province – ROK

After that event, I did fall into line a bit and for while. She had shamed me to be sure, shamed me to the core. I was no longer just failing my wife, but I was now also failing my mother again, it seemed.

I devoted myself to not going out too often, not spending too much money, teaching more classes, and trying to find different kinds of work to round out my resume for when we moved to Canada.

The plan, as we had agreed when we got married, was to stay in South Korea for five years, save as much money as we could for a down-payment on a house in Winnipeg, and then we would move down to her home city and stay there for a year, so that she could be near her family for that last year in Korea.

Not surprisingly, at least to the reader I'm sure, life improved for us both during this time. We became closer and were very happy for a while, in my estimation.

In an effort to stay home more, I became a devoted online MechWarrior, going by the handle of CDW_Lonewolph, and this game really kept me out of a lot of trouble (Thanks Albert!), as I was fairly successful at it, if I recall correctly.

I did begin to drink more at home, but life was not crazy anymore, and we settled into a good rhythm.

Later that year, after I had mulled over and over how to become a better husband, I decided that now was the time to have the child that we both had been wanting, and later that year, we conceived.

There are certain events in your life that you remember because your highly evolved brain, completely independent of you, says, "Damn! We need to remember this so that it does not happen again."

And then there are moments in your life of pure joy, that really, in the evolutionary sense, do you really no good in remembering, but you remember it forever.

That was what the birth of my first child was to me; a moment of pure joy upon the dark, dark canvas of my life, and for that first year at least, I believe that I did an okay job at being a devoted father.

I think, anyhow.

After the birth of our first child I was energized, and I began to think like the head of a family. Lee and his Korean wife had opened and English academy some years back and they were doing quite well. Lee made me a very respectable franchise offer, but my wife would have none of it. She held the strings on the bankbooks, and there was no way in hell that was going to happen.

I gave up after about three months, but kept looking for some other opportunity.

The next year, after speaking with my wife, I took a high school ESL teacher position outside of Seoul, in quite the small town of Gwangju (est. pop: 200,000) in Kyoungi Province, not to be confused to the much larger city of the same name that my wife came from in South Jolla province.

My plan was twofold; 1) Get a solid paying job that was guaranteed money, as relying on private lessons was hit and miss, and negotiating the sometimes unpredictable traffic on my 400 CC Honda was dangerous, and we had purchased a vehicle from a friend as this seemed the safer route for a family man.

The other half of the plan, my longer term goal to become a better husband, was to get me out of Guri City where we lived, as it was still only a forty-minute taxi ride to Itaewon, and I was known to head out late at night after playing several hours of MechWarrior and getting very drunk, and not returning home until the wee hours of the morning.

All my buddies still partied, and so it was just too easy for me to head out any given night that I got too drunk. I really missed my friends, and I missed being popular.

In the days that followed, my darkness again returned, and would increasingly take over my life.

15:01 – 27 June – 2020
My Hostel Bunk – São Paulo

The last four days or so of writing this Part II has been quite different than writing Part I. The stories in Part I wanted out of my head with so much force that I could neither type fast enough, nor scribble notes effectively enough, to get it all out the first time through. I find that I am constantly returning from writing Part II to Part I to add another story, or to input additional details into one of the stories, or to add slight nuances here and there so that the reader may better understand the context of that story.

But writing Part II so far has been more like doing a black-and-white 50,000-piece puzzle in the dark, while using only a box of matches for light, and with only a very vague idea of what the big picture actually is, for I was drunk for most of those years.

The pieces of the puzzle are each a memory from that time in my life, and if I focus very carefully on a particular piece, that memory becomes clearer, and I can begin to pick out the finer details of that life event and get a better sense of what it is, and how each lends itself to the overall picture.

I'm finding that I must make notes of particular memories whenever they surface in my mind, and, as more details about a particular memory come to me, I must return to that particular puzzle piece and add more details to it until the memory becomes ones again complete.

This is a slow process, but I understand why this is the way it is, as I understand how my brain works now, and rather than try to force the memories to reveal their hidden secrets, I take breaks whenever I feel like I need one. I also do my part of the hostel renovation that I'm providing consultation, on in return for free bunk and board.

I am only producing about a page a day, but I understand that I am chipping away at a thick dam of time and intoxication and trust that eventually, if I chip out the right piece, the blockage will collapse and I will remember everything at will.

The Remainder of 2003 to the End of 2004
Gwangju City – Kyoungi Province – ROK

I had been working at the new school now for a few months, and my only friend in the school was a Korean man about my age of smaller stature, but huge of heart.

One day, I mentioned to him that I had heard that the real estate market was booming near the town where the school was, Kwangju City in Kyoungi Province. He offered to take me apartment shopping as it were, and after about a week I found the perfect specimen.

I prepared an elaborate presentation for my wife which went off fairly well, and we ended up purchasing our first home, a new 42 Pyeong (about 1500 square feet) apartment on the fourteenth floor of a high-rise apartment building.

The view was amazing.

Now, getting farther away from Seoul sounded like a brilliant idea to me at the time to be sure; wishing to be more responsible, it surely would stop me from going out late nights/early mornings when I got drunk, and I would be a better husband and father, and life for my family would be grand, and I would no longer be a failure as a husband.

However, as the weeks and then months passed, and my loneliness intensified, my days became darker, and at nights I did the only thing that I knew could keep the darkness at bay, I drank more and more. And here began the years of steadily decline into alcohol abuse for me.

I wouldn't go see my friends in Seoul, and so every Friday and Saturday, I drank at home. First six beers, the ten, then fifteen, and then often up to twenty five-hundred millilitre beers a session.

That's ten litres.

Then it became Friday though Sunday. And then Thursday though Sunday. that had basically been my partying cycle in Korea up to this time, and it appeared to have bonded itself to the very cells of my body and brain.

Now I would never understand, much less admit it until after I returned to Canada, but I became a high-functioning alcoholic during those years, which means that I feel that I fulfilled the most basic responsibilities of a father and husband; we went shopping weekly, visited local parks often, we visited with my wife's friends and family. I acted like a sullen or petulant child most of the time, but I was present.

I could go a day or two here and there without drinking generally, and when I did drink, I could control it to a point, especially if we were with family and friends.

As a result, I did the bare minimum that I could do for my family, which was at times to simply be in the house. I didn't kid myself; I knew that as for as the parental responsibilities went, with the exception of being the sole bread-earner, their mother was almost completely unaided by me throughout the time that we lived together in Korea.

She did try to fight with me in the early years, but my fury just took over faster and faster and she soon sagely opted for peace in the house most time, and would just let me do what I really wanted to do: drink beer and watch movies.

A National Holiday
Gwangju City – South Jolla Province – ROK

This was an earlier one of many national holidays that we drove down to my wife's hometown to spend between two and four days with her family.

From the very beginning, at least once they learned of the existence of a foreign boyfriend only after I had proposed, they accepted me into their family and not one of them ever treated me ill. They afforded me every honor of being a senior male member of the family and gave me great leeway when my foreign rudeness, seemingly constant anger and childish petulance surfaced, which was a common occurrence.

On this particular visit, I had brought my new laptop computer to keep me busy during the majority of the time that we would spend here. I participated where appropriate in family events, but I never really ever conversed with the individual members of her family, with the exception of the rare occasions when my wife's brother or brother-in-law might take me out for a drink, for it was quite well known that I loved to drink, which was quite acceptable in Korean culture, as well as many others around the world.

In any event, the particular dominant dysfunctional characteristic that I was displaying to all this particular visit was anger. I was deeply angry, though by the time that I am writing this story, I really can't remember why. It could have been simply because it was summer, and the mosquitoes had been biting me all night. It never ever really took very much to set me off. But I would never rant and rave in front of her family like I might at home; I would simply remain sullen and petulant the entire time.

After waking the morning after we arrived at her parents' home on that particular trip, I pulled out my new notebook and continued setting it up from the night before.

Suddenly, one of those pesky mosquitoes that kept me awake all night buzzing in my ears, landed on the wall next to me sitting cross-legged on the bed. I leapt to my feet in an instant, furious at it, and bounced all over the bed trying to slap the little bugger as it flitted along the wall and up to the ceiling.

And then, I realized that I'd just stepped on the screen of my new notebook computer.

Instantly fearing the worst, I dropped down off the bed, and sure as h-e-double-hockey-sticks, there was a sizable mark across the screen.

I was instantly furious at myself for this sheer stupidity. I violently punished myself by punching myself in the head multiple times and then switched to punching myself in the upper thigh about a dozen times, hard. I had learned in quite detail from the bullies in elementary school that this was called a *Charlie Horse*. This is quite different than the *Snake Bite*, which was often done on my forearms until the skin was red and flaking.

As my leg gave out from under me and I collapsed to the ground, my wife entered and alarmed, asked what was wrong.

Deeply furious with myself, I show her the damage that I did to the computer, and I remain sullen and petulant in the room for the remaining two days that we visited.

And this was only one of any number of such events.

And yet they accepted me, and never overly chastised me, and never thought any less of me that I ever learned.

And I love each and every one of them to this very day, and always will.

When it came to my professional life, this was where I really excelled. Momma didn't raise no fool, and I've always had a good head on my shoulders, in my estimation anyhow. Excelling at my professional life made me feel barely competent at the rest of life overall; yes, I sucked as a son, as a boyfriend, as a fiancé and as a husband, but the only things that kept me from being a total waste of oxygen were the facts that I believed that I was a bare-minimum functioning father, and I that was a highly-sought after business professional. Jiyeon, my friend and the recruiter that I worked with for the last nine years of the time that I was in Korea, always maintained, to me at least, that I was over those years consistently the most hired and highest paid of all of her contractors.

So, for the first ten years of my professional career, I learned how to do business the Korean style; I dressed smartly, I spoke the language, I understood and participated in the culture. I bowed crisply to those of higher stature and age than myself, I accepted and gave alcoholic drinks in the Korean style when out socializing, and was generally well accepted by that society. Unlike in my personal life, when I had a specific role to play in my professional life, like a waiter, or a performer, or a businessman, I could talk to anyone, at any time, about anything, and be a highly engaging conversationalist.

It was only when I had to be myself that my social anxieties reared their ugly heads, and still do occasionally to this very day.

In my time in Korea, I was fortunate enough to teach ESL at all levels from kindergarten through on to grade twelve, university and in business. I worked first as a teacher, then as a public speaker promoting English language programs around the country for a Seoul-based consulting firm, and then I became a program consultant, designing, implementing and managing a corporation-wide English language program.

After the high school and for the remainder of my time in Korea, I teamed up with my recruiter to help her take her company to the next level. She had a sizable network of both employers in Korea and contractors around the world, but had very little web presence or established organizational policies and processes.

Already good friends at that point, I valued her constant friendship and support throughout my time in Korea more than words can express.

Chapter 20

The Spring of 2004 to Spring 2005
Gwangju City – Kyoungi Province

By this time, just over three years into our marriage, my wife has become quite used to my drinking and temper tantrums. The little boy in me is constantly out and about these days, his red-hot fury instantly palpable at any perceived threat or insult from the woman, and thus default authoritative figure in my life at that time, my wife.

Now I say default because she never measured up to the original authority figure, my mother. Which was not necessarily a bad thing, nor would it have been productive; she just was fundamentally unable to instill the terror in me that my mother could with a mere glance.

Oh, to be sure, many of my previous partners at some point or other had tried to take that hands-on-hips, feet shoulder width apart and stern glower, with which they intended to communicate to me that they were about to explode and that the shit was going to really hit the fan. But even in the heat of a huge argument, no matter how furious or guilt-ridden I felt, as soon as I saw any partner do this, I would immediately burst out laughing. In genuine, honest-to-Buddha, gut-rolling laughter. Because I knew what they were trying to do; they were trying to look scary, and they were trying to intimidate me, to dominate me and my will in that moment, and whenever they did that, I laughed, and laughed, and laughed.

For what they just couldn't understand, was that I had seen some of the worst demons that have ever trod this planet, and as hard as they might try, they simply had not the barest flicker of that evil in them.

Beginning at the birth of our fist child through these years, and in fact to the very day that my tenure in Korea ended, in all sincerity, my wife was a diligent housewife, an absolute hero. All her focus was on simply trying to keep a civil, smooth-running household while taking care of one young and angelic, and one old and furious, child.

And so here I humbly introduce, without blame, what would be for me, the first real nail in the coffin of our marriage.

In Korean culture, as I understand it, it is not odd for the husband and wife to sleep apart, especially when a baby or two is in the picture. Traditionally in Eastern cultures, the responsibility of the wife after marriage is to manage the household, which includes taking care of any children.

However, this is not the case in most western families as I have experienced it, and my wife and I had talked about this several times before the birth of our first child, and it was particularly important to me that we sleep in the same bed.

I thought that I had explained this very well to her, and that we had come to an understanding.

Rather than going the traditional Korean route of the mother sleeping separately with the offspring, we purchased a nice crib, and as per the Western style, we would let the baby get used to sleeping in it, and we would be one happy family.

After the birth of our first child and when the two returned from the hospital, our beautiful baby spent the first night in the crib, as per the plan. The baby, and thus mother, had a fitful night, as was to be expected when getting used to a new place to sleep, such as I feel to this very day sleeping in a strange place. But as we had discussed, this was to be expected and could go on for several nights, weeks, or longer.

After the second or third night though, she could not take the baby crying anymore and exited the bed, took the baby and slept on the floor in the living room.

I thought nothing of it.

Until she did it the next night, and the next.

From then on in the marriage and for the greatest majority of the time that we were together, she slept separately with the children from me, and I considered this a rejection of me on the deepest of level.

I pleaded with her many times over the next few years, to no avail.

And as time went by, and my loneliness and existential feelings of failure grew, and I drank more and more to self-medicate, one could hardly blame her for not wanting to sleep with a drunkard.

If that was the first nail in the coffin of my life in Korea, my work during those darkening years was the second.

263

At this time, corporeal punishment was still utilized in the public-school system in Korea as the go to disciplinary method for students all the way up through grade twelve. As soon as the tenth and eleventh grade students at my new place of employment discovered that I would not cause them any type of physical suffering in any way (this was anathema to me), which was basically days into the school year, they all pretty much stopped listening to me entirely for the remainder of my tenure at that school.

I would hate arriving at that school each and every morning for those two full years, including summer classes.

I was also gaining quite a bit of weight from my ever-increasing beer drinking, and so wanted to get active doing something. To this point in my life, I had probably gained and lost up to fifty pounds five or six times, first starting sometime after I started pounding beer and chicken wings after most shifts when I was making money hand-over-fist as a steakhouse server. I'd heard that some of the male teachers played badminton on a regular basis, and like any typical North American, I had dabbled in racquet sports over the course of my life, mainly racquetball, tennis (never did learn to serve) and some badminton.

I began showing up to watch and was soon kindly invited to play.

In the beginning I was very patient. I knew that these guys were far better than I was, and it would take me some time to catch up.

But as the weeks and months wore on, to be sure, my skill did improve, but like my days with my friend Chris playing that NHL hockey game, I could never quite win. And this brought out the furious child in me immediately every time, and he ranted, and he raved at each missed shot, stomped on the ground or tossed his racquet in the air, much to the amusement of the other teachers.

I played with them for about a year and eventually realized the damage that it was having on me emotionally and stopped playing, but by then it was too late.

The furious child was now almost in complete control.

The child was petulance and fury; when he was out, Mom backed away from him. He could hit things and she would not care. He could yell and scream, no words, just howls of existential frustration at simply having been born in this time and place, and she would never refute them.

The furious child was the one, still very young, that threw my cousin's toy truck into the bushes at our grandfather's house that time when we were about six, for some reason that I cannot recall.

He was the also one that punched little Billy Chambers in the nose when he called me Hardon right in my back yard when I was about eight. Perhaps that's why I felt safer to defend myself. He had presumedly heard it from some local schoolmates of mine.

He was a year younger, I believe, and somewhat smaller than I was.

As he turned and ran the twenty feet or so to his duplex's side-door holding his bloody nose, I caught a shadow move slightly in my room through the open but screened in bedroom window.

It was my mother, and her face was all shadow.

I didn't have the paralyzing fear of her yet that I would have in later years, and I remember two specific thoughts in my head; I regretted having caused suffering in Billy out of anger, and I wondered how my mother would react to this violence in me.

I had never done, and thus she had never seen me do, anything like that before.

She never said anything about it.

I vowed to never cause that type of suffering again.

It was also the furious child that was the first one that asked the question that all facets of my personality would at minimum ponder, if not lament outright, innumerable times throughout the coming decades: "Why is this existence so long?"

If the system was in jeopardy and I was not getting enough dopamine via activity which was more responsible, which was what I swore to do to myself each and every morning that I woke up, head pounding from the night before, then the little boy would step in sometime during the day, afternoon, evening or night, sometimes instantaneously

266

full of rage, but most times deceptively disguised as feelings of deepest sadness and dismal failure, to lull me into such a great disgust at my mere existence as to let him take over.

And once he did, he would quickly resolve any current problem the only way we knew how; alcohol had always made us feel good. If I was in the middle of an argument when he took over, we would simply flee the scene; we would grab the car keys and off to Itaewon we went, often not returning to the house until late Sunday.

And once in Itaewon, we would do whatever was needed to get that dopamine fix.

Fall – 2004
Kwangju City – Kyoungi Province

I distinctly remember the first time that I sat down with my wife, at my request, to begin talking about what preparations we might need to make for moving to Canada.

She was washing the dishes and I asked her to come and sit down and talk with me in the living room. She eyed me suspiciously but agreed. We sat on the couch, and after a moment I started with the opening I had prepared.

"So, I thought that now might be a good time to talk about when we might move to Canada. Next year will be five yea..."

I trailed off as she simply stood up and walked out the front door of our apartment.

I waited for about an hour, and then decided that maybe one more year would be manageable.

Late that year we conceived our second child.

We both knew that we wanted another child, both before our first was born, and then most certainly after experiencing the massive joy that she brought into both of our lives. So, when our second came, we both felt blessed and ecstatic.

Which, by the way, is still how I feel every single day about this wonderful human being that she is becoming, more and more of, each and every year.

Chapter 21

The Spring of 2005 to Spring 2006
Gwangju City – Kyoungi Province

"There are essentially only two drugs that Western civilization tolerates: Caffeine from Monday to Friday to energize you enough to make you a productive member of society, and alcohol from Friday to Monday to keep you too stupid to figure out the prison that you are living in."
- Bill Hicks

I signed on for a second year at my high school, hoping that the first year was just to get settled and that I would do much better as a teacher that second year to maintain control of my classes.

And I did try much harder; I inquired with the other teachers, experimented with different non-violent disciplinary methods, but it was all to no avail, and by the end of the first term at the beginning of summer (the Korean school year goes from March to December), it was all that I could do to make it all the way through the six hours or so of classes that I had every weekday. I pointedly counted the minutes of each day off, starting the second the first bell of the day rang.

I drank most evening and nights and, as my world became darker and darker, the furious child wanted his way more and more often; I was isolated of the English language and of any friendly face, my sister had gotten married and had two children, my father had retired, my mother's mother almost passed away a number of times from a large number of health issues that would have killed an elephant, and so I did the only thing that always made me feel better.

I drank.

During this time, in the space of about two weeks I want to say, I lost two friends who were very special to me, Duff in Canada and Holidayz in Korea.

Holidayz was a few years younger than I was, but had such a constant and incredible energy and positivity about him that everyone he met loved him immediately. I certainly did. I had not experienced death in my adult life to this point, and the death of those two friends, at that time, really shook me to my core and added considerable weight to my already overloaded psyche.

I had stopped taking the taxi into Seoul; it was for too expensive now from where we lived, given that it took an hour on the expressway to reach Itaewon.

But I realized that didn't mean that I had to stop going; we had a car after all.

Sometimes at midnight, sometimes at 02:00, sometimes at 04:00, when the wife had gone to sleep with the children and when I had drunk enough not to care about any possible consequences, I drove into Itaewon. I had gotten a DUI last summer, but had been pardoned by the Korean President after about nine months into my one-year suspension, along with 10,000 other people or so that year, and my Korean driver's license was reinstated.

Getting the DUI didn't slow me down though, I just got "smarter".

I began staying out later and later, longer and longer, refusing to drive home during the very strict hours that the Korean police did their highly effective traffic blockades, searching for intoxicated drivers first early in the evening, then late at night, and finally early in the mornings as people drove in to work.

I would sleep in the car, on a rooftop, or under a bridge, wherever I could find a quiet place to lie down for a couple hours or so, and then drive home in the late morning.

09:52 on a Normal Saturday Morning

"On a long enough timeline, the survival rate for everyone drops to zero." – Fight Club (1999)

I awoke sweating profusely in my tan sportscoat that I typically wear to work.

I looked down and found myself stretched out, lying on my right side on the roof of a low-story building towards the beginning of Itaewon Street (I don't think that was the actual name of the street, if it even had one; it was just how we referred to it at the time). It was midday and the sun was blistering hot, and the cement of the roof around me had focused the intensity of the heat.

It had to be over forty degrees where I had been sleeping.

I awoke because my spidey-sense was tingling; someone was coming up the stairwell to the roof; at least two people, for I could hear an older male-voice speaking.

Then everything came flooding back.

I had started the Friday night at home, fully intending, as always, to not go into Itaewon, but rather stay home and take the family to the park tomorrow. I had even promised my wife (who was pregnant with our second bundle of joy) that I would before she went to bed with our growing healthy baby.

But these days, my promises were just farts upon the wind.

But then that would highly insulting to farts.

I remembered that at some point in my drunken stupor, likely after 02:00, right around when I finished my tenth five-hundred millilitre lager, I decided, consequences be damned, that I deserved a good time and I drove the thirty minutes or so into the city (traffic was always faster at night...the commutes were easy sixty to ninety minutes of inching along in bumper-to-bumper, four lane-wide, five kilometres an hour traffic).

I parked the vehicle near my favorite starting place and on my way to the front doors of the tavern, who did I run into but our main ecstasy hookup from years back.

I stopped him because I wanted to see if he had any product, and we chatted four about ten minutes.

Now, five years ago or so when I first met this fellow Canadian who was about my age, he was quite the brilliant conversationalist. He had majored in political studies as I had, and so our discussions about current and past world events was always very enjoyable for me.

But on this particular night, and for clearly some time beforehand, that highly engaging person that I knew from five years ago was no longer there.

In his stead was a man around my age, who was unshaven and whose sported unkempt hair, dark and sunken eyes, and massive pupils that darted about seemingly constantly. I think that I may have even detected a slight twitch in his face from time to time, I could not be sure.

But what struck me the most was the clear, considerable, chronic or acute (I had no way to know) drop in his IQ and speaking ability. I thought for a few minutes that he was just exceptionally high, but then I realized, no, while he was high, there was much more going on.

Then it hit me.

He loved E just as much as any of his clients did, and as a dealer, he paid only a fraction of what his clients did for it. Most of the time that I was in that scene, one pill cost the equivalent of fifty USD. I'm sure he only paid dollars for each pill, if that. And so, like mine, his E use had increased over time, however, he had not been limited in his excesses financially like I had been and was, and what I was witnessing here was the possible result of long-term excessive ecstasy abuse.

Saddened for him, I cut our conversation short, for I had business to attend to.

Product changed hands, and I bid him adieu.

09:52
A Rooftop in Itaewon

Some twelve hours later, I awoke suddenly on the sweltering rooftop and immediately recall all this, and additionally remember a scant two hours or so before (the sun had already been up, but not so hot) when I had picked this particular building on purely a gut feeling.

I then climbed the stairs and when I got to the top, as if I had been there many times, I felt along the top of the ledge just above the door, and sure enough, there was a key there. I stuck it in the padlock that latched the door to the roof closed, opened the padlock, removed it from the latch, hooked the padlock over a conveniently-placed nail on the wall, opened the door and after a quick survey of my temporary residence, closed the door behind me.

I then sat down cross-legged on the then only warm cement, and proceeded to partially consume the cheeseburger meal that I had purchased about thirty minutes previous.

I hungrily downed a few bites, took a long gulp of soda, and exhausted, stretched out on the rooftop and promptly passed out.

About two hours later, as the door to the rooftop slowly opened and I groggily stood, an older Korean gentleman, about sixty years of age, questioning why the door was not locked, stepped through the doorway, and was closely followed by a younger couple in their mid-twenties.

I slowly gathered that he was showing them the rooftop to one of the apartments that I had passed on the way up the stairs earlier.

As I stepped nimbly around the three of them, through the open door and down the stairs, I heard the older gentleman ask me how I got up here, but I remained silent and simply descended the stairs, and returned to my vehicle parked some ten blocks away.

I unlocked the driver-side door of our four-door white sedan and climbed stiffly in, closed the door, started the engine, and guiltily started the one hour or so drive back home.

10:41

"So this is death. Dark. Cold. All alone. In death there is no second chance. So that's what you think about when you're dying; the real value of all that you've done with your life. And all that you might have done. If only you'd a second chance." – To End All Wars (2001)

My spidey-sense explodes to maximum alert and I am instantly wide-awake and, despite all the chemicals that I have downed mere hours before, I am completely clear-headed and instantly aware of where I am and what is happening.

I had fallen asleep while driving, eyes wide open.

Quick-as-a-cat, I gently jerk the steering wheel briefly to the left at the last possible second before my vehicle slams into the right-side guardrail lining both sides of the expressway. I then guide the vehicle back across an on-ramp merging lane, and re-enter the traffic lane that I had drifted out of only moment before.

Okay, no big deal. It has happened before, once in particular on the drive back to Winnipeg from Dauphin one year, when I borrowed a friend's vehicle and that Ukrainian dancer and I took in a country concert.

But that time, I had not drifted in my lane.

This time, not only had I drifted to the right and completely out of my lane, but I had completely crossed one of the right-side merging on-ramps that are built on to the expressway every few kilometers or so.

A fraction of a second later, and I would have crashed my vehicle.

But this paled beside the fact that vehicles entering the expressway merged into the traffic from that on-ramp, which extended the expressway at that point only roughly fifteen meters to the right of where normally the guardrail would be, and roughly one hundred meters forward, before merging completely into the expressway.

On any other stretch of expressway where there didn't happen to be an on-ramp, I would have crashed into the wall.

And there was even more.

Typically, semi-truck driver's park their massive vehicles on the far right-side of these on-ramps to eat, rest, etc. For most of the drive back, I do not believe that I noted another on-ramp where there were no vehicles parked.

Even though I awoke and saved myself at exactly the last possible moment, I was only alive because 1) there was an on-ramp precisely on that one-hundred or so meters stretch of expressway, through which my vehicle safely drifted, and 2) no vehicles had been parked on this particular on-ramp on this particular day, at this particular time.

Keenly aware that I should be dead, I focus on the road and staying awake, intent on getting home to my family safely. I arrive at the massive apartment complex, park in our parking spot, quickly kill the ignition and remove the key, promptly exit the vehicle, round the back of the car and squat right in front of my passenger-side front tire.

It takes me two seconds to locate the mark.

A barely visible, two-inch, very slight scrape along the outside edge of the tire's plastic hubcap.

I believe that the speed I was going at the time I awoke was ninety kilometers an hour. I typically go the speed limit at this age; I don't want to get a speeding ticket.

In a split second my mind calculates the chances that I should be squatting here at this moment, looking at this mark on the tire where my car had already contacted the cement barrier at the very instant in time that I awoke.

I hang my head.

Not in shame, but in deep thought.

Chapter 22

The Remainder of 2006
Gwangju City – Kyoungi Province

"You've had a near life experience." – Tyler Durden, Fight Club (1999)

I stopped driving into the city when drunk after that event. It shook me that much.

I knew that I had been afforded a glimpse into what the future held for me if I kept on this path.

I grew desperate. I still drank every night, but I stayed in my bedroom, watching movies, chatting with friends back home, mainly Craig, the kind man-boy who changed my life in high school. Our chats over those years gave me a link that I sorely needed to support from back home.

I knew that I had to get everyone out of Korea.

I just had to.

By this time, I had been working with my friend and recruiter Jiyeon for several months at least, helping her to develop organizational policies and procedures, a training package for new ESL recruits, and a new website for her company.

I'd decided not to return to the high school. Since my recent near-life experience, a single meme had been bouncing around in my cerebrum; The future's not set. There's no fate but what we make for ourselves.

Yes, I watched a lot of Arnie movies. But this was pretty much what that meme that had entered my thought-stream had said.

I should be dead. What use for the universe if my story continued on from this point? It would not get better. There wouldn't be any happy ending. that death would have been as good as, and as painless as any other, and my life insurance would have provided financial support to my family.

But my life had <u>not</u> ended there.

This I chose to view as a miraculous save by the universe, if you will, that a hockey goalie can wait an entire season for just one chance to make. If this was not just a random experience (Because what fruit can come of that tree?), but rather a conscious decision by a power greater than myself, which I had always believed in, to change the most convenient instance of my death, then what else about my life could be changed?

"If the universe has decided that my story is not over, then what is the purpose?", I asked myself for the first of probably millions of times over the next many years.

Why had this occurred? That would have been the perfect ending for my life thus far. A fiery crash. And if my life <u>should</u> have ended there, then a decision was made that there was yet value to the universe in having me continue to live this life.

That was logical to me. It made sense. Logic had always had a voting seat at the command table of my psyche;

when you have a split second to either get punched in the eye or kicked in the nuts, decisions like this become virtually automated and based on what makes the most logical sense in terms of physical damage, which was sometimes to just let them kick you in the nuts.

After my near-life experience however, the prospect of my death entered the inner dialogue that occurs moment by waking moment of each and every day of my life, amongst the dominant members of my psyche who have a seat at the command table that runs the whole show.

It was at this point in my life that my entire psychic command system first considered, and then very quickly unanimously acknowledged, that the worst thing that could happen to us was not pain, as we all had believed until that moment, but rather death out of intoxication leading to heedlessness, for then categorically, I would be a failure as a father.

My contract with Jiyeon kept me very busy for the next many weeks and months, which was not the reason that I signed it though. And it certainly was not to keep me from drinking; HAHAHAHAHAHA. No. That never entered my mind. Sure, my wife had very carefully asked me many times over the years if I thought that maybe I might have a problem with alcohol, to which I would usually scoff and say, "I only drink beer."

The reason I took on the challenge was threefold; 1) I felt strongly that I had some sort of karmic debt to this person who had helped me so much and been my friend for so many years, in this country where foreigners are not always looked upon with the kindest of eyes, 2) I knew that I would need more experience on my resume for if/when I was able to move my family to Canada, and this job would add that vital experience, and 3) we had an office in the city very close to Itaewon, and I would have somewhere to crash, and thus would not need to drive the expressway home when drunk anymore.

As the reader should hopefully interpret, I am nowhere near to seeing the forest through the trees yet. But the issue of driving drunk was important to resolve, because I needed to be alive to have a chance of becoming a decent father.

But there was more.

Before the near-crash I had existed just to be a failure, but if a decision had been made by a higher power to not left my life end where it would have been most convenient to at that point in my life, then my existence must have some further use to the universe, which meant of course that I needed to be alive to realize it.

I had no delusions that the universe had kept me around for a purpose that would be beneficial or even enjoyable to me in any way; no, for even I could see benefit in having an example of failure always around for others to see and learn from.

And I was never one to say no to anyone that asked me for help.

People like me rarely got opportunities to earn genuine gratitude.

"I used to have an appetite for my life, and it's just gone."
— *Elizabeth Gilbert*, Eat, Pray, Love

Even though I believed that my life purpose had intrinsically changed somehow, my darkness went absolutely nowhere.

It would be over those next few years that I became, what I later described to the first of a number of mental health professionals that I would visit over the upcoming decade, as being borderline suicidal. This is my own definition, which to me meant that I never actually became suicidal; I never began to plan to take my own life, but I could imagine, and did quite often, how I was likely to die, and I believed that there was no way out of this dismal life I had created, except death.

I don't think that I could have hated who I was any more and still have been able to live with myself, for then perhaps borderline suicidal would simply have become suicidal.

Up to that point, the two choices that I had allowed myself to consider were to stay in Korea for the rest of my life, which was never part of the bargain, or leave my children, which since a child myself I had sworn over and over throughout my lifetime that I would never do.

It was just not an option. I would not abandon them to the childhood that I had experienced. Until I did that unimaginable thing, I still had not completely failed as a father, and that had considerable value to my fragile ego in a life where I had failed at most everything else that mattered to this world.

I crashed more and more often at the office, sometimes after nights out in nearby Itaewon, but more and more simply just to be alone. I had realized that when I was alone, I felt less guilt and shame for what I was, felt better as a result, and could therefore think more clearly.

Ever since the time that I first began to think for myself as a human being, I had always preferred to let my thoughts roam free, unbound by limitation if you will, for this was most often where my greatest ideas were born; out of seemingly nothing.

I had long ago learned that if I tried too hard to solve a problem in my life on my own, very few ideas that I had ever generated myself ever worked as hoped. You see, I couldn't come up with any really useful ideas using my conscious brain, but if I let my mind relax and go where it wanted to, sometimes what could pop into my mind from seemingly nowhere could be pretty radical.

For example, it was in that office near Itaewon that the idea to not do a third year at that high school flashed into existence from my subconscious mind.

I remember clearly that I was standing at the wide second-story office window that opened onto the shaded street below, which had tall trees along both sides. The area was close to Gangnam, one of the many affluent areas of the Korean capital. I simply loved to stand at that open window, close my eyes, listen to the light traffic passing by, enjoy the birds singing in the sweet-smelling summer trees, as I picked up bits and pieces of lives passing under my perch.

It was during one of these many quasi-meditations that I would start making in my life on a very regular basis in this kind of setting and others like it, that the idea first entered my mind; Why must I continue to work at a job that makes me absolutely miserable? Hadn't I once dreamed of working for the United Nations because, as my father had at many times sagely advised me, I wanted to do something that I enjoyed?

The more I dwelled on it, the more logical it sounded.

And then sometime in the weeks that followed, Jiyeon approached me to request my particular skill set in helping her solve some frustrating challenges that her company was grappling with.

I liked to solve problems (I had made the connection very early in life that solving problems, even extremely simple ones like reorganizing my bedroom furniture, provided very nice little serotonin hits), and I loved it when people actually thought that me, Micheal Harding, that punching bag, that failure, might be able to help them in some way.

From that point, solving problems became my first wholesome, self-prescribed antidepression medication.

I'm somewhere around five years old when my mother is setting out a just-filled bowl of dog food for Sheba, her gorgeous German Shepherd.

Suddenly, out of nowhere, she barks at me.

"Don't eat the dog food, Micheal. Its for the dog."

I do not recall if that was actually my intention at the time, however, as my body and spirit had not yet been lashed into near oblivion by this likely already in some ways broken, or at least partially broken woman, I yet possessed a modicum of strength in me, in the form of spite.

So, when she turns back to her precious dog, I grab a meager handful of those dried bits of whatever from the large white plastic pails that she keeps it in, and shove them in my mouth, taking care that she doesn't see (I have already stated that I've never been even partially suicidal).

To my surprise, the dog food didn't taste that bad.

And it instantly made me feel...good.

And this is how dog food became my first addiction.

It started as a self-prescribed prescription for feeling good, which I got from that brief, childishly innocent moment of spite. I remember immediately taking another handful. And then another.

And that quickly graduated into a daily habit.

In time, that dog food addiction evolved into a food addiction, first during our time in that haunted house and from our very own kitchen fridge that mother told us to leave alone (Sis, we should have listened about the tabasco sauce...), and then after, from the garbage cans at school.

Then it became a sugar addiction, and then a video game addiction.

And then friends.

And then girlfriends.

And finally, alcohol, drugs and nicotine.

Chapter 23

The Beginning of 2007
Gwangju City – Kyoungi Province

"If you do what you've always done, you'll get what you've always gotten." – Tony Robbins

Very slowly over an indeterminable period of time, my brain began to function increasingly better.

Perhaps because I had been drinking less, perhaps because I spent more quiet time at the office, or even possibly from the additional dopamine that I was getting from the cigarette smoking that I just decided to take up one sunny day here in the office.

But most likely, it was a result of the combination of all three to varying degrees.

The thing is that I don't really know when or why my brain started to work. All I knew at the time was that I could think more clearly most days, especially those that I didn't drink too much, and most especially when I was at the office.

And thus my conscious brain began ruminating over what, at least at that time, it believed to be my largest life-issue; living in Korea.

I was preparing again for my annual prostration before my wife, but each year she always responded the same; "I'm not ready to talk about it."

Given sufficient meme exposure, most should be aware that one of the definitions of insanity is doing exactly the same thing over and over again, but each time expecting a different result.

"Okay..." my subconscious brain said one day when I was blissfully enjoying a cigarette at the office window, just letting my mind wander where it willed, "...is it possible to break the overall plan into different phases? Say, for instance, instead of simply having one phase for this project, moving to Canada, we break it up into two phases, the first being to move across the country to the wife's hometown, Gwangju in South Jolla Province, so that she can spend that last year with her family, as we promised her."

I knew that she was as miserable, if not more miserable than I was, both in our marriage and at being mostly across the country from her family, and I thought that if I presented it to her just the right way, she might leap at the chance to move us all to her home base, the root of her power, near her parents.

Then I would figure out after that just exactly how I would go about accomplishing Phase 2: Moving my family to Canada.

But for now, one phase at a time please.

The presentation went swimmingly.

Within weeks the four, of us moved to my wife's hometown, and thus I began the very quick but painful final countdown to the single most heart-breaking moment of my entire life to date.

The Spring of 2007
Gwangju City – South Jolla Province

True to my word, we moved close to my wife's family; we were a mere five-minute walk away.

And that became a problem for me.

Because, of course, I hadn't stopped drinking. Drinking was not a problem per se, and even _if_ it was (my wife had planted that seed inside my head more than once, and it germinated...thank you, for that among so many other things...), I had cut down considerably to be sure.

However, against all my assumptions and expectations, the more time that passed by in this city with the in-laws, the darker my world became. And I knew that it was my fault., because I couldn't stop drinking, even though I was so close to my goal for the first time ever.

Yeah, sure, I could put off the cravings for a day or two here and there, but inevitably my vision became too weighted down and I needed a dopamine fix.

So any time that I couldn't resist that first one, I drank to oblivion.

I had pretty much completed all the hard work by this time with Jiyeon, and private classes is this smallish city didn't pay anywhere near what they did up in Seoul. But we were able to quickly locate a small job in an English school, and so was able to bring enough cash for us all to live on.

It also took me mere days to find the local expat hangout, and once I heard the beautiful language of English being spoken to me again, it became my only hangout.

02:13
A Non-descript Very-early Morning in Early Summer – 2007

I was out again at Speakeasy with my buddy Luke, a newly arrived Canadian teacher that I took under my wing for a short time. It was really nice to have a connection like that for me in those dark final months in Korea.

The weekly trivia game had finished some hours before, and I was chatting with a nice Korean gentleman about my age. He offered to buy some soju, but Momma didn't raise no fool, and I stuck to my tried-and-true beer.

He then suggested heading to another location, and since he had been especially congenial, and given that he only looked to be about one-hundred and sixty pounds, and I weighed more of a beer-tilted two-hundred and five pounds, I didn't feel that he posed any threat to me.

However, I guess that in my drunkenness I misunderstood him, because I had thought that we were heading to another drinking establishment (I hadn't been able to find a late night one there in Gwangju yet), but instead we'd arrived at a public bath house, which commonly were open around the clock throughout the country.

So, what the hell I said, as I could definitely use a relaxing hot bath.

We entered the bathhouse and my acquaintance paid for us both, for which I was appreciative, and we went in and threw our clothes into separate lockers in the men's room. He wanted to go to the cold-water bath, but that was entirely unappealing to me, though an important part of the bathing culture in Korea as I understood it, and we parted ways.

I found a nice secluded spot in the hot water baths, sat down with my back against a wall hip deep in the nice hot water, and promptly fell fast asleep.

After all, drinking was hard work.

08:43

I gently awoke sometime later, still sitting upright in the open area bath.

I looked around briefly, but my acquaintance was no where to be seen. I panicked for a second, before I remember that I had locked my clothes and wallet in a separate locker.

I returned to my locker and saw that the locker next to mine was empty, so I got dressed and caught a taxi home.

09:13

When I arrived home, my wife was in hysterics.

She had thought that something had happened to me, which wouldn't have been the first time, to be sure. She advised me then, that her father got very worried when she called their house first thing in the morning upon realizing that I had not come home.

She then informed me that her father had called the police in his genuine concern for my wellbeing.

I blinked uncomprehendingly at her.

Then I remembered that she had never ever mentioned anything about my overdrinking or depression to her family, throughout the entire course of our relationship.

Ever.

So, naturally, this was all brand new to them.

My spidey-sense began to tingle.

My wife promptly called her parents, who then ostensibly called off the cops and then headed over to our fourteenth-story apartment unit.

When they arrived, they were solemnly issued into the living room by my wife, where I was already sitting cross-legged on the floor in the Korean style.

Then they all sat down.

What occurred over the next forty minutes or so was a very thorough and well-overdue lesson to me in the unfettered power of the in-laws. They advised me, led by my father-in-law, who I loved, respected and admired, that in no uncertain terms, this type of behavior was not becoming of the husband of their eldest child, and if this continued, they would not permit her, or their grandchildren, to move to Canada.

Checkmate, my brilliant wife.

Apparently her momma didn't raise no fool either.

20:44 – 18 December – 2007
Our Apartment – Gwangju City – South Jolla Province

I am absolutely hammered again, and my wife and I are arguing something fierce.

She has called her sister over for support and they are both standing before me, my wife with her hands on her hips, staring at me defiantly, yet a mere shadow of the previous demoness that I had escaped. Her sister was standing a few feet behind her and off to the side, seemingly hunkering in the doorframe to the extra bedroom, as if very much wanting to be anywhere else.

I'm losing the battle in Kwangju, and I know it.

I can feel it in the pit of my stomach every single waking moment. I do not have a square on the chessboard to move to safely. If I drink, I act badly, and when I act badly, well, blood is thicker than beer.

And I cannot resist the drink. It's the only thing that lightens the darkness.

I'm outnumbered, outgunned, and outsmarted.

And I'm furious at that.

Yet at the same time, I'm absolutely desperate. I know from where my inner voice has always spoken deep within my mind and chest equally, that if I do not leave here soon, I will die here.

Suddenly, from no place that I can fathom in my drunkenness, a thought comes to me; if I will die here, then I must leave this place. That is the lesser of the two evils.

And if I cannot leave my children, then I must make my wife throw me out of our home.

For good.

Then, years later after I had returned to Canada to live without my children, at least I would be able to console my self with the knowledge that she had ended the marriage, not me.

So without a second though, I think of the very worst thing that a husband could ever do to a wife.

"I've slept with at least twenty prostitutes in the back of our family car in Itaewon." I calmly tell my wife.

She does not react in any way. She just stares blankly at me.

I think that perhaps she did not hear what I said, so I begin to repeat my horrifying false testimony.

Faster than one could blink, so fast that I never saw it coming, she slaps me hard as fuck across the face.

I see nothing but red and stars.

And I am instantly furious. Like so many years ago at that bar when I lost control of my rage, and I shoved my then-girlfriend when she threatened to have me tossed out of there like I was a nobody to her, I raise both my arms to shove my wife.

But then I freeze.

For I have had an epiphany; I have been playing this life and marriage game, unbeknownst to me, severely emotionally and intellectually handicapped, for many reasons that I would not begin to unravel for years. My family-devoted wife would <u>never</u> leave me. That <u>never</u> had been an option for her. She would take any of the worst shit that I could every dream up, because for her, the honor and sanctity of her family meant far more than any suffering that I could ever cause her.

I grabbed my wallet and keys and left the house.

For a beer.

And to think.

20:11 – 22 December – 2007
E-Mart Shopping Centre – Gwangju City – South Jolla Province

"It's only after we've lost everything that we're free to do anything."
- Tyler Durden, Fight Club (1999)

My wife and I were on the down-escalator, and she was

standing next to me behind a shopping cart full of Christmas presents for our girls.

I had told her yesterday that, for my health, I couldn't stay in Korea anymore and was going back to Canada, with or without them.

Her swift response;

"We are staying."

That was the smarter decision on her part.

I'd already purchased a return ticket to Canada with some side-money that I'd recently earned though recruiting with Jiyeon, and departure was set for three days after Christmas.

At that moment, my wife was lamenting that we were spending too much money on presents, because I will need it when I leave.

I told her not to worry about money, because it would be the last happy Christmas that the girls would have for a while.

My wife hung her head.

"Self-improvement month. I guess somebody gave me a wake-up call. I just wanted to apologize to you. And to let you know that apparently my capacity for self-sabotage wasn't boundless after all. The real question is, why did you ever put up with me?" – Eddie Morra, Limitless (2011)

The taxi is waiting outside.

We've said nothing to the girls yet. Neither of us knows what words might sooth what is coming.

All four of us are taking the elevator down in complete silence. Not even our youngest, just shy of two and a half years old, makes a sound.

The children sense that something is very wrong.

The elevator door opens and they three exit the elevator so that I can remove my single suitcase. It occurs to me at that moment that I am leaving with one bag, whereas just over a decade ago, I had arrived in Korea with two.

All that time, and what did I have to show for it? I felt that I was leaving with less than I had arrived here with. And with so much heartache having been suffered by the four of us in between.

My heart is straining to the point of disintegration in my chest, I can feel it. And I do not know if my fragile mind will survive that.

I walk quickly to the waiting taxi. I open the driver-side passenger door, throw my suitcase in first, glance over at my wife, and my two God-blessed beautiful babies that I have loved with all of my soul since the very second that I set my eyes on their angelic faces, and who need me, their father, to help them grow up safely in this horrifying, nothing-but-suffering producing world.

Its too much for me. There are no words in any language for a moment such as this. Tears are streaming down my face and I am physically unable to speak.

I simply turn and get into the waiting taxi, close the door, and tell the driver to go to the airport. And then I try my very hardest to not look at my family as the taxi pulls away, but some things, no matter how excruciatingly painful one knows they will surely be, one simply cannot resist doing anyways.

And here I am at the single-most heartbreaking thing that I had ever witnessed in my entire life up until this very moment, and beyond.

I look back, and my wife has just told our daughters that I am leaving, and presumedly that I won't be coming back for a long time. My youngest, sitting in her dark-colored stroller, not really understanding at all what that means, bravely raises her little hand and waves at me in the taxi.

But my oldest is over four years old now, and she loves her father with a power far hotter than a billion earth suns, and as my gaze switches to her beautiful dark eyes, I can see plainly through the windows to her soul, as that had once been me, that she knows what this means, and that her little heart is breaking.

I turn quickly away, but it's too late; I've already seen the pain in her soul, and the look she gives me in a desperate silent plea to not leave her will be forever seared onto my soul. I understand that my daughter believes that I am abandoning her, and that she doesn't understand why, and I know deep in my being, that just as I did when my parents separated, that she will blame herself.

It is at this moment that I realize that I have finally failed ultimately, as I always new that I would; I have failed my children.

My heart shatters into a billion, tiny, magma-like, scorching pieces of excruciating grief.

PART III: My Return

Chapter 24: Rock Bottom

"It begins where it ends. In nothingness. A nightmare born from deepest fears coming to the unguarded. Whispering images unlocked from time and distance. A soul unbound touched by others but never held. On a course chartered by some unseen hand. The journey ahead promising no more than my past reflected back upon me. Until at last I reach the end. Facing a truth I can no longer deny. Alone as ever." – Dana Scully, The X-Files

Many old timers in alcoholics anonymous (AA) will tell you that, unless you hit rock bottom, you are not desperate enough to walk through the front door of a meeting.

As the theory goes, once you hit rock bottom, once you get to that place in your life where you are lower than you have ever been, and your very core self is so shattered that you do not recognize the dark, sunken, glazed and haunted eyes staring back at you in the mirror in the morning, this is the best time to start rebuilding yourself from scratch.

You don't necessarily <u>have</u> to hit rock bottom, but it does provide one with more shattered pieces of a soul with which to begin the long process of rebuilding it.

I had not hit rock bottom in Korea, rather merely removed myself to an environment significantly less conducive to suffering.

My worst was yet to come...

The Beginning of 2008
Winnipeg – Manitoba – Canada

"Stop thinking of what you intend to do. Stop thinking of what you have just done. Then, stop thinking that you have stopped thinking of those things. Then you will find the Now, the time that stretches eternal, and is really the only time there is." – Robin Hobb, Royal Assassin

I had no plan for when I returned home.

All I had, and all I really could have handled at the time anyhow, was the simple goal of getting out of Korea. But as I had learned from my any experience in teaching English that first year in Korea, you rarely, if ever, even need a plan. It can help, sure, but sometimes you get better results by just going on gut instinct.

And so that is what I did.

By the time the plane landed in Winnipeg, I already had a quasi-type plan; find work, get an apartment, start a career.

That was it. Simple, but you gotta start somewhere.

These were the immediate challenges before me that I felt rank the highest, according to what western society says one must attain to be considered well-adjusted. However, as Jiddu Krishnamurti, a contemporary Indian philosopher once stated; "It is no measure of health to be well-adjusted to a profoundly sick society."

But I wouldn't figure that out for many years yet.

I still had not considered to this time that my drinking might be in any way related to the countless poor decisions that I had made, over the course of the last thirty-eight years, that had slowly eroded the stability of my core self.

And most certainly I was not ready to consider that there was any existential link between alcohol and my darkness.

I simply believed, as ever, that I was just a complete failure at life.

End of discussion.

I stayed with my mother for a number of weeks in a spare room in the basement of her home.

My wife and I chatted now and then by phone. Nothing significant per se in terms of our relationship, as mainly I wanted to be able to talk to my babies. Occasionally, the topic of the future of our family came up, and though nothing concrete was ever really discussed, decided or agreed upon, it was clear to both of us that this option was still on the table.

My drinking lessened considerably after leaving Korea, I hypothesize for the following reasons to varying degrees:

1) I was staying at my mom's house, so getting drunk was out of the question.
2) I had very little money. I had left all our funds in Korea.

3) A lot of pressure was released upon the decision to leave Korea. The absolute bottomless emptiness that had been my almost constant companion for years now, had receded somewhat. Things were far from right, to be sure, but I think that first step away from the environment where I first became profoundly ill, made a significant difference in my overall physical and mental disposition, if at least temporarily. Spiritual disposition was another matter entirely.

I simply concentrated on just moving forward, to keep thinking about the future, how I was going to build a home for my wife and daughters if, somehow, it worked out one day that they all moved to Canada.

If something can be imagined, then it can be achieved.

After all, I had imagined getting back to Canada and had kept that in my mind most waking moments for the last few years, and there I was.

And then, the unthinkable happened.

Within mere weeks of landing Canada-side, I received a Facebook message from the girl who broke my heart mere weeks before I left Canada a decade previous.

And she wanted to meet me.

What happened between me and this woman is not necessary for this part of the story, but suffice to say that I made a life-altering connection.

Sometimes, in the past, when people treated me in ways that caused suffering in me, what they did to me was not really about me at all, but rather about them, about their life, and about their particular set of life-challenges that that they were running up against, or like me, banging their head against at a frequency directly proportional to the intensity of the translucent darkness I felt daily on my mind and soul.

By the time that we finish our first conversation, I had not forgiven her; rather, I had realized that there was nothing to forgive. She had only done what she felt she needed to do while trying to make life-affecting decisions. I had hated her, and thus caused suffering in my own mind, body and soul, because I did not understand that some things are not about me in this universe.

We instantly become the best of friends, and since then, I have considered that brief but emotionally intense time together with her as one of the greatest treasures of my life.

Today, she is married to an equally amazing Winnipegger, and they have co-created one of the most beautiful children that I have ever seen.

After everything was done, he and I agreed that, had circumstances been different, we likely would have been good friends.

I hold in my heart for their whole family the most wholesome and compassionate of love and well wishes.

March – 2008

A life cannot be thought good which is harmful in its impact on others, or which results in a perversion of the possibilities and capacities of the person living it. A choice of life has to be able to stand up to scrutiny, a fact that rules out irresponsible, destructive, wasteful lives as good."
- A. C. Grayling, The God Argument

I was not drinking that much at all, but my darkness during these early days after my return to Canada was so very heavy upon my soul. But I'd realized that a significant portion of the darkness was guilt; guilt for my many failures, and guilt for my many lies.

After about three months in Winnipeg, my darkness grew too heavy for my psyche to be able to operate effectively, and I knew that I needed to release the pressure somehow.

I decided that the best way to address the guilt was to accept complete responsibility for the part that I played, and so I decided to write my wife a very long letter outlining the breadth of my failures to her. My base rational was that if she saw me at my worst, but still accepted me for all my failures, then she was a keeper.

I sent the email off, fully understanding and ready to accept whatever potentiality may come, and received a prompt response.

She did not need to read the letter. She wanted our family to be together, and so all was forgiven.

I was elated.

A number of days later, I got a second email from her.

She advised, despite her previous decision, that she had to know what was in the letter, and that she and my daughters would not be coming to Canada.

Period.

That was the smarter decision on her part.

"Sometime, when you least expect it, you'll realize that someone loved you. And that means that someone can love you again! And that'll make you smile." – Homer Simpson

I quickly landed a job at the airport just a few weeks after I arrive back home, working as a check-in agent for a small airline service company. The pay was decent, and it kept me busy.

After a few months I was promoted to supervisor, which meant that I should have been feeling better, but as the beginning of summer rolled around, my darkness returned intensely, and my drinking increased considerably.

I had my own place by this time, my mother having prompted me to move out of her place after a few weeks by telling me that I was going to have to pay five hundred dollars a month rent, which was a good chunk of what I was making at the time. She would house many friends and family members over the decades and it always ended the same way; mother's darkness would get too much for her to handle, and she would sometimes literally kick them out on to the street.

No one was exempt. But most everybody who knew her, knew that going in, so it was never a surprise, at least not when she did it to me.

But when she did it to her own mother? Well, that's a different story entirely, and there are only two people still living that were involved in that fiasco, my mother and her youngest brother, both of whom would rather see the family torn asunder than act like example-setting family elders.

June arrived that year and I was suffering horribly from loneliness, and so I decided that it was time to change things up and get back into the dating scene.

All attempts at communication with my wife had been met with silence, and since I understood that one highly effective way, at least in my experience, of forgetting about a recently entombed relationship was to start a new one, dating seemed an appropriate decision.

I wanted desperately to move forward in my life to get better, whatever that meant to me at that time, and I correctly perceived that meeting someone new might just give me that forward momentum that I needed.

I would join a number of dating sites over the following decade or so, as I felt that this mode of finding a life-partner to be the most efficient, given that one could review hundreds of potential partners before going on a single date. Meeting that many people by conventional means was basically a crap-shoot, and despite the greatest feedback that I received over the years from my dates and others being that online dating is insane, I still believe that this mode of partner-searching is the most efficient one out there in this age.

Then again, I had developed one skill that many others might lack, that of being able to read between the lines, which I had developed over the those years of working directly with Jiyeon and having reviewed hundreds, if not thousands, of applications from people wishing to teach in Korea.

By comparison, reading between the lines of online dating profiles was piece of cake, and I met some of the most amazing women on the face of this planet over that decade. Each and every one of them taught me or gave me something of themselves that I vitally needed, perhaps known to, somewhat suspected by, or completely unbeknownst to me, during the time together that the universe very kindly gave us.

The very first, and ultimately the one that helped me to start my long climb back to sanity itself, and, against all the wishes of her heart, let me go when it was time to, was Jessica.

Late May – 2008
Winnipeg – Manitoba

"You met me at a very strange time in my life." – Fight Club (1999)

Within days of joining the first of many online dating websites, I was matched with this simply brilliant, captivatingly beautiful, green-brown-and-gold eyed actress/feminist in a Canadian city somewhere west of Winnipeg.

The words "long-distance" had lost any meaning to me at that point in my life; I was desperate to meet anyone that rose to my long ago self-acknowledged impossibly-high standards, which I make no apologies for; I once read in a book that one should always shoot for the moon, and if you fall short, at least you will rest eternal amongst the stars.

Jessica and I linked up and quickly graduated to chatting by messenger, and then by video.

And then we fell madly in love. A highly romantic love. We redefined what romance meant to me, at least.

During one online conversation that occurred mere weeks after our first contact, we decided that we were each sufficiently enamoured with the other to make a pair of visits, first me going out to meet her in her hometown, and if everything went well, she would come out to Winnipeg later in the summer.

The first trip went swimmingly; the moment that our gazes touched as I descended the escalator at the airport, was as charged as when I first met that previous girlfriend in the basement of that restaurant in early 1997, and we immediately began planning the next trip for early to mid-August, I want to say.

As I had love back in my life, my darkness predictably became virtually undetectable.

Life in fact was grand all around for me because, assumedly, I had been successful at getting the things that are supposed to make one happy, according to our society; I've got a highly intelligent, kind and gorgeous girlfriend, I've earned a promotion at work, I've purchased a lightly-used SUV, I'm renting a super-yuppyish condo, and drinking $20 bottles of red wine like I'm addicted or something.

There was no question that I should have been happy.

And so I was.

For a while.

Late July – 2008
Winnipeg – Manitoba

"The imagination. It's there to sort out your nightmare, to show you the exit from the maze of your nightmare, to transform the nightmare into dreams, that become your bedrock. If we do not listen to that voice, it dies, it shrivels, it vanishes. The imagination is not our escape. On the contrary, the imagination is the place we are all trying to get to."
- Six Degrees of Separation (1993)

Jessica arrived on schedule, and the next few days were filled with absolute bliss for us both.

We were out and about everyday as I took her to all the wonderful must-see locations in what I will always consider to be my hometown of Winnipeg.

On day four of her seven-day visit, the unthinkable happened.

I got laid off from my airport job, along with the entire staff. Our office's only airline contractor shut down overnight, stranding tens of thousands of highly perturbed tourists in various hospitable locations around the world, and there simply was no more work for us.

Immediately, my perfectly reconstructed world began to hum, like the atoms of a crystal might when a high-frequency sound beam is pointed at them. But my problem-solving skills were quite evolved by this point in my life, and my brain, for the first time, interpret and applies to that current situation a parable that I first heard in university.

The reader may recall my professor at university, Professor St. John (pronounced Sin-jin), and it was very early on in my first semester in university, taking that fateful Introduction to International Relations course, that I heard him explain for the first time of many times that the Chinese character for crisis was almost exactly the same as the character for opportunity.

It just depended on how you looked at it.

That afternoon, as Jessica and I talked at my condo about what I my options were, like I had done with increasing success over most of my life, I let my subconscious mind "guide" the rest of the command table if you will, for that's when the more radical ideas typically come to me.

It was likely that I even heard a replay of Professor St. John in my head telling the class, "Crisis and opportunity are one and the same, merely viewed through different lenses".

Suddenly, a thought popped into my mind; my job had ended because my time in Winnipeg had come to a close.

I was on a month to month lease. I would be financially stable for the next few weeks (I had received two weeks of severance pay from my employer), and I was in love with an amazing being that had her own place in another part of the country.

317

Recalling my contemporary existential viewpoint, that the universe may yet had some purpose for my continued existence, I made the conscious choice to believe that my firing was not random event, but rather a gentle push by the universe in the direction that it desired me to go.

Three days later, Jessica and I drove out together to her hometown in my loaded SUV.

"Grief is a way of loving what has slipped from view. Love is a way of grieving that which has not yet done so." – Stephen Jenkinson, Die Wise, 2015

The first thing that Jessica did upon her arrival home was introduce me to the world of yoga.

I didn't like it at first, because, of course, I thought that I looked like the most ridiculous person ever to try it, especially in the black, full-length, bell-bottom spandex yoga pants that she had bought for me and insisted that I wear. I understand now that for most of my life I have suffered from different social anxieties, one being that I just cannot look stupid or unlearned of anything in front of people that I do not know and trust, else that would potentially be enough to make me a target to those who preyed on weak people like me.

However, sometime months later, I would find yoga a very effective tool for improving my physical, mental and spiritual health, and I still practice today.

But at that time, yoga was a no-go for me.

After being in that new city for only a few weeks, I was not really interested in trying new things anymore, anyways. Things with Jessica and I were swell, but I hadn't yet been able to find work, and even though I quickly landed interviews at a number of good opportunities, I didn't quite make it over the finish line.

I was able to land a job serving tables quite easily though, at the local franchise of the steakhouse that I had worked with in Winnipeg throughout university, and so was able to pay day-to-day expenses once my severance pay ran out.

And then, one day, completely out of the blue, I got a phone call from back in Winnipeg.

My mother's mother was dying, this time for sure.

I returned to Winnipeg immediately, and was able to be by her side when she passed peacefully. She helped raise my sister and me for almost a decade after our parents separated, and truth be told, I loved her as a mother.

Over the next few weeks and then months, my darkness gradually returned for reasons that I could not fathom at the time, and I returned to the only things that I knew that worked against that dreaded weight; alcohol and drugs.

21:18 – 28 December – 2008
Jessica's Condo

I'd been trying unsuccessfully to get a hold of my wife in

Korea for a few days so that I could talk to my girls at Christmas.

My wife had started letting me talk to them a couple months previous, and I called every couple weeks or so just to hear the love in their voices over the thousands of kilometres of intervening communication cables. As I self-medicated more and more by primarily drinking, speaking with my daughters was increasingly the only thing that seems to lift the heaviness that my blanket of darkness was, once again, slowly engulfing me within.

I was about to hang up the phone yet again, when suddenly my wife answered and relayed to me a very brief but non-negotiable message; She had decided not to let me talk to our daughters anymore, because she had grown weary of deflecting their days-long barrage of questions after each call about when I was coming home.

I nodded my understanding as I hung up the phone.

It was at this point that I believe that I suffered my first full mental collapse.

I hung my head.

Jessica came in after a short time from the other room where she had gone to give me some privacy, and immediately asked what was wrong.

When I didn't answer, she came over and knelt down on the floor directly in front of me, where I had not yet moved in the chair by the phone.

Emotionless, I quickly related the synopsis of the call, stood up, calmly collected my wallet and keys, turned and told her that I needed to go get a drink, and quietly left the apartment, closing the door softly on my way out.

21:39

I exited the beer vendor nearest Jessica's condo and calmly walked back to my SUV parked in the lot about thirty feet away, barely registering the beautiful but increasingly falling snow.

I rounded the rear driver-side bumper of my SUV and came to an abrupt halt as I saw three of what I took, by their attire, to be homeless gentlemen, sitting on the curb at the front of my vehicle, and who immediately made to get up and gone.

"Do you guys want some beer?" I simply asked.

All three who were in the various stages of standing up, stopped and stared blankly at me for a moment, and then what I assumed to be the thirstiest one in the group grinned toothlessly and said, "Fuck yeah!"

Sitting right there on the curb in front of my vehicle, we quickly demolished the twelve that I had bought, and I offered to go grab another.

But instead, they had a different suggestion.

"Do you wanna get some crack?"

My response: "Fuck yeah!"

"Do you have enough money, man? We're kinda broke at the moment..."

"How much is it?" I inquired politely.

"Sixty bucks for a rock."

I stood, reached into my pants pocket and pulled out last night's tips and handed it to one of them, and he quickly departed and returned in a foggily short amount of time.

We all climbed in the backseat of my SUV and lit up.

"So, what's there to do around here, guys? I'm new in town."

I was thinking that they would suggest a club or something, but instead, they suggested we drive to a buddy's place and drink and smoke more. that was exactly what my doctor had ordered, so I immediately exited my vehicle, climbed in the driver's seat, fired up the ignition and we departed post-haste.

I noted as I pulled out of the parking lot that the two-lane-each-way asphalt street was covered in about three inches of heavy snow, more where previously passing vehicle tires had dug ruts.

I pegged it to the maximum speed allowed, sixty kilometres per hour. Now, I'm a Winnipegger through and through, so I know how to drive in deep snow, especially when drunk and high, and I had one hell of a sports utility vehicle, so I intentionally pushed the speed limit in order to get to my next hit.

I did not notice that the vehicle about fifty feet in front of us had come to a stop in order to turn left.

The abrupt intensity of my spidey-sense instantly focussed me to total and complete alertness, and my mind took a screenshot of the scene immediately before us and quantumly processed it.

We were about fifteen feet or so from the rear bumper of that poor gentleman's burgundy-red mini-stationwagon when I slammed on the brakes, but quantumly, my brain assessed that my all-season radials would not grab the cold asphalt enough to stop in time in that snow, and so I spontaneously changed tactics and applied the gas a touch and cranked the steering wheel to the right, just in time to hop the snow-rut and clear the stationary vehicle's rear-right bumper.

As I wrestled my responsive SUV entirely into the inside passing lane and drew even with the passenger-side door of the still stationary vehicle, I turned my head momentarily to the left and locked eyes with the driver of the other vehicle, as he stared in absolutely astonishment back at the four bums staring at him in what was probably a stolen vehicle, for all he knew.

Almost immediately I cranked the steering wheel back to the left, as not twenty feet ahead was a parked car in the lane, and the sport suspension package leapt the vehicle to the left, back over the snow rut and cleanly into the left-side lane.

I gently applied the brakes to slow the vehicle down, as I had needed to apply a fair bit of torque to be sure that we cleared the deep ruts during that little maneuver.

As I brought the SUV back down to the speed limit, I glanced to my right, and all three of my passengers' mouths were hanging open in disbelief that we were all not dead, or at least mangled in a two-vehicle wreck right now.

I simply turned my head back to the road and gassed it, hoping that I had enough money for more beer and crack in my bank account.

29 December

I returned to Jessica's place sometime early afternoon the next day, looking worse than death apparently, for Jessica gasped in shock when I entered her condo.

I recall indicating that I was in no condition to talk, and collapsed on the bed in the spare bedroom.

13:17 – 31 December

I slept the rest of that day and all of the next one too.

New Year's Eve I arose and somewhat dazed, I exited the spare room and Jessica immediately asked if we could talk. She wanted to know what was going on with me. I told her that I was fine, and we began getting ready for the party that night, to be hosted by one of her theatre friends much later in the evening.

Before the party though, Jessica had a late afternoon show to perform.

I went with and had a not-insignificant number of beers while watching her hilarious, roughly two-hour show. I relaxed somewhat, and my fractured mind began the sometimes weeks long process of slowly gathering itself back to operational capacity.

But right now, the furious little boy was in charge, as he almost always was when we have suffered any severe trauma.

17:51

*"Women who seek to be equal with men lack ambition." –
Timothy Leary*

After the show, myself, Jessica and a few of her theatre friends went to a local tavern to celebrate; an older James Lipton type actor had announced that was his last show.

As soon as we entered the tavern, I spotted two very nice pool tables, and since I loved to play pool, I did so.

Jessica headed off with the rest of her friends to their respective restrooms.

About ten minutes later I was joined at the pool table by Jessica, who was laughing with great mirth. I was chalking my cue and trying to decide on a shot, so I was only half-paying attention to her when she, ample chest heaving for air, related with a huge smile on her gorgeous face that she has just flashed the man of the hour.

Now, I was raised by two incredibly strong women, and have always understood that a woman's body is her own to do with as she determines is most appropriate for her life and/or existential paradigm. This is the innate ability of any being, whether consisting of one biological cell and having the ability to simply discern helpful proteins from unhelpful proteins, or, as in the case of the evolved human body, which is comprised of an estimated thirty trillion individual cells, and having a brain with the capability of processing a billion billion calculations per second.

This affords each and every individual human being on the planet the ability from birth, in vastly varying and increasing degrees, to interpret and store a mind-blowingly colossal amount of sensory and experiential data. Thus, every mature, educated human being on the planet should understand the most basic mental constructs of individual freedom of choice and the sanctity of one's own human body.

So I, Micheal, certainly understood that if Jessica made the choice to flash her naked breasts at her much-loved and respected retiring colleague, that was her choice to make, and if I had any issue with her choice, then I needed to look within myself first, because I factually possessed a statistically insignificant amount of the data on the issue compared to that which Jessica had collected, stored and likely processed billions of times throughout her life.

So, the proper response should have been something to the effect of "Oh. I wouldn't have done that, but then again I don't possess a modicum of the data that you do about your life, so the logical and socially ideal thing for me to do would be simply congratulate you, as you seem to believe that what you have done is wholesome and appropriate to your own existential paradigm, of which I know statistically and factually nothing."

But I didn't say that, because I was not in control anymore.

The furious child was, and he was so enraged that she has shared with another man that which he, in his perpetually immature mind, incorrectly judged to be for his eyes only.

I played pool and did not talk to Jessica for the rest of our time there.

20:17

We arrived at the party some hours later, and it took me about twenty minutes to locate some ecstasy.

My mind blanked here for a while, for the next thing I knew, I was being asked to leave the party because I was aggressively hitting on a young colleague of my girlfriend.

But I was done taking orders from anyone in this life, and I simply stood my ground.

First one, then two, then three, then four, then five guys are required to pin me to the ground. I wasn't striking out at anyone, I just refused to be pushed around by anyone or anything anymore. That was the only thought in my mind. I didn't want to physically hurt anyone; that had never been me.

I was just not going to cooperate in being thrown out of that house.

And so I simply resisted without violence.

At the time, I was about 215 pounds, and I was no weakling anymore, and it took them about three or four minutes to remove me from the front hall of the residence, once they gave up trying to calmly talk me down. They were all good guys, and I'm grateful that the universe decided that perhaps I didn't need any more lessons in physical pain at that point in my life, but only psychological pain, and they deposited me softly on the property front lawn.

It was at this point that Jessica's mother arrived by taxi, having been alerted to the situation some time ago by cell phone by her daughter.

As soon as the maternal figure appeared, all the fury went out of me, and I allowed Jessica and her mother to remove me from the scene, as the fifty or so revellers slowly trickled back into the house.

Nothing was said the entire taxi ride and Jessica and I departed the taxi at her condo, and her mother went home.

Once we arrived inside, Jessica demanded an explanation.

I broke down sobbing and told her that I didn't know what I was doing anymore. I told her about my previous evening and advised her that I was nothing but trouble for her, and that she should make the smarter decision and get rid of me.

She told me not to worry about it, that things were not so bad, and that we could still work things out.

I collapsed on the bed and promptly passed out.

12:44 – 1 January – 2009

I woke with my head absolutely pounding, and groggily rose and stumbled out of the room.

Jessica had gone to work, so I sat down on a chair and tried to get my thoughts together for the day.

And then I remembered everything, and the searing pain in my chest and mind was unbearable, so I started in on the first medicant that could find, a forty of vodka.

16:41

I leave the condo and drive to work, as I have a shift at the restaurant.

As soon as the on-duty manager smells me, she knows I am drunk and politely instructs me to go home. The obstinance of the previous evening has left me, and I sullenly return to my vehicle.

I first cry, because I believe that I have likely shattered the only thing that I have left to tie my psyche however precariously to sanity; my professional image.

And instantaneously, the furious child takes control.

We start the vehicle and pull out onto the main street, having no particular destination in mind.

As I pass through the first busy intersection in the middle lane of the three-lane street (the lane farthest to the right is full of parked vehicles), a vehicle abruptly enters my lane from the right-perpendicular street that has a red light, and scoots in just ahead of me as I clear the intersection, barely missing my right-side front bumper.

Furious at being thusly cut-off, and I lay into my vehicle's horn.

The vehicle ahead of me, a two-door sedan of some color is all I remember, slows to a halt about three feet in front of me. There are two people in the vehicle, and one looks to be a adolescent of about fourteen, but that does not matter to the furious child. He taps the gas lightly, brings my SUV front bumper up to the rear bumper of the offending vehicle, now stopped directly in front of me.

Fully intending to push to vehicle forward down the street, as that crazy old man had done to me in my Camaro in the spring of 1997, I floor it. But its winter, and the streets are still snow and ice from the storm a few days ago, and my vehicle tires simply spin, not going anywhere.

I have no concern for the occupants of the vehicle; my mother always told me that you get what you deserve, and they had cut off the ultimate failure at life, so...

I'm not sure how long I have been sitting there, uselessly spinning my tires at this busy intersection, trying to push this vehicle over the edge of the world, but at this point in time, the police arrive.

"Interesting" is the one word that slips from my mouth as I watch the two police officers approach my vehicle, hands on their holsters.

I stop pressing the gas and turn the ignition off.

I hear one of them yell for me to exit the vehicle, hands high in the air, but I don't move.

The same voice yells again for me to exit the vehicle with my hands in the air, but louder and more insistent this time.

My inner voice speaks to me.

"Get out of the vehicle." it says inside my chest and mind simultaneously.

I open the driver-side door, step out onto the snowy street, and simply stand about one foot off of my vehicle's left-front quarter-panel.

"Hands in the air!" is the welcome that I am greeted with.

My hands are hanging limply by my sides; I was not told by my inner voice to raise my hands, so I do not. I am done letting people push me around. I am not wanting to hurt anyone; that is not me.

But I will not cooperate anymore.

The officers stand motionless about twenty feet or so somewhere in front of me; exactly where, I don't know for sure, because my eyes are unfocussed on the crowd of people on the sidewalk, just about ten feet away.

The officers hold for a few moments, presumedly assessing that I am not yet enough of a threat for them to draw their sidearms, and one starts slowly circling round back of me. His partner, still in front of me, predictably orders me again to raise my hands into the air to distract me from the intentions of his partner.

Now, Momma didn't raise no fool, and the bullies in the playground had been pulling this shit on me since grade three, and I know exactly where this is going.

He is going to slip in behind me, and try something.

That's fine, I say to myself. Whatever happens, happens. I don't take orders from people anymore.

I hear the footsteps long before they reach me, and I just stand there, waiting.

The burly officer tackles me very nicely...my football coach at that one summer camp I attended would have been proud. His momentum carries us both to the ground directly in front of my vehicle, and the officer rolls away nimbly and jumps to his feet.

His partner, having closed in a few feet, repeats his order to stay down.

I calmly regain my feet and again just stand there, arms hanging limply by my sides.

I'm tackled hard again.

My head hits the side of a parked car, and my face is thrust into the twelve-inch deep or so pile of snow between that car and the next vehicle parked ahead of it.

"Good one again!" I think to myself.

"Stay down!"

I stand up.

I'm tackled a third time.

And then a fourth.

And then on the fifth tackle, which I felt no more than the previous four, my inner voice tells me to stay down.

I stay down.

21:09

I was sleeping on the floor of my holding cell in the fetal position, when I was unceremoniously awakened and released on my own recognisance.

In the taxi ride back to Jessica's condo, I would read in the police report that after the officers placed me in the back of their police vehicle, on the way to the station, I had continuously and violently smashed my head into the seat headrest of the passenger seat in front of me, all the while crying and saying two words over and over;

"I'm sorry."

I had also urinated in my pants while standing, after they had locked me in the small cell.

16:13 – 2 January – 2009

"If, as one fares, one does not find a companion who is better or equal, let one resolutely pursue the solitary course; there can be no fellowship with the fool." – The Buddha

Jessica came into the spare room where I had passed out after handing the police report to her and nodding to her mother standing anxiously in the living room, and gently shook my shoulder.

"Micheal, you have to get up. We need to talk. Now, please."

I groggily made my way out of the bed and into the living where she was standing about four feet in front of me, with her arms crossed in front of her.

Her mother stood emotionless just behind her and to the right.

I focussed on Jessica.

"You can't stay here anymore", she said bluntly.

I smiled slightly to myself.

It was the smarter decision on her part.

"When do you want me to go?"

"Now." was the polite response.

I hung my head and returned to the spare bedroom, and began to pack.

After about forty minutes, I had jammed most of my meager belongings into my SUV parked in the building underground lot, noting once again that I was leaving with less than I had arrived with.

I turned around at the driver-side door to look at Jessica one last time.

She smiled warmly and simply said, "Take care of yourself."

I nodded and climbed into the vehicle, and started the longest fifteen-hour drive of my life.

Chapter 25: Detox and Recovery

The Beginning of 2009
Winnipeg – Manitoba

*"I have been a seeker and I still am, but I stopped asking
the books and the stars.
I started listening to the teaching of my soul." – Rumi*

I would not have cursed any being to be inside my head for the next fifteen hours.

I was physically, mentally and spiritually spent. I was still slightly inebriated, and I still had trace amounts of ecstasy and crack in my system.

I'd broken an angelic heart and surely created many a horrifying rumor in her small but highly-talented artistic community, and I was going back to beseech the support of the one parent in my life that I had felt for decades did not have my safe and protected existence at the forefront of their intentions.

How do I know that I'd hit rock bottom?

I called my mother for help.

"And then, something happened. I let go. Lost in oblivion. Dark and silent and complete.
I found freedom. Losing all hope was freedom." – Fight Club (199)

As soon as I arrived at my mother's new house in Winnipeg, only two doors down from my sister, her husband and two children (*snicker*), I immediately followed the advice of both my mother and my sister, and less than an hour after my arrival, we all three departed the house, and my mother drove me directly to the Main Street Project, a centrally located alcohol and drug detoxification facility in the city.

After the required three days of detox, of which the entire time I either slept or stared listlessly at the ceiling, I was kindly advised by the facility management that I needed to make a decision in regards to which provincial addiction program I was going to choose.

I had previously been provided with information on all the choices in the province, and I decided to take some of Grandma's sage advice from decades back, when she used to take care of my sister and me during the summers that my mother abandoned us at her home in the country and was ostensibly off studying at university.

"If you are going to do something right, do it right the first time." she would say.

I knew that if I was going to get better, which my inner voice told me must be my sole focus at that point in my life, though of course having no idea at all regarding exactly what that meant, I'd decided to take one of the longer programs, a twenty-one day residential program offered by Anchorage, the addiction treatment program of The Salvation Army.

I wholly committed myself to learning how I ended up in that addiction treatment program and how I could ensure that I never went back here again. I attended all the required classes, seminars, counselling sessions and mandatory AA meetings, and I learned a lot about addiction, its causes and its treatment.

At one point very near to the end of the residential program, I broke down crying during one of my many counselling sessions with an absolutely amazing spirit named Maureen. She had just told me that the causes of many addictions reach all the way back to childhood, and I began to cry, remembering those terrifying years.

I was able to find some release after that, and decided that I needed to being making amends to people that I had hurt most recently. The damage that I did in Korea was another matter entirely, and one which I had avoided thinking about as much as possible.

After some heart-felt consideration, I wrote a letter to Jessica's mother, apologizing for the pain that I had caused her daughter. Jessica and I had chatted a fair bit by phone for the first week or so that I was in treatment in Winnipeg, and while she readily forgave me for what had transpired in her hometown and between us, eventually she told me that she needed time alone.

I never spoke with her again.

I then wrote my manager at the steakhouse that had very kindly hired me, to apologize for showing up drunk, and then not showing up at all.

I also decided to write my mother a letter, telling her that her somewhat rough disciplinary methods that she had employed throughout my childhood may have affected me negatively to some degree.

I remember talking with her about the letter a few weeks later over coffee and cookies in her kitchen.

She smiled a fake smile, you know, the one where the lips smile but the eyes do not.

Her simple explanation: "Yeah, that's how I was raised."

"Whatever the mind can conceive and believe, it can achieve." – Napoleon Hill, 1937

A couple weeks after my graduation from the Anchorage alcohol addiction program, predictably, I'm sure by now even to the reader, my mother had me move out of her house by indicating she was going to charge me rent.

I first rented a room for a few months on Osborne Street North, just a few doors down from where Chris and I used to sit on the roof some nights and chat about whatever fascinating thoughts he was having that particular evening.

I also got a job at the River & Osborne Safeway. They wanted me to join their management program, but managing a grocery store was not the thing for me.

Cashier was much more my speed.

I attended AA weekly and enjoyed it a fair bit. I had made a number of friends at Anchorage, and most of us continued to attend the AA group some of them revived shortly after we all graduated. We all had been through hell together as the saying goes, and I learned that talking about my life challenges in a setting where I trusted those present was very helpful to me.

I would not make the larger connection on that for almost a decade.

I also saw a psychologist every two weeks or so for some months, whom I was very kindly linked with by my former Anchorage counsellor, Maureen. She and I even met for coffee some weeks after I graduated, and I remember her many wise and kind words of encouragement over those weeks of the program with much love and appreciation.

Somewhere towards the end of the six months that Dr. Vanderwater very kindly provided me *pro bono* with my first extended exposure to mental health care, in which he basically just listened to whatever I would talk about, he said something to me that left me profoundly thoughtful.

I can't recall exactly how it came about, but I was telling him about my childhood and relating the barest inkling of the suffering that I had experienced, and at the end, I wrapped up the story by saying something to the effect of, "But I survived."

His compassionate response to my suffering flairs gratitude in my heart to this very day.

"You deserve more than to merely survive."

Spring 2009

"Find joy in everything you choose to do. Every job, relationship, home... it's your responsibility to love it, or change it." – Chuck Palahniuk

My state of mind improved dramatically over the next many weeks and I set about rebuilding my life.

Again.

The first thing that I decided to work on was a career. We all need money to live.

I decided that I wanted to start in the non-profit world, because it was important to give back to your community, and I figured that good talent might be hard to find for organizations such as these, that cannot compete against profit-making or public-funded organizations.

I was quickly hired by the local chapter of a national health charity organization as provincial program manager. I would work there for almost three years, and I absolutely loved all of it.

My Executive Director would even generously offer to promote me to director if I would stay at the very end, and I was always very grateful for that kindness, and the many more before and after that, both to me and my family.

January 2010

As the winter kicked into third gear in ever-frosty Winterpeg, I mutely celebrated one year of sobriety, and I was in a pretty good place.

I'd learned how to deal with cravings somewhat and I'd attained a consistent level of clarity in thought that I normally only rarely got to, and so both conscious and subconscious minds were working on a number of issues around the clock.

I was still very lonely, though blessedly my darkness for most of that time hung back a respectful distance, and I often found myself wondering whether my daughters remembered me at all, as it had been over a year since I had last been allowed to speak with them.

But I quickly brushed those thoughts out of my mind, as I understood that I needed to concentrate on myself.

I'd been able to regain some control over my life since I had stopped drinking, and the clarity of thought was quite enamoring. However, I was not feeling any happier really; I only felt better the way that one would naturally feel better when one stops constantly banging one's own head against a cement wall. So really, what I was trying to say was that I was feeling somewhat less hateful of my existence, but still a universe away from actually being able to believe that it had any real purpose or value to me.

I took the bus everywhere I went as my driver licence had been suspended, but I expected to have it reinstated sometime in the fall, and a vehicle would be very handy getting to work, which was about an hour by bus away from where I was currently renting a basement room in a house, not too far from my previous place on Nassau Street North.

I had also finally gone to court in Winnipeg in the summer regarding the extra-provincial incident, and was charged with *driving while intoxicated, resisting arrest* and *assaulting an officer*.

When I arrived at The Law Courts bright and early that summer morning, clean cut, shaved and wearing a suit, and spoke with the prosecutor for the first and only time, he took one look at me, then advised that he thought that dropping the assault charge was appropriate, if I plead guilty to the two other charges.

I smiled and shook his hand.

April 2010

"Nothing is worse than having an itch you can never scratch." – Blade Runner (1982)

There were two major beer vendors within walking distance of the twenty-five-unit apartment building that I was now living in and managing in the area of Confusion Corner. Following the example of one of my best friends, I had decided to apply for a resident manager job so that I could cut down on my largest living expense; rent.

At the job interview just a few months previous, one of the managers was also in AA, and he seemed to be impressed with my resume, and simply asked if I was attending AA meetings, which at that time I was, and had every intention of continuing.

But everything that has a beginning has an end, and that includes sobriety at least some of the time.

As the weeks and then months went by with me sitting all alone in my two-bedroom apartment, with only a mattress and a TV in the living room, my thoughts increasingly centred around alcohol.

Now, to be sure, this was a planned return to drinking. I had learned a lot about addiction, alcohol and more than a little about my psychological make-up, and born within me was a soul-pledge that I would not believe anything that I read or that I heard, unless I reasonably confirmed it somehow for myself. I no longer trusted either the intentions or professed knowledge of anyone in the world. Period.

It was not that I suspected everyone of lying or being out to get me all the time; I had just decided to only trust my inner voice from now on in my life.

This would have a profound affect on my rate of self-healing.

Additionally and finally, for the curious, I did not fall off the wagon because of some occurrence in my life. I in fact noted, very quickly after the thoughts began to surface more consistently, what was going on in my addicted mind, and I forestalled my return to drinking a number of weeks, advising myself that there was no rush, and that I had time to consider the implications very carefully.

In the end, I decided that there was no way that I could attend that George Thorogood concert without having at least one beer.

That would have been sacrilege.

Chapter 26: The Reunion

The Beginning of 2011

"The message is clarion clear: to think for oneself is essential to the good life because what flows from doing so is one's own. If others do the thinking for one, or if orthodoxies do it, one's life is not one's own. The good and well lived life is not a servitude, but a device to one's own chosen values. So the train of thought goes: freedom is what makes it possible to create meaning in one's life, and the creation of meaning in one's life is the good life itself."
- A. C. Grayling, The God Argument

Time passed, and I engrossed myself in my non-profit program work.

Now that I was drinking again and, while surely having monthly rough patches, I was able to cut back considerably on the beer. By cutting back considerably, I meant that I drank an average of about a twelve of beer a night on the weekends, and at most six or so the nights preceding work.

That's roughly four litres a sitting on weekend nights, and 2 litres give or take on weeknights.

By contrast, when I was at my worst in Korea, I was drinking upwards of 10 litres, four or five nights a week for years. So, yeah, I had cut back. However, I had not yet clued into the fact that its not necessarily how much you drink or how often, but that you have that first drink at all.

And yes, I know that they always say in AA that a thousand beers is never enough, but one is too many, and like so many other proverbs like that in life, while I had understood the meaning of the words, having English as my first language, I did not understand the thousands upon thousands of years of human suffering that was the genesis behind the grammatical composition.

Work was going fantabulous and that really lifted my spirits; if I wasn't much of anything else, I at least had value to my employer.

As the months passed though, my thoughts returned more and more to my two beautiful daughters whose photos I had up all over my, by this time, completely furnished, two-bedroom apartment. A friend very dear to me sidelined as an interior designer and was quite successful at it. She busted her butt for weeks, dashing all over the city to one quaint housewares store and then to another, looking for the perfect fashions for my abode.

However, the spare bedroom was still complete empty, as I had hopes for that.

Money was also plentiful, as was my ever-rising credit limit. I prided myself in that I had not missed a single debt payment since returning to Canada, but I was again unwisely steadily increasing my debt. Budgeting was not a skill that I had yet developed, among so many others that I sorely lacked.

Somewhere during the summer, when my guilt and loneliness were becoming too intense, I decided to send a communication out to my wife in Korea, not really expecting her to even receive it, as I could readily imagine a scenario where she had blocked me on all of her social media platforms, including email.

However, to my very pleasant surprise, she responded fairly promptly, if my sense of time is accurate even a smidgen, and we were soon talking fairly regularly on the phone again, every month, give or take, though she did not let me speak with our children, which was actually perfectly fine with me, as I had loftier goals.

You see, I was not going to put myself out there to her again just yet; I'd had too may trust issues with my wife over the years, as I'm sure many marriages experience, but my thoughts were that if I could be honest and clear about where I was in my life in Canada, and if she did not hate me down to the very fibres of her being yet, she may eventually inquire as to where things are between her and me.

At which point, I planned to tell her that I wanted them to move to Canada to live with me.

She never asked.

28 December – 2010

"I dream. I dream I am floating on the surface of my own life, watching it unfold; observing it; an outsider looking in." – Robin Hobb

Its early morning, and I'm calling my wife late in Korean time. I don't want to wait all day.

I've been pondering and pondering for weeks and weeks, and I have finally arrived at a heart-wrenching decision; my wife no longer has any interest in our marriage, and thus the best thing to do is just get it over with, so that we both can move on with our respective lives.

I plan to advise her that I am formally filing for divorce on the first business day of the new year.

She answers the phone fairly quickly, likely having been provided advance notice by myself via email that I was going to call.

We chat pleasantly for a while about our girls and Christmas in Korea, and then I decide that enough polite time has passed in the conversation to get to the point of my call.

I select a convenient pause in the conversation, and as I am drawing in breath to begin my prepared notice, my wife suddenly interjects.

"Why haven't you come to Korea?"

I'm stunned by the suddenness and bluntness of the question, not to mention the eerie timing. Literally half a second more and I would have begun the legal demise of our marriage.

"What do you mean?" I ask.

"Why haven't you come to visit us here in Korea?"

I'm slow in comprehending the larger intimation here, but I do grasp it after several silent seconds.

I say the first truth that pops into my head. "I haven't had the money."

Her immediate response: "Well, how about I buy you a ticket."

My response: "Fuck, yeah!"

Mid-January – 2011

A few short weeks later, I landed at Incheon International Airport and hopped on the train up to where Don had lived for about a decade. As ever, he was as solid as a rock and offered me his spare room to sleep in. We played Cribbage and talked about life in general, and the next day I took the highspeed train down to Gwangju, South Jolla Province.

I arrived at Gwangju Station in the early evening. I remember that the sun was just beginning to set. I hopped in a waiting taxi outside the station and headed to the meetings place, a library that they all spent a lot of time in, near where they were currently renting.

The taxi let me off at my destination, and I turned my head left and right a few times to get a sense of where I was compared to the directions that were already provided to me by smartphone.

Rather than locate the library itself first, I spotted the three of them standing in the entrance to a modernish building. There was no light above them to light their features, at least none that I could see from across the small asphalt road, but there was a brightly lit room directly behind them.

At least I thought that it was them, for two of the silhouettes definitely resembled my wife and my eldest, but the third child standing beside my eldest I did not immediately recognize, until I remembered that I had been away from my youngest for more time than I had been in her life.

I walked across the road and into the building entranceway, held my wife's hand warmly for a moment, and then immediately knelt down in front of the two most beautiful things that I had ever seen, my daughters.

I hugged them both to my chest, as tears streamed down my face.

"Leave off sniffing the carcass of your old life-do you enjoy unending pain? There is no shame in walking away from bones. Nor is there any special wisdom in injuring oneself over and over. What is your loyalty to that pain? To abandon it will not lessen you. – Robin Hobb, Fool's Errand

My wife and I decided that we would put whatever had happened before behind us for the sake of our children, and on 24 May 2011 they all arrived in Winnipeg, and move into the two bedroom apartment that I had secured almost a year and a half previous in beyond hopeful anticipation of this moment.

I had lovingly decorated my daughters' room in pink and with a thousand-sticker mural of a cheery blossom tree on the wall.

You should have seen their little eyes light up with pure joy the first time that I opened the door, and let them peer into their own private room.

Things actually went very well those first three month after they moved to Canada, and the relationship between my wife and I was actually heading in a very positive directly.

However, somewhere towards the end of the summer, something occurred between my wife and me. What exactly occurred is not of any importance, but it caused me to lose all faith that my wife had my best intentions in her heart. As the reader may well understand by now, when I had lost trust in the primary female figure in my life, the romance part of the relationship ceased to be for me.

I tried as hard as I could to let it go, but my darkness returned like a shot to the stomach and my drinking thus as well, and somewhere towards the fall of 2012, I recognized that I was returning to my pre-program drinking ways, and had already decided that things would not get that bad again.

Near the end of September of that year, my wife and I separated for the last time.

Chapter 27: Losing the War

Fall 2012 to Mid-Summer 2013

"To laugh often and much; to win the respect of intelligent people and affection of children; to learn the appreciation of honest critics and endure the betrayal of false friends; to appreciate beauty; to find the best in others; to leave the world a little bit better, whether by a healthy child, a garden patch, or a redeemed social condition; to know even one life has breathed easier because you have lived. This is to have succeeded." – Ralph Waldo Emerson

My wife and I coordinated my move out very well, and I took a second resident manager position over and above managing the building that my family was living in <u>and</u> my now full-time job as an analyst with the Government of Manitoba.

I needed to keep my expenses down; on top of all the debt that I had already built up by furnishing the apartment for my family's arrival from Korea last year, I also foolishly furnished my second apartment about a five- minute drive away from them. And then on top of that, I was also paying child support to my wife in accordance with federal law, which support alone accounted for almost a third of my income.

For only the second time in my life, I decided to take a very close look at my finances, and quickly determined that I would only be able to make the minimum payment on my credit cards for the foreseeable many number of years, and would not be able to start making a dent on the capital until my children turned eighteen years old and the federal child support requirement ended.

Unless, of course, one or both of my daughters went immediately into university and continued to live with their mother (I didn't like the chances of that), then I would have to continue to pay child support until they were twenty-five.

I consulted with a bankruptcy trustee, and on their advice, decided to declare bankruptcy for the second time in my life.

Again, a failure.

Or was I?

Sometime in the last few years, I had come to realize that I was only a failure at something if I gave up trying. I had named myself a failure as a father when I left Korea, but here I was, still trying at it, and that reinforced just enough the core belief of mine that what can be imagined, can be achieved. And so I imagined that instead of being a failure at managing my finances, I had merely lost another financial battle, but not the financial war.

I went online and taught myself about budgeting, and once I was discharged from bankruptcy a number of years later, I kept a very detailed budget for many years, and to this day, do not owe a single dollar to anyone or anything.

I recall that at that time, I pondered considerably over how much to let my children know about my particular life issues and how I was dealing with them. Previous to this time, I had defaulted to telling my children exactly what my mother had told me and my sister about her personal struggles throughout our lives, absolutely nothing, and had gone so far as to actively lie to them to hide the fact that I had human frailties.

But, as I had swore to myself many years previous that I would not fail to be at minimum present for my daughters whenever they needed me to be so, I had also promised myself many years previous to this promise that the abuse in my family, in my line at least, would stop with me; I would never cause any of my children physical or mental suffering in any way, simply because they exercised what reasonable adults would consider to be poor judgement.

So, from that point on, I told my daughters basically everything.

"Problems that remain persistently insoluble should always be suspected
as questions asked in the wrong way." – Alan Watts

As the weeks and then months passed, my loneliness and thus my darkness returned.

My drinking slowly increased on the weekends and occasionally on weekdays, but I was now fully engaged in seeking to control my urges to drink. I believe this to a be a familiar battle among those who at minimum abuse a chemical substance at some point in their lives. And since I believed that what could be imagined could be achieved, I imagined that I could control the cravings.

Now, I am sure that the reader can envision life issues where this control approach would be very successful, but as there are exceptions to every rule, addiction cannot be addressed though the method of control, because, as humans, we are fundamentally and necessarily designed to fail, and thus failure at controlling the urge to drink is essentially unavoidable.

And for me, as I can't speak for any other human being, with failure came depression, and with depression came a significant increase in my base need to counter that depression with the only thing that had consistently worked throughout my life, at least on a short-term basis; alcohol.

And once I over-drank, I became more depressed.

And I always over-drank.

It was a vicious cycle, that when combined with a firm belief in the possible realization of the imagined, could drive a person quite to the edge of madness.

In those many months, I tried scores, if not hundreds, of different tactics and strategies in my sorely misguided effort to control how often and how much I drank, every single one of which ended in failure.

Towards the fall of that year, my conscious mind began to grudgingly consider the possibility that control may be out of my ability, at least at this time of my life. As I had learned from my marriage, sometimes I just had to admit that I didn't have the knowledge, experience or capability to accomplish a particular goal, and while, at least for me, everything that could be imagined could be achieved, that concept had to be set aside, at reasonable times, by a reasonable mind, with the understanding that there <u>was</u> a way to accomplish the goal, but that it, at least for the time being, was beyond my current knowledge, experience and capability to successfully achieve.

Then I decided to try something that I had learned in government; if the question you are asking does not return the answer that you expect or need, then try changing the question.

And so I looked at the question before me as it were, and made one small change; if I could not control my drinking, then could I stop my drinking?

And thus, the war continued, just on a different front.

After hundreds of battles to quit drinking over the rest of 2012, and as the Christmas holidays approached, my darkness was particularly heavy upon my psyche. There is a mental illness called Seasonal Affective Disorder, or SAF, whereby during most of the year, an affected individual may feel quite normal, but when a certain season approaches, usually but not necessarily winter, their depression increases in varying amounts.

I loved winter. Always had. Winterpegger. Life-long Winnipeg Jets fan.

But the season that <u>had</u> always negatively affected me since my late teens was a holiday season, and by that I don't mean solely the Christmas holidays, but anytime that family typically gathered in Canada, such as at Thanksgiving.

I never really understood why, until recently that is. Family gatherings were always a happy time for me, so why was I more and more depressed the closer that one got?

I began to think about when else in my life I had felt as good as I did at say Christmas, and then it hit me; I had also felt safe and free in Brandon whenever there were parties at our house on Westaway Bay.

Okay. So, what was the connection?

As it turned out, it was very logical, at least to me.

All throughout my abused life with my mother, she rarely if ever punished me at events where there were a significant number of other family and friends. Oh, I got spoken to quite harshly, and occasionally sent to my room, but never, to the best of my recollection, was I ever physically struck at such a gathering.

So, anytime that there was a family event, I knew that I was safe.

I didn't know why I was safe. I didn't even know that I knew that I was safe.

But I was safe.

"Why?" I asked myself aloud one day, probably a few months before I would start writing this book.

And then everything clicked.

I've known now for some years that my mother is a narcissist to the extreme, at least in the estimation of myself and a number of other family members. How she is viewed by others, was and continues today, to be an existential core concern for her.

She must always at minimum appear as if she is the perfect mother when any person of any significance in her life is around. So, I believe that deep inside herself, she knew that beating a defenseless child was wrong, or at least not acceptable to vast swathes society, and so she refrained from it completely at these times, and my body and/or unconscious mind figured it out decades before the rest of us would, that we could be a normal child at these events.

And I suppose to everyone who has known me since I was a baby, it certainly must have appeared that I was a normal child, for I danced, played with cousins with great enjoyment, got tickled by aunties, and played hide-and-seek with fun-loving uncles. I got to stay up until the wee hours, I could eat all the sweets that I wanted, I got included in card games that the adults played, and all the family loved one another, and so these events had been little pieces of heaven in an otherwise terrorized childhood.

Since that time and unknown to me though, every year after my childhood, right on through to today, when a traditional Canadian family holiday or other similar event rolls around, an additional weight comes upon me, and takes up residence on top of whatever normally occurring darkness might be there already.

In years past, I have remedied this quite effectively with self-prescriptions, but now, as I believe that I fully understand the entire process of this particular type of suffering, when these feelings predictably arise throughout the year, I simply acknowledge their existence, locate and identify in my mind the physical and mental processes at work, acknowledge that these are normal functions of my psyche, and watch the until the feelings complete their temporary lifespans in full.

Everything that has a beginning, has an end, and that includes feelings and emotions, as I would begin to learn in the greatest detail later on in the new year.

"I think you appreciate that there are extraordinary men, and women, and extraordinary moments when history leaps forward on the backs of these individuals. That which can be imagined can be achieved. That you must dare to dream but that there is no substitute for perseverance and hard work and teamwork, because no one gets there alone. And while we commemorate the greatness of these events and the individuals who achieve them, we cannot forget the sacrifice of those who made these achievements and leaps possible." – Dana Scully, The X-Files

As Christmas of 2012 neared however, I had not yet made any of these vital linkages, and my drinking was getting progressively heavier, despite my new goal of quitting.

But what was different at this particular time in my life, was that by that time I'd successfully ended one pattern of behavior that had significantly affected my level of darkness, and thus how much I drank; my marriage.

I also had sixteen months of sobriety under my belt, and so my brain's logic told me that if I could affect things in my life that deepened my darkness, and thus my drinking, as my marriage had, that meant that I could also affect other changes in my life that lessened my darkness, and thus lessened my drinking.

Consequently, just before Christmas, days before in fact, if memory serves, I joined an AA group for professionals (medical professionals, legal professionals, public figures and such), and put together another three months or so of sobriety, before I fell off the wagon again.

But that time, I was not going back to drinking. I had been successful at quitting drinking again. For only about ninety days, sure, but a day without drinking alcohol is a successful day for an addict, and thus I firmly believed that if I could quit drinking for that length of time via one method or process, such as AA, then logically, I could get and stay sober a different way, if I only could imagine that other way.

From my religion studies that last year at university, I had come to believe that no religion has the entire right or wrong of it, and that told me that no one method to sobriety had the entire right or wrong of it either. Afterall, neither AA nor its sister groups has the entire right of achieving permanent sobriety, else everyone that walked through those doors would never abuse their poison of choice again.

But what a good group of these types did do, in my mind at least, significantly further ahead of most any other addiction treatment or therapy, was provide a safe, non-judgemental, confidential, empathetic, and mutually beneficial environment, for both old-timers and newcomers alike, to come to get sober, to stay sober, to get sober again, or just to think about getting sober.

AA has a lot of it to be sure, definitely something needed by all substance abusers at least some of the time, and those months in that group enabled me to reset my drinking a bit to a more manageable level, for a while.

Every time I attended a meeting, I learned something about sobriety, addiction or my mind and how it functions, that I did not know before that meeting.

Today, I know that at every AA meeting I ever attended, I discovered one more piece of the puzzle for forging for myself a path to permanent sobriety, and so even when I "went back out" over the next year, I always attended meetings when I felt the pressure of my drinking and thus my darkness got to great.

After all, you are not a failure until you give up, and I had failed at many things, but this one thing that I knew that I must not ever give up on. For that meant that while I did not give up on finding a path to permanent sobriety, I felt that I was still a functioning father, and that had meant more to me than my existence since the day that my first child was born.

Chapter 28: Orthopraxy

Mid-Summer – 2013

"I think that a man does what he can until his destiny is revealed." – Nathan Algren, The Last Samurai (2003)

I was really fighting that summer. Fighting against the cravings for alcohol that wracked my body and mind anytime that I was not at work.

But why not at work?

In my professional life, I was successful. I'd risen in classification within my unit and my Executive Director, an absolutely brilliant legal and political mind and not uncompassionate soul, trusted me and gave me the leeway in my work to take my previously narrowly defined role within the department, and expand it an appropriate and pre-approved degree. This added much learning to my position, and if I was learning something, I was fulfilling a being's most basic purpose for existence, and so never had any desire for alcohol until I got home at the end of the workday.

But at work only. I was failing miserably at quitting drinking any other time.

I would go in patches; a couple days here, a couple days there.

Come Friday though, and my body, my mind, my heart and my very soul raged full of frustration, anger, pity, hate, and pure loathing at whatever it was in my psyche that I couldn't identify, much less shake off, that made me so sad, so lonely, and thus so needing of a drink.

I also was not attending any AA meetings regularly anymore. I had fallen off the wagon a few months back, and just felt that I needed something more than AA, but I don't think that I could have voiced that at the time if I had been asked; it was just a sense that I had.

I got my girls only two days a week, which I rarely if ever miss, but when they were not with me, well, as a slight variation of the popular song goes, ain't no sunshine when they're gone...

At the moment, I was driving the two of them out to the lake. Every summer since my girls had come to Canada, my sister and I got together and rented a cabin (or rather she did all the work and I brought her nieces out), and our four children usually have a great time. For me, it was always my favorite time of year, as I got to spend usually an entire week or more with my daughters, and I could enjoy the pleasant fiction that I was a normal father.

But I was not a normal father right at that moment, and I was furious with myself.

I was supposed to take my girls out yesterday to the cabin that my sister had rented, but I called around noon and told their mother that I was not feeling well, which was technically true.

But the stark reality was that I hadn't been able to go to bed, because I couldn't stop drinking and watching movies the whole night.

While that is not uncommon on the weekends, I had rarely if ever done it when I had responsibilities to fulfill the next day, such as ensuring that my daughters got to enjoy being with their cousins for a whole week at the cabin.

It's always been a family tradition on my father's side.

"You shouldn't smoke these. They'll kill ya." – Eric Draven, The Crow (1994)

Ever since I began to really drink heavily in Korea during those first years of my marriage, my binging evenings would basically go like this, on the nights that I did not go out:

I'd go the nearest convenience store (only in Korea can you buy a bottle of Dom Perignon any time of the day or night at your local 7-Eleven) and buy six beers, cuz that was all that I was going to be drinking that night <u>for sure</u>.

Then I'd barricade myself inside the bedroom at the computer, chatting with friends back home for a couple hours, and then, because I haven't clued in yet and wont for many years, that a thousand drinks is never enough, let alone that one is too many, I'd head back to the store for another six.

When I got back to the apartment, I would sometimes listen to music first for a while, but always the next few hours of the night were primarily consumed by watching movies.

This first session of movie watching usually included old or new favorites, and then when I'd finished the second six of beer, I'd go out to the convenience store for round three.

On my return, I would watch specific movies where I identified with the main character, or where the movie seemed to have a message from some sort of higher power specifically for me.

I would watch these movies scores, and sometimes hundreds of times.

When the beer was again gone, I would make a fourth and usually final trip to the store, but I would not go directly back home after this last beer run, which was usually around 04:00.

When we lived in Kyoungi Province Gwangju, there was an expressway that we had to walk over to reach the side that the convenience store was one. I would sit for hours at the top of that primarily metal pedestrian overpass, watching the traffic go by underneath, drinking beer and smoking cigarettes for hours, just trying to figure out how I could get out of Korea, other than dying.

At other times, during these wee hours of the morning where the color of the sky matched the shadow all around me, I would lean out of our fourteenth story apartment, staring at the ground not that far below, and imagine my mangled and lifeless body lying there in a pool of blood and guts.

When I had had enough of that meditation, I would go back to the apartment and drink beer and watch movies, where anything was possible, until I passed out.

In my twenties, it was such movies as Braveheart, where the hero dies for love and for his people; The Crow, where the hero comes back from the dead to avenge his and his lover's murders; and Dances With Wolves, where a Union soldier, wearily sick from all the suffering that he has seen in war, finds love and acceptance with one of the last American Indian tribes.

Then in my thirties it was The Matrix series, which contained many connections to eastern thought, in which I had always been interested, where Keanu Reeves brilliantly plays the hero that lives in the computerized simulation that is our world, and chooses to see the world for what it really is.

Then there was The Last Samurai where the main character, an alcohol soldier who is horrified at the suffering that he has seen and caused in war, somehow, all the way across the world from where he was born, and against all reasonable odds, finds love and peace by choosing to live his life by the Japanese philosophy of Bushido, or The Way of the Samurai.

Then there was Fight Club, a nothing short of brilliant movie that tells the story of a severely depressed man who is subconsciously able to completely change himself from a button-down, Oxford-cloth wearing, IKEA nesting, spiritually defunct shell of a middle-aged man, into a philosophically-enlightened warrior for change.

And finally, there was Man on Fire, where Denzel, as always, nails another of what I consider to be an Oscar-worthy performance as a minimally functioning alcohol former CIA operative, who decides that the only meaning that his life has left, is to avenge the death of a little girl whose safety he was charged with and failed.

I suspect that it will be very easy for the reader to understand which themes I related to and for what reasons, so I shall not drill down any further on that.

Mid-Summer – 2013

"The Great Way is not difficult
For those who do not discriminate.
Throw away likes and dislikes
And everything will become clear."
- The Third Patriarch

But it got worse.

Not only did I not pick them up and drive them out yesterday because I drank and watched movies all through the night, despite my best intentions of going to bed early, I drank beer and watched movies all day, evening, night and early morning of today until about 07:00, called their mother and said I would be late, and then crashed another couple hours.

So at this point, I was driving down the highway, the sun was blazing, I was barely sober and absolutely exhausted, and I was furious with myself, because the day was already half over and my daughters had been waiting anxiously for hours by the time I rolled around.

I felt burning guilt and disgust with myself and hate for my weakness and inability to figure out how to break free from the drink.

After about ninety minutes, we arrived at the cabin and unpacked the truck.

All four cousins went off to see the water, my sister chaperoned them, and I crashed in the cabin for a couple hours of much needed sleep and reprieve from my thickening darkness.

A Few Months Previous

"Don't be sorry your darkness is gone. I'll carry it for you, always. I'll keep it with mine."
- Dexter Morgan

After about three months of grieving the second end to my marriage, I returned to casual online dating because I was bone-crushingly lonely, and also had clued into the fact that I drank far less when I had the approval of a prominent female figure in my life.

I am also beginning to understand deep in my chest somewhere, that every woman that the universe graces my path with, leaves me with a learning intrinsic to my progress along my very, very long path back to health, whatever that meant exactly.

Over this time and on until I would stop dating in life completely somewhere after I met Misa, I would learn the following lessons; Chantelle taught me that it is possible to break free of an addiction without AA; Ginger taught me that someone can abuse alcohol as a result of post-traumatic stress disorder (PTSD); Theresa made me re-evaluate my basic assumptions about how people worked, including myself; and in late spring of 2013, Lisa gave me one of the greatest gifts of my entire life, a door to a wholesome orthodoxy that would eventually lead me to within a hair of my ultimate goal in life; to get permanently sober.

What was it exactly that she gave me?

If I remember correctly, she was walking through a bookstore one day some months after we met, saw a book on a shelf, and as she related to me, a voice inside her told to her buy that book for me.

So she did.

Mid-Summer – 2013
Our Rented Cabin – One Hour Outside of Winnipeg

"Lead me from darkness to the light,
lead me from ignorance to knowledge,
lead me from bondage to freedom,
lead me from death to immortality."
- The Upanishads

I awoke face-up on the couch in the cabin where I had collapsed about two hours ago, judging by the sun, which was still high in the Manitoba solid blue sky just outside the window by my head.

I just lay there for a long time, staring up at my darkness, hovering just above the tip of my nose, and barely an inch away from smothering the life from me. I could feel that I was hanging over the precipice of a return to my darkest days in Korea, and I was really, really scared.

If I couldn't stop drinking, it would eventually cost me everything, of that I had absolutely no doubt.

I turned my head to the left to peer around for my backpack that had my cigarettes.

I easily spy it right across the little cabin living room from me, leaning up against another sofa, and atop it, exactly at my eye level, sandwiched between four shirts, was the book that Lisa had given me a significant number of weeks back.

It had been sitting on the bottom shelf of the bookshelf in the living room of my two-bedroom apartment since she gave it to me. I remembered then that during my haste to pack, I had grabbed the book and thrown it in my bag in case I needed anything to pass the time.

I hauled myself off the couch, fetched the book, and returned to the couch to sit.

I looked at the front cover of the book, as I had done many times on my couch in my living room, wondering whether it held for me the tools that I needed to quit drinking, which cost of not doing would eventually be, well, everything.

The book was titled "One Breath at a Time: Buddhism and the Twelve Steps", by author and Buddhist monk Kevin Griffin. It detailed his journey from an alcohol musician to Buddhist monk, and how he was able to both quit drinking and rebuild his broken psyche by following the principles of Buddha-Dharma, a very old far-eastern philosophy of life.

By page five I was googling local Buddhist organizations, and the very next Friday, at precisely 18:25, I walked into the Dharma Centre of Winnipeg, founded and headed by Lama Gyurme Dorje, or more affectionately known to his students as Lama Gerry, or simply LG for short.

Two hours later, I emerged from that humble little building a Buddha-Dharma Practitioner for life.

"You should sit in meditation for 20 minutes a day, unless you're too busy, then you should sit for an hour." – Sukhraj S. Dhillon

For the next five years, I rarely missed a weekend listening to and learning from this beyond insightful, sincerely caring and at times cantankerously hilarious teacher, about a way of living that I felt had been right at the edge of my thoughts my entire life.

Its also important to note that Buddha-Dharma is not a religion, or an orthodoxy, which can be loosely defined as a way of believing, but rather an orthopraxy, or a way of living.

Historically, Buddha-Dharna practitioners and teachers alike do not proselytize, and so that is all I will say about Buddha-Dharma itself. If the reader is interested in knowing more, they already have all the information necessary to begin that journey.

However, what I am going to lay out here, as succinctly as I can, is what my five years of study under a qualified Buddha-Dharma instructor taught me.

Meditation: *Anapanasati*, the meditation on in-and-out breathing, is the first discourse expounded by the Buddha, if he in fact was a real person born in Ancient India some three thousand years ago, as the many legends and surviving documentation strongly assert.

But if he was born, the Buddha was not born a Buddhist, as one of Lama Gerry's favorite discourses begins, but rather a human prince by the name of Siddhartha Gautama. This man, if the stories are to be believed, was able to, through perfecting Anapanasati and practicing Metta (another type of meditation where the practitioner sends universal love (or in Pali, Metta) to all beings, awaken spiritually, or to put it another way, he became enlightened, that is, understanding of the very nature of reality itself.

Thus, he became the Buddha.

I can't speak for others who have practiced Anapanasati for any not-insignificant amount of time, but what one of the primary results that occurred in me and increased over time, was that by focussing all of my attention on a single spot on my face, and bringing that attention back to that spot each and every time that I noticed that my attention had unavoidably wandered for hundreds, then thousands, and then tens of thousands of times, was that my ability to focus on a particular issue or thing, such as my constant cravings for alcohol that had I wanted to understand very badly for many decades, became razer-sharp.

Advanced Orthopraxy: The "Dharma" in Buddha-Dharma can be roughly translated as "universal truth" from Pali, the language that was spoken in the region and at the time that the Buddha is thought to have been born, and thus it is largely accepted that if he was born there, he likely spoke Pali, at least if I remember my lessons correctly.

And as I have already set out, an orthodoxy is a way of believing, whereas an orthopraxy is a way of living, just as AA is an excellent orthopraxy for living sober.

Essentially what Buddha-Dharma sets out, in a very logical and structured way, are the methods that the Buddha developed to awaken (attain enlightenment), and the set of principles, called "The Eightfold Path", that if practiced under the guidance of a qualified teacher, should result in the lessening of that individuals suffering, and at minimum, a varying degree of advancement along the practitioner's path toward enlightenment, or toward understanding the very nature of reality itself.

As a result of following this path under the regular tutelage of Lama Gerry, I became increasingly able to recognize the things in my life that were causing me suffering in some way, whether it was physical, emotional, existential, or any combination of the three.

For example, within months of beginning to meditate and apply The Eightfold Path to all aspects of my life, I rebuilt my eating habits from scratch, I quit drinking for the first year completely, and I returned to volunteer work.

Then when I did eventually return to drinking and consulted with LG, I took his advice.

Instead of fighting the urge to drink, which typically would be a days-long battle when the cravings became too strong, I just sat back, focussed on the present moment, and really paid attention to what happened to me physically and mentally when I drank.

In time, I learned all about myself, my body, my mind, and how they work. I learned, among many other things, exactly what a craving is, how one starts, the process that it goes through in my body and my mind, and eventually I learned that I can just sit back and watch most any craving and, if I am focussed appropriately on the moment, as I seek to now be each and every waking moment of my life, I can follow that craving through its entire lifecycle, from the very moment that it enters my awareness, all the way through to the very moment it completes its cycle, and until it disappears from my mind and body, completely.

Chapter 29: So Close, Yet so Far

Late Spring – 2017

"Randomness has consistently generated the most interesting and fulfilling, if sometimes brief, romances of my life." – Micheal Harding

For about five years, through daily meditation and applying my ever-increasing understanding of and skill in the Buddha-Dharma orthopraxy, I increasingly developed a calmness of mind and clarity of thought that enabled me to discover, understand, and take appropriate and effective steps to address, most of the remaining physical, emotional and existential suffering that I had experienced at some point in my life, and had kept buried deep within my psyche.

I read book after book after book on world history, ancient anthropology, the history and make up of the universe, quantum mechanics, the human body, self-healing, and leading a wholesome life in the footsteps of Buddha.

My production at work exploded. At one point towards the end of my time serving the friendly people of my fine province with the Government of Manitoba, for a very short period of time at one point mind you, I was carrying out all of my responsibilities as a legislative and policy analyst with my unit, I was working half-time with the transformation team that was leading the department's organisational and governance restructuring, and I also took on for two weeks, the role of Acting Acting Administrator for the Manitoba Health Appeal Board.

I also met and moved in with one of the most empathetic, funny, brilliant as well as beautiful professional psychologists ever to practice in Winnipeg, Misa.

Every person with mental illness can benefit from a Misa during their recovery. When things again turned bad for me, and they did turn very bad, perhaps the worst arguably, she differed from most every other woman that I had ever partnered with before.

For, when all of the calm, focus, peace and serenity that I had built up over my five years of Buddha-Dharma study and practice, and with which she had mostly seen me act, started to inexplicably disintegrate, and I restarted drinking heavily again to medicate my returned and intensifying darkness, instead of sending me packing, she accepted my bad and my ugly with my good, and allowed me the space that I needed to work things out for myself, with the sole condition being that I continue to actively try to work out my issues in some way, such as through AA.

After meeting Misa, I read another stupefyingly fascinating book on existentialism by psychologist and author Michael Newton, called *Journey of Souls: Case Studies of Life Between Lives*. This book would cause me to rethink my entire existence, through the lens of my eternal soul progressing through hundreds, or even thousands of lives, in order to learn and grow.

This brilliant book would provide me with the final mental concept that I needed to make sense of everything that had every happened to me, including my suffering.

December – 2017

"Close only counts in horseshoes and hand grenades." – *Frank Robinson*

Mother retired a few years ago from a successful career in the Manitoba Civil Service, and had been enjoying herself immensely oil painting; I'd told her that she should display and sell her many paintings that she had lying in storage under the house, but she refused to gift anyone, despite many such family and friend requests.

She travelled abroad when she could, though she still took care of our youngest sibling with down-syndrome, who by then was thirty-one years old. Mother perhaps did her very best as a mother with that one, for she was, and is, nothing less than a being of pure love and joy.

Mother had once again resurfaced after disappearing for around six months. Somewhere towards the end of 2017, she simply vanished without a word to any of her children, with the exception of our sister with down syndrome.

Through rumor and inuendo that flowed through the family over the following many months that we searched casually for her, for that was not an uncommon occurrence, we were finally able to confirm that she had been located at a mental health treatment facility somewhere outside of the city.

Once we knew where she was, mother then decided to contact all of her children separately, including me because she and I were on really good terms again, given the advancement of my Buddha-Dharma practice.

After she contacted us all though, we three eldest siblings immediately connected with each other, to take the few individual pieces of what she selected to tell each of us, and put it all together, in an attempt to determine for ourselves what the real story was.

Once mother started accepting guests again, which was about six months after she resurfaced (she didn't see any of her grandchildren in over a year), I took it upon myself to spend as much time as I could with her, trying to be a calming presence in her life.

I picked up groceries for her every couple weeks if she needed, and I sat and chatted with her for hours over coffee at her home, and emotionally supported her in her allegations that she was injected with an antibiotic, without her informed consent, during a late-night emergency room visit for chest pains, somewhere right before the time that she inexplicably disappeared.

Her mental state over these many months was extremely erratic, and she self-admittedly often makes no sense at all.

I was going to AA now and then, but I knew that I had hit a wall there. I only went to a meeting when I was desperate to not go out drinking, or I needed the temporary reprieve from my quickly returning darkness that the permanent smiles and free coffee at a meeting always brought me.

But despite the best that I had learned over the last decade to keep my drinking to a minimum, and thus as least harmful as possible for me, my drinking over the last six months or so had been increasingly intensifying, and I had no idea why.

My life was essentially perfect; I was engaged to marry a brilliant and vivacious woman who loved my two daughters like they were her own children; we had a beautiful home; my career was picking up and I'd finally been successful in qualifying to interview for a director-level position; I had no debt and owned my SUV outright, and my future looked bright according to what society had to say.

So why was I drinking almost uncontrollably, again and straining my engagement with Misa to beyond reasonability?

So engaged thus in that never-relenting search to become mentally and spiritually healthy, since I finally felt that I had a very good idea of what that might look like through my Buddha-Dharma studies, that I decided that I needed to look past Buddha-Dharma.

Misa, whom I loved as an equal in life, and who I had never once doubted had my best intentions in her heart and soul, had kindly mentioned to me, once or twice over the last year, that she felt that I might benefit from some professional mental health care.

I decided to trust her on that.

The next week I met my psychiatrist for the very first time.

He immediately suggested that I consider going on anti-depressants.

I listened to him.

Chapter 30: Everything That Has a Beginning, Has an End

Late Spring – 2018

"You are seriously fucked up, have you looked in the mirror lately? You need professional help."
- Funboy, The Crow (1994)

I saw my psychiatrist weekly over the next twelve months.

When I first walked into his highly nondescript tiny office, besot with stacks of files, in very early January, he smiled kindly and simply asked why I had come to him. I hadn't really prepared for that question, so I said the first truth that came to my mind.

"I haven't been able to quit drinking or smoking, though I have been desperately trying for several years."

His simple response; "Well, that's a great place to start."

However, by this time, my drinking had not improved as I had originally hoped it would, but I wasn't considering ending the sessions because, well, as Grandma had always said, if you're going to do something right, do it right the first time.

Besides, I had been taking anti-depressants for some time now, and my darkness was significantly thinning.

So I kept going, needing desperately to do it right.

Suddenly, I had a breakthrough; just as my partner had been softly suggesting over the past few months, it was whenever some drama happened with my mother, which was about every two weeks or so, that I seemed to crash emotionally and return to all but constant drinking.

I had initially scoffed at her suggestion, but she was successful in at least lodging it in my subconscious mind, and for all I know, was worked on every waking moment until that very breakthrough in session with my psychiatrist.

At Misa's sage suggestion, I mentioned this in the next session that I had with Dr. Anderson, and we began to peel back the layers of why that might be so.

Within weeks, I suffered my second full mental collapse.

"Every man's got a devil, and you can't rest til you find him." – Top dollar, The Crow (1994)

It's just another day that I have called in sick to the office this week, and am siting on our backdoor steps in a private area of our backyard at the side of the house.

I'm on my seventh beer, and its only 14:00. I've been drinking every night and day since arriving home late Thursday evening, after visiting with my mother at her home, whose physical and mental health are again declining visibly.

My mind is now locked on the perpetual questions of my existence thus far; What is wrong with me? I sit all day on these steps, or in front of the small brick firepit I recently built out back with my father, using leftovers we found in the garage when my partner and I moved in last July, continuously ruminating on this question as I drink beer after beer and smoke cigarette after cigarette.

Suddenly it hits me, like a ton of bricks.

I have been hurt by a lot of people over the course of my entire life, and I have never said anything to anyone, must less the person that hurt me. All of that pain is still in me; I can feel clearly now every individual black, soul-piercing razor-sharp shard of it in the center of my chest, battling desperately to work its way to the surface of my very being from where I have hidden it deep down in my psyche for decades, in some cases.

And what has my spiritual practice taught me to do instinctively by this time in my life? I examine the pain very closely.

Instantly my hand, seemingly of its own volition, reaches into my jeans pocket and pulls out my smartphone. For the next ten hours I call, email or message anyone that comes to my mind that I have unresolved issues with.

I start with the girlfriend that broke my heart and which led to me fleeing overseas for a decade, then my friend Don in Korea, then my sister, and then a number of former heartaches and other friends.

Every singe person that I unload on with absolutely no warning, and with varying degrees of intensity and pain hidden deep inside me for years and years, responds in a way that instantly heals that wound that developed as a result of their humanity.

I then call my father.

I think that I started with a text something like "Hey old man, did you even know that I was bullied for my entire childhood because you weren't around?"

His response within seconds; "Oh Mike I'm so sorry. I really fucked up."

We would chat for hours and hours over the next many months, and when first I told him by text from Brazil that I'd decided to share my story with the world, again within seconds, his response came back.

"That's great. I'm sorry I didn't do more."

My response to that response:

"Dad, you were there when it mattered most. You know how I know that you did everything that was necessary? I finally got it right."

And then I call my mother. She picks up the phone immediately.

I honestly don't know how I started, but I didn't receive the same response as I had from my other parent.

She advises me that she is not yet feeling well enough from her ongoing illness to help me at this time. She says that we can talk when she is feeling stronger.

Wordlessly, I hang up the phone.

Mid-August – 2018

"You will continue to suffer if you have an emotional reaction to everything that is said to you. True power is sitting back and observing things with logic. True power is restraint. If words control you that means everyone else can control you. Breathe and allow things to pass."
- Bruce Lee

As the days passed with no communication from my mother, and then turned into weeks, and then months, I drank pretty much constantly out by the firepit in the back.

I further attacked my fiancé at the most innocuous perceived provocation, who while being very supportive of my clearly fragile state of mind, must for her own sanity sleep at her parents' place a number of times.

I was stone sober though this Year though when I picked up my girls on a typical beautiful Manitoba summer day, and we drove out to the cabin that my sister had again rented for the week.

I'm not in control of my multiple mental illnesses per se, namely being depression, anxiety and addiction, but my mental training over the last many years has resulted in me easily being able to not drink when I must not.

But whenever I can, I drink.

We arrived at the cabin and unloaded the truck.

My brother had already arrived from out west with his family and had occupied the next cabin, and my sister and her kids were in the larger one beyond that.

As soon all the work was done, my daughters took off to find their cousins, and I took up position right in front of the communal fire and cracked the first of many beers that I would drink that week.

However, unlike all the previous times over my entire life that I have drunk in an effort to self-medicate particularly acute occurrences of depression, rather than trying to resist for as long as I could first, I quickly made the conscious decision to let me body drink as much beer as it desired, and I, being separate from my body and my mind as I understood things, would just simply sit back and observe what happened.

And so I drank and visited pleasantly with everyone.

Later that evening, after I finished the first twelve, I went back for another.

My eldest sister, my brother, his girlfriend, my youngest sibling with Down Syndrome and all of our kids of varying ages were sitting around the fire, and the adults and older children, including my daughters, were discussing the topic of our summer; my suffering and the family head's complete radio silence when it came to me.

Unlike our mother, who tried to hide every human weakness that she could from her children and anyone else of any import whatsoever in her life, shortly after I started attending the Dharma Centre of Winnipeg, I had made the conscious decision to be completely open with my daughters about the fact that I suffered from depression and addiction, and I made no effort to hide my suffering from them over those years.

Further, I had talked openly with them whenever it seemed appropriate to do so, about my successes, my failures, and my never faltering commitment to get as healthy as I possibly could for them, and for myself.

On this particular night at the cabin, surrounded by only those that loved me, I was very interested in what my older sister and brother thought about the horrible things about our mother, that had started coming out of me a week or so ago and into our family group chat containing the five of us, including our mother.

About seven nights previous, I had been sitting by that fire again in our backyard, drunker than a skunk, and I suddenly snapped.

I lost it.

Again, seemingly of it's own accord, my hand reached into my jeans pocket and took out my smartphone, and I started unloading a textual tirade of anguish, fury, insults and provocations at my mother for all of my siblings to see.

Why? I wanted to call out my mother and show her what she had made of her eldest child, and I wanted my closest loved ones of appropriate maturity to witness what she was going to say.

Which was nothing at all.

And what did my elder sister and brother have to say about what I have been saying to and about our mother?

"Do what you need to do."

And so I did.

Several times that week at the cabin in fact, and then I continued on into the first half of November.

I remember remarking to my psychiatrist sometime later, after relating to him the story of that entire week at the cabin, regarding the brutality of the things that I had written to and about my mother.

"Pain. Its ugly going in, and its ugly coming out."

He nodded in agreement.

15 November – 2018

"I'm not frightened. I'm not frightened of anything. The more I suffer, the more I love. Danger will only increase my love. It will sharpen it. It will give it spice. I'll be the only angel you need. You will leave life even more beautiful than you entered it. Heaven will take you back and look at you and say; Only one thing can make a soul complete, and that thing is love."
- Friedrich V. Schiller, Love and Intrigue (2006)

Four days before my forty-ninth birthday, and about one-hundred days after the walls fell that had been holding in all of the physical, psychological and existential suffering that my mother had, in her humanity, branded in perpetual excruciation on upon my very soul, was mostly spent, I decided that enough was enough.

I posted thanks to all my Facebook friends for their many birthday wishes, and vowed to the world that by my fiftieth birthday next November, it was my intention to be the heathiest that I had ever been physically, mentally, emotionally and spiritually.

And I took my last drink of alcohol.

21:55 – 23 December – 2018

Thirty-four days after my birthday and thirty-seven since I'd stopped drinking, I decided to open the card that I got in the mail that past Friday. My birthday was some time ago, so I had just tossed it on the marble counter, but I spied it lying there as I went to the refrigerator for another diet soda, and figured I'd open it.

I removed the card from the envelope, tossed the envelope in the garbage, and as I was walking around the corner and back to the living room where I had been watching TV with Misa, I stopped cold in my tracks.

The birthday card was from my mother.

And she had sent me, of all things, a fifty-dollar gift card for an upscale social club downtown.

On the card, she had simply written, "Enjoy!".

Now, my mother very well knew through the family grapevine that I had quit drinking, and this "gift" made me, not the child within, instantly furious. If she had really wanted to send me to a restaurant that I would surely enjoy, she and every other member of my family had known for two decades what restaurant was my all-time favorite, and I was positive that she wouldn't have sent me that gift card to a food and alcohol establishment that I had never heard of, much less been to before.

I applied my subconscious mind to the task immediately, and I got back an instant answer.

"She is still very angry at me for the things that I said to and about her over the summer. This must be her way of making sure that I do not forget the things that I said.", I offered to Misa.

She was a psychologist after all, and had very successfully operated her own private practice for many years, and I had always trusted her deep knowledge and intuition on these types of issues.

She pondered for a moment, and then slowly nodded her head. "There is some merit to that, from what I have seen of her these last couple years."

My hand, seemingly of its own accord, reached into my pants pocket and I pulled out my smartphone.

"I'm calling her." I announced as I located her number.

The phone rang only once and my mother answered, but upon hearing my immediate insistent demand for an explanation as to why she would send me a gift card to a place that has a reputation in the downtown business community as a great place to go for drinks and socializing after work.

After all, she used to work only blocks from this place before she retired.

Mother hung up the phone.

I looked at Misa and I made an instantaneous decision.

"I'm going over there."

I grabbed my jacket out of the front hall closet, and as I was preparing to leave, Misa spoke in a very carefully neutral tone.

"Are you sure that you want to do this?"

I knew instantly what she was worried about. She was worried that I was going to freak out as usual when something occurred like this with my mother, and as I only had a few short weeks of sobriety, she feared for me.

I immediately stepped forward and gently took her in my arms.

"Don't worry. I got this." I said as I gave her a tender kiss on the forehead.

And with that, I departed for my mother's home.

00:13 – 24 December – 2018

"This is your pain. This is your burning hand. It's right here. Look at it."
- Tyler Durden, Fight Club (1999)

I walked the ten minutes or so to my mother's house in Transcona from the nearest bus stop.

About sixteen months previous, I had decided to sell my SUV to pay off some growing debt that I had to my father, and to commute to work and pretty much everywhere else in the city by mountain bike. It was one of the many better decisions about my life that I had been making, since I had become a dedicated Buddha-Dharma practitioner just over five years ago.

I walked down her street and up to her front door, and rang the doorbell.

No answer.

I knocked.

Nothing.

I then rationalized that I never told her that I was coming, and so likely she was nervous about answering the door at that late hour, as most people likely would be.

So I walked back around the double garage and down the short sidewalk at the side of her stucco-forest bungalow, reached up over the tall wooden back gate, lifted the latch, pushed the gate open, and let it slam shut fairly noisily.

I knew that her bedroom was located right on the other side of that wall, and if she was in bed, she was most certain to hear it.

I then trod onto her back wooden deck, making sufficient noise as to alert her that someone was out there, figuring that she would take a peek out her bedroom or kitchen window and see me there.

I waited for about twenty seconds, and then, just as I expected/hoped, I saw movement in the kitchen, through the one of two kitchen windows on this side of the house. I took a step closer to the window and peered in, and sure enough, it was my mother, and she was carrying a chair to the kitchen from her bedroom.

"Wow," I said to myself. "She wants to talk."

I was stunned. I couldn't believe that it had been that easy. I just had to show up at her home, when instead all I had been doing was calling, texting, messaging and emailing.

I followed her as she walked to the kitchen back door, still carrying the chair in both of her hands, and as she leaned forward towards the door.

I stepped forward expectantly for the door to open.

But the door did not open.

I glanced quickly to my left through the same kitchen window, and I saw my mother walk back into her bedroom without the chair and close the door firmly behind her.

And then, without even looking through the kitchen door window, I already knew that she had placed the chair that she was carrying with the chair back against the door, and jammed the chair back top rail under the doorknob, a trick I had seen my mother use over my entire life when she didn't want someone to get into the house.

My quantum brain very quickly calculated what had just happened.

She was not scared that someone was trying to break into her house, because my sister and/or her husband and two children would have been summoned immediately; they were only two doors down.

She also wasn't turning on the other lights in the house because she was not concerned about who was outside her home.

She just didn't want that person in her sanctuary.

It was at that moment that I realized the heart-breaking truth that had been before me my entre life; my mother was profoundly mentally, physically and spiritually ill, and she would never let anyone in her home, her heart, or her mind to see her weaknesses, her frailties, or her humanity.

She would never let me in.

I remained another twenty minutes in the her backyard to be sure that the police had not been called, and that my sister's family all remained undisturbed while visions of sugar-plums danced in their heads, and then I walked the five kilometers to McDonald's at Regent Casino, entered and ordered a small coffee, and sat in a warm booth for the next two hours, meditating on those events.

Then I called a cab, and went home to bed.

Seven days later, I quit smoking for good.

Chapter 31: The Present Day

*"If we have souls, they are made of the love we share.
Undimmed by time, unbound by death."*
- Jack Harper, Oblivion (2013)

That's it.

That's my story.

Its been six-hundred and six days since I quit drinking alcohol permanently.

I still get teeny cravings from time to time, but they have no affect on my judgment or decision-making process anymore, for I finally understand what a craving is, and that everything that has a beginning has an end, and whenever one comes, I just sit back respectfully and observe the entire lifecycle of the craving in my mind and body.

The answer never was to fight with or control the cravings, but rather to accept them as a necessary and important part of me, with a specific purpose. I say respectfully because every individual facet of my personality now understands the value of our cravings; they signal the rest of us when there exists an issue of mental health for us to address.

I believe that I can truthfully claim that I have addressed all of the major issues in my life to date that previously limited my advancement in my orthopraxy and in life in general, and I am at peace with all of my extended family and friends, both past and present, that choose to remain in my life.

My mother still has not contacted me to acknowledge and accept her part in my suffering, so that she can begin the process of acknowledging how causing that suffering in me caused suffering in her, which is the second step on the path to optimal physical, mental, emotional and spiritual health.

Misa and I decided that the immediate future held other wonderful things for each of us, and we've each gone our own way, though we remain the best of friends, and always will be.

I have continued to apply the eightfold path to all aspects of my life.

In early fall, after much soul-searching (pardon the pun), I resigned from my position with the Manitoba Civil Service, and now only spend my time and resources on the projects and programs that I believe are the most wholesome for me specifically, and for the world in general.

After Misa and I parted ways, after much discussion with my father and my daughters, I decided to leave Canada, and currently am of no fixed address in São Paulo, Brazil. I came here briefly at the end of 2006 to visit with Chris, and something about the people and culture really stuck with me, and so when things in Canada were percolating just right in the summer of 2019, I decided to return to this amazingly rich and cultured country, which I feel was the most wholesome choice, for it has resulted in this book and the redefining of my vocation, not to mention my further emotional and spiritual healing.

And speaking of healing, I don't believe that it is every really over in life. I still take prescription anti-depressant medication, but I have hopes of getting off of that as well. I am very interested in the latest research surrounding psilocybin and DMT, the spirit molecule, which more and more strongly suggests that these substances, when properly administered by a qualified professional, can be very effective in the treatment of PTSD, addiction and depression.

Graham Hancock, one of my favorite authors, has written a number of excellent books on the subject.

Now I can truly say that it is well with my soul, for I understand that nothing in my life happened that was not supposed to. I now understand that there was never anything that needed to be fixed inside me per se, for it was all part of my initial life-journey from birth to self-healing, the same initial life-journey that we all start at birth and so few of us truly ever complete.

No human being who has breathed air has not experienced suffering, and though we all suffer from different causes and to different degrees, the worst that we each have ever suffered, regardless of our skin color, is an equally soul-rendering anguish.

And finally, I no longer feel alone, and I never will again, for now I understand that there has always been one being in my life that was always there for me without fail; my biggest supporter, my number fan, the one that would make me laugh when I was sad, the one that would always listen to me with sincere interest and concern when I needed an ear, and who always provided deeply thought-provoking insights when I seemed to need them most.

I mean, think about it. Recent science suggests that the brain is in fact an organic quantum computer. Scientists even posit that they are narrowing down on exactly what part of the human brain is responsible for the subconscious.

And if there is any place in the human brain that operates quantumly, I posit as a layman on the subject, that it would have to include at minimum the human subconscious.

And what other being most likely, according to my particular existential paradigm, should at minimum also operate quantumly?

Why, my soul of course.

To my mother,

I now understand what that little five-year old boy in that car repair shop did not so many years ago when we first left the city.

It is not my purpose in life to make you happy. And it is not my purpose in life to love you.

I no longer love you as a son should normally love a mother; you beat that out of me many decades before I would ever understand enough of you, or value enough of myself, to acknowledge that.

That little boy that you caused to torturously suffer still exists in me, and he always will, and no matter how much I learn and understand about myself and him, and the suffering that we experienced over all of those years, he can never forget, and he will always feel that pain, and that fury.

And as my Buddha-Dharma practice experience has been thus far, one cannot feel both fury and love at the exact same time, and so he can never love you.

However, I do have a much more useful love for you, though it be more humanical; I love you as Lama Gerry taught me to love any being that is suffering; with as much loving compassion as I can muster.

I do not need your forgiveness, just as you do not need mine. I understand now, with my particular existential view, that your soul agreed to play this role for me in this lifetime, and for that I thank you greatly, Mom.

For I do now believe you when you said that what was coming next was going to hurt you more than it hurt me. I'm not sure if in fact that was the case, but I do believe now, with all of my mind, heart and soul, that the horrible suffering that you inflicted next, regardless of your intention, did in fact hurt you more than you, or I, will ever be able or willing to admit, much less understand.

As I would feel for <u>any</u> being that is suffering, if there is anything that I can do that is both wholesome and appropriate, that might help you to begin to identify and address that suffering that your past decisions and actions have caused within your mind, heart and soul in this life, I'm here.

Your son,

Micheal

"Imagine that everything that your life and your death mean is decided by how you live and die, while you live and die. If the meaning of life isn't necessarily anything at all, then try to imagine that you have to make meaning instead. Imagine that the meaning of things, especially of human beings, is itself a made thing, and imagine that you can make meaning every day."
- Stephen Jenkinson, Die Wise, 2015

Manufactured by Amazon.ca
Bolton, ON

14166855R00236